THE ART OF
MARRIAGE

THE ULTIMATE BOOK ON HOW TO
CREATE THE PERFECT MARRIAGE

THE ART OF MARRIAGE

THE ULTIMATE BOOK ON HOW TO CREATE THE PERFECT MARRIAGE

Ruki D. Renov

Mekor Press

Published by Mekor Press, a division of Menucha Publishers
copyright @ 2013 by Ruki D. Renov

All rights reserved

ISBN: 978-1-61465-1314

No part of this publication may be translated, reproduced, stored in a retrieval system, or transmitted in any form or by any means, electronic, mechanical, photocopying, recording, or otherwise, without prior permission in writing from both the copyright holder and the publisher.

Distributed by Menucha Publishers
250 44th Street
Brooklyn, NY 11232
Tel/Fax: 718-232-0856
www.mekorpress.com

Cover Illustration: Gadi Pollack
Cover Design Concept: Laya Perlysky
Cover and Book Design: Avi Stahler avistahler@gmail.com
Editing: E. Flam

Printed in Israel

To my extraordinary parents,
Rozi and Morty Davis/Davidowitz,
who taught me to write, to laugh, to believe, to
appreciate, to care, to share, to understand, to give,
and most of all, to love.

To my beloved husband, fabulous children, their
wonderful spouses (who are like my children), and
delicious grandchildren, who fill my home, my heart,
and my life with warmth, with excitement, with
Torah, with music, with joy, and with boundless love.

And to HaKadosh Baruch Hu, Who gives meaning
to my life, Who gives me strength to face my
challenges, and Who has blessed both me and my
family with so very much to be grateful for.

TABLE OF CONTENTS

Introduction 11

Part One: Pre-Marriage

1: Know That Hashem Is in Charge 17
2: Be Educated 19
3: Date the Right Type 21
4: Strategy. 23
5: How and Where to Meet 28
6: Date to Find the Right Person 30
7: The Search for Perfection 33
8: The Dating Period 37
9: Recognizing the Right and Wrong Person 46

10: Signs of Abusive Behavior................ 66
11: Research........................... 70
12: The Right Person Is Not a Perfect Person..... 76
13: Rejection.......................... 80
14: Go Out........................... 84
15: Your Family's Attitude.................. 87
16: Older/Younger Dating.................. 90
17: Should I Settle?..................... 93
18: Committing........................ 105

Part Two: Marriage

19: Let the Marriage Begin................. 111
20: First Disagreement.................... 117
21: Dealing with Differences................ 122
22: First Year......................... 134
23: Ingredients for a Successful Marriage....... 142
24: Men and Women Are Different........... 150
25: The Need for Self-Esteem............... 165
26: Boundaries........................ 184
27: TLC: Talk, Listen, Care................ 196
28: Love Each Other.................... 235
29: Share Responsibilities................. 242
30: Major Issues: Sensitivities and Insecurities .. 251
31: Different Backgrounds and Outlooks....... 257

32: Discover Your Personality 265
33: Can a Person Change? 270
34: Character Counts 278
35: Common Interests or Disinterest? 287
36: Common Values and Goals 291
37: Stay Emotionally Involved 295
38: Appreciation 300
39: Share Your Lives 306
40: The Little Things Make a Big Marriage 313
41: Compromise 317
42: Anger 320
43: Refine Your Focus 328
44: Trust 330
45: Forgiveness 332
46: Attraction 336
47: Pregnancy 340
48: Children 342
49: Financial Issues 345
50: In-Laws 357
51: Commitment versus Divorce 384
52: The Medical Advantages of Marriage 403
53: Don't Compare Your Marriage 407
54: Grow Old Together 411

Bibliography 413

INTRODUCTION

When I mentioned to someone that I was writing a book about marriage, he cleverly asked me, "For or against?"

Jacob, ninety-two, and Rivka, eighty-nine, are excited about their decision to get married. Strolling along while discussing the wedding, they pass a drugstore.

They enter and Jacob addresses the man behind the counter, "Are you the owner?"

The pharmacist answers, "Yes."

Says Jacob, "We're about to get married. Do you sell heart medication?"

Pharmacist: "Of course we do."

Jacob: "How about medicine for circulation?"
Pharmacist: "All kinds."

Jacob: "Medicine for rheumatism, scoliosis?"

Pharmacist: "Definitely."

Jacob: "How about heating pads?"

Pharmacist: "Of course."

Jacob: "Medicine for memory problems, arthritis, jaundice?"

Pharmacist: "Yes, a large variety. The works."

Jacob: "What about vitamins, sleeping pills, Geritol, antidotes for Parkinson's disease?"

Pharmacist: "Absolutely."

Jacob: "You sell wheelchairs and walkers?"

Pharmacist: "All speeds and sizes."

Jacob says to the pharmacist, "Wonderful! We'd like to register here for our wedding gifts, please."

People, young and old, want to and should share their lives with a partner in marriage.

In the beginning there was nothing. Then G-d said, "Let there be light" and there was light. There was still nothing, but now you could see it better.

After reading this book you may still be in the same position as before, but hopefully you will understand your situation and your options more clearly. Of course, in order for the suggestions in this book to be effective, people must be open to the possibility of change and growth.

This book contains many jokes that poke fun at husbands, wives, and the institution of marriage. Although these are serious topics, I believe that approaching all aspects of life with humor makes every experience more enjoyable and less burdensome. Laugh your way through the pages. Hopefully, each of you will emerge from your reading more knowledgeable about and better prepared for marriage.

The information is appropriate both for those already married, and for those who are preparing themselves to have a rewarding marriage in the not-too-distant future. Since choosing the right partner is the key to a successful marriage, a quick review of choosing your spouse, a topic covered in great detail in my first book, *The Art of the Date*, is included. Of course, I have also included new insights, stories, *divrei Torah*, Torah thoughts — and plenty of new jokes!

If you are already married, part 1, "Pre-Marriage," is sure to give you excellent ideas for advising singles, as well as offer you insight into your own marriage. If you do not think you need to read part 1, feel free to enjoy the jokes, which are written in bold, and skip directly to part 2, "Marriage." This way, even if you feel you are not making progress in your marriage, you will benefit by feeling that you are making progress in your reading!

Part One
Pre-Marriage

1: Know That Hashem Is in Charge

Yossie was late for an important meeting and couldn't find a parking space. Looking upward, he said, "Please, G-d, if You give me a parking space I will donate $500 to *tzedaka*, charity." No parking space materialized, and Yossie was desperate. Again, he looked up to heaven and said, "Please, G-d, if You give me a parking space I will give $5,000 to *tzedaka*." Still, no parking space appeared and Yossie thought he would go crazy. He couldn't be late to this meeting! He cried out, "G-d, please help me! If You find me a parking space I will give $50,000 to *tzedaka*." Suddenly, a car pulled out of a spot right next to Yossie. In great relief Yossie looked up to G-d and said, "Never mind. I found a space on my own."

Recognize that Hashem is running the world.

I joined a Don't Worry Club. When I called up and asked, "When is the next meeting?" a voice answered, "Don't worry!"

It is difficult to select a suitable spouse when you are feeling stressed. Take the attitude that Hashem is in control, and put yourself in His hands. Of course, "G-d helps those who help themselves," so you must do what you can. Keep a positive and upbeat attitude, believing that Hashem will make it happen for you at the right time and with the right person.

Hashem blessed us with the gift of prayer, not because He needs our *tefillos*, or prayers, but because it is our most precious tool to connect to the Almighty. Beseech Hashem for help in finding your true *bashert*, soul mate.

Put your trust in Hashem. *Ein od bilvado*, there is no one but Him. Finding your *bashert* is a challenge, but realize that everything Hashem does is for your own good. Therefore, if Hashem gave you this challenge, you must trust that it is for your benefit.

The first step to a good marriage is finding the right spouse. Search for your mate with a relaxed attitude. Too many people start dating anxious that they are bound by a time limit. This causes needless worry and the inability to make proper judgment calls. Relax and be assured that Hashem is handling everything.

A Jewish telegram: "Start worrying. Details to follow."

2: Be Educated

Marriage is the only sport that requires the trapped animal to buy the license.

In order to acquire almost any skill we must take lessons, devoting time and energy to learn the ropes. You would not allow a child to cross the street without teaching him to look both ways. You would not send a fighter into a boxing ring without showing him how to block and punch. You would not strap skis on a person and send him down a mountain without instruction. Yet there are no required courses to master two of life's most important skills: how to build a solid and healthy marriage, and how to raise well-adjusted children.

The government does not permit you to drive without passing a road test, yet it does allow you to ruin your own and other people's lives by creating a reckless marriage. In order to dissolve a marriage, people spend years and pay fortunes, subjecting themselves to undergoing psychoanalysis, being drilled by lawyers, and answering an infinite amount of questions in civil court and *beis din*, Jewish court. Yet before marriage, people barely delve into their own feelings. Premarital classes and psychological counseling should be required to ensure a person's readiness for this institution.

John had a maddening compulsion to tear paper. His wife finally took him to a therapist, who soon cured him.

The grateful wife said to the therapist, "What did you say to finally cure him?"

The therapist said, "I told him, 'Don't tear paper.'"

Marriages can be greatly improved if couples are simply told what is involved, what to expect, and what they should and should not do. Although religious individuals take *chassan/kallah*, groom/bride, classes with excellent instructors, many classes are not comprehensive enough. Ideally, these classes should cover all aspects of marriage and relationships, and it is best if they are given by people who have psychological as well as spiritual training. Organizations such as the Shalom Task Force provide excellent premarital classes.

3: Date the Right Type

Whom you date determines whom you marry. Dating is an art. Recognizing whom to date, whom to avoid, how to date, how to communicate, how to evaluate the relationship, how to enjoy the person you are dating, and how to make that person like and appreciate your fine qualities are all vital to your dating experience.

Sifting through your dates to determine who is your Mr./Mrs. Right is an even greater art.

Two pirates meet.

"My G-d, Angus! What happened to you?"

"Oh, you mean my pegged leg? I was at sea and a shark bit it off, so I got a peg."

"Okay, but what happened to your arm?"

"Oh, you mean the hook? I was in a fight and a young

swashbuckling pirate cut it off, so I had to get a hook."

"But what happened to your eye?"

"Oh, I was at the beach and a gust of wind blew sand in my eye."

"Listen," said the first pirate, "I can understand about your losing your leg and I can understand about your losing your arm, but I do not understand how a gust of sand could cause you to lose your eye!"

"It can if it's your first day with the hook."

Despite their lack of dating and marital experience, people still like to choose the right person to marry on their first go-around. You just need to be careful so the wrong person does not get his/her hooks into you.

4: Strategy

Three men, Giovanni, Isaac, and Joe, are sentenced to twenty years in prison. The warden asks each one what he would like to take into the cell with him. Giovanni asks for a wife.

"Granted."

Isaac asks for a telephone.

"Granted."

Joe asks for a case of cigarettes.

"Granted."

The cells are then locked. After twenty years they are released. Giovanni comes out with his wife and twelve children. "Thank you so much," he says to the warden. "I am so happy. I have a great wife and twelve wonderful bambinos."

Isaac comes out and says to the warden, "Thank you so much. I used my phone to make unbelievable trades on Wall Street and I am now a wealthy man."

Joe comes out and says to the warden, "Can I have a match?"

Plan a strategy to help you achieve your goal of a first-rate marriage. Develop an understanding of who you are and what qualities in another person will fill your needs and further your growth. Then you can determine what you are looking for and what you need. Don't be rigid. Your vision of what you think you need should not be etched in stone. It is only a guide.

Step one is to be aware of who you are. Columnist George Will describes the most dangerous person as "the one who does not know what he does not know." Without a full understanding of your own makeup, personality, attributes, ideals, capabilities, sensitivities, and objectives in life, it's hard to assess what type of person is right for you. Be realistic about yourself. Understand who you are, recognizing your needs. After you come to know and value your own essence, be certain that you understand and appreciate the person you are choosing to marry, and that s/he knows and appreciates you as well.

Develop and educate yourself, and you will be attractive to yourself and to the man/woman of your dreams. Then continue, by dating people who have also developed themselves intellectually, emotionally, and spiritually.

If you don't know where you are going, when you get there you'll be lost.

— *Yogi Berra*

Striving to improve one's character is essential in a proper marriage; good *middos*, character traits, build a marriage, whereas negative traits are harmful to a marriage. Rabbi Zelig Pliskin refers to marriage as a *"middos workshop"* wherein one should continually grow and observe progress. Preparing oneself for marriage should be an important stage in one's growth.

What's the name of a face lotion developed for Jewish women?

Oil of Oy Vey.

Examine yourself physically. Are you the best you can be? Can you improve your appearance? Visit a gym, see a nutritionist, update your hairstyle, whiten your teeth, redo your makeup, change your glasses, or put on contact lenses. Have someone help you revamp your wardrobe. Even small changes make a difference in how you look and feel about yourself.

Work on improving your attitude. Warmth appeals to people, so learn to smile. Read books and take courses on happiness, to develop an upbeat outlook and an appreciation for what you have, while avoiding anger and jealousy. Developing a positive sense of self will not only help you during dating; it will also help you build a better marriage. One who exhibits a *simchas hachaim* — a zest for and an enjoyment of life — is most appealing.

Remember, we never get a second chance to make a great first impression. Are your interpersonal skills all they can be? Are you comfortable with people, or do you feel shy and introverted? Are you possibly too loud and aggressive?

Are you a good conversationalist? Think about your communication skills. Speech and communication classes or assertiveness training courses may be important for you.

Are you uncomfortable on dates? Practice dating. A boy should know where to pick up his date, where to take her, how to get there, where to park, and how much to tip. Always have your date's phone number in case a problem arises beforehand.

The mother said to the little girl, "You mustn't talk all the time, dear."

The little girl said, "When will I be old enough to?"

If you are nervous, plan some topics of conversation. Prepare a few good stories and even a couple of jokes. These will help you break the ice until you feel more at ease.

Ironically, deciding whom to date can be more difficult if you have too many choices. Mrs. Schwartz went to Toys R Us with her nine-year-old son, Benny, and told him he could pick out one toy. After hours of trying to choose between all the toys, Benny returned home empty-handed and crying.

When it comes to dating options, most men have too many while women have too few.

Although you must retain a standard, keep an open mind about meeting different types of people, because you never know who will appeal to you. Allow yourself to be introduced to many individuals, by many people. People don't always meet their intended in the way they imagined.

A frog telephones a psychic hotline and is told, "You are going to meet a beautiful young girl who will want to know everything about you."

"Great," says the frog. "Will I meet her at a party?"

"No," says the psychic. "Next year in biology class."

5: How and Where to Meet

A *shadchan*, matchmaker, sang the praises of a particular woman to an excited young man, and then brought him to meet her. Yankel took one look at the girl whom the *shadchan* had so eloquently praised, and recoiled.

"What's the matter?"

"You said she is young," whispered Yankel, "but she is forty if she is a day. You said she is beautiful, but she looks like the back of a bus. You said she is shapely but she is fat enough for two! You said…"

"You don't have to whisper," interrupted the *shadchan*. "She's also hard of hearing."

Try every means available to meet eligible prospects. Go everywhere you can and network with everyone you know. Allow people to fix you up on dates. Welcome suggestions from friends, relatives, coworkers, and *shadchanim*. Encourage everyone to look out for you.

Go to places such as appropriate parties and social events, school, work, and shul where you are familiar with the type of people that are in attendance. Many reliable organizations run events where singles have a chance to meet each other.

Many successful matches have resulted from Internet dating. There are legitimate and trustworthy sites for Orthodox Jews, with excellent success statistics, that are worth visiting. Many have online *shadchanim*. It may be worthwhile to break out of your box and widen your horizons by trying online dating, but be careful to choose only reliable sites with sterling reputations. Don't be the type who says, "I don't do those things." Give yourself the most opportunities possible to meet the right person.

Today, even in the non-*frum*, nonreligious world, matchmakers have become popular. Looking for a spouse who fits your requirements has become a complex job. Most matchmakers conduct interviews; some even do background and financial checks, verifying age and employment, social and organizational involvement, and religious affiliation to match the demands of their clients. Some matchmaking services will coach individuals on proper dress and etiquette, as well as offer image consultants and personal trainers.

A woman visits her rabbi in Israel. "Yankele un Yosale are both in love mit me," she says. "Who vill be the lucky von?"

The wise old rabbi answers, "Yankele will marry you. Yosale will be the lucky one."

6: Date to Find the Right Person

There are two categories to cliff jumping: first place and stuff on a rock. You don't get a second try.

Unfortunately, some people enter marriage with a "Who cares?" attitude: *If this doesn't work out, I'll get divorced and take another stab at it.* But that's not how it works. It may be ridiculously *easy* to get into a marriage, but it is extremely *complicated* to get out of one. Divorce is not simple; it is often a war where both sides are torn to pieces emotionally and financially. Be careful whom you date and whom you marry. When you are dating for marriage your attitude should be: *I am dating to find the right person to share the rest of my life with me.*

A man comes home, agitated after seeing his doctor.

"What's bothering you so much?" his wife asks.

"The doctor said I have to take a pill every day for the rest of my life."

"So what's the big deal?" asks his wife.

"Well," he says, "he only gave me three pills."

Remember, you are choosing your partner for life, and hopefully that will be for a long time.

Whom you marry influences every aspect of your life, from your perception of yourself to your ability to move forward in a productive way. Self-esteem is vital, and a spouse who nurtures that is a blessing. Even if your self-confidence is healthy, it will be affected by how your spouse makes you feel.

You must feel good about yourself in order to feel good with someone else. Build your own self-esteem; your perception of yourself should not be solely dependent on what your spouse thinks of you. If you lack self-esteem you will easily take offense and misinterpret much of what your spouse says. You will attack rather than calmly understand. You will not be able to compromise for fear of being compromised (see chapter 25, "The Need for Self-Esteem").

You should like your date, but it is even more important to like yourself when you are with your date. Someone who allows you to be yourself, admiring and appreciating you as you are, builds your confidence and helps promote your growth. In turn you will do the same for him or her.

We know of not a single case where the enemy has successfully used camouflage against us.

— *Army general*

Never camouflage who you really are. Fooling your spouse into marrying you is unfair to your spouse and to yourself. If you are usually sensitive, don't pretend to be thick-skinned while dating. If you have a tendency to be serious and intense, don't fake being lighthearted and laid back. If you are meticulous, don't imply that you don't care about details. If you have issues with your intended's family and friends, let him/her know now, rather than suddenly distancing yourself from them after marriage. Don't act sweet and demure before the wedding, and tough and aggressive after. Don't act happy and forgiving before, yet be upset and jealous once you are married. It's misleading to be a big spender before the wedding day and a tightwad afterward, or pretend to need nothing before and then be demanding after you are married. Don't tell a person you love him/her exactly the way s/he is, and then spend your life trying to change him/her. Marriages that are based on false impressions and dishonesty usually don't survive.

My father said, "Marry a girl who has the same beliefs as the family."

I said, "Dad, why would I want a girl who thinks I'm an idiot?"

— Adam Sandler

7: THE SEARCH FOR PERFECTION

A guy is sitting alone at home when he hears a knock on the front door.

When he opens the door, he encounters two sheriff's deputies who ask if he is married and, if so, whether they can see a picture of his wife.

"Sure," answers the guy, showing both deputies a picture of his wife.

They look carefully at the picture, and then one of them gravely says, "I'm sorry, sir, but it looks like your wife's been hit by a truck."

The guy says, "I know, but she has a great personality, is good with our kids, and makes an amazingly delicious cholent!"

Perfect is the enemy of great. Don't keep searching for perfection, because you will never be satisfied. You will always think something better exists somewhere else.

Benny married Shari, a woman he thinks is beautiful, but he wonders what he will do if he eventually sees someone who is even prettier. Certainly Shari will age and may not look as beautiful as women thirty years her junior. Claire was happy when she met Morey, whom she considered a charismatic businessman. Later Claire heard someone speak who seemed even more dynamic. Should people never settle on a partner, continually searching for perfection, or should they decide that they do not need "the best"?

No one remains the best forever. Sooner or later, someone better looking, smarter, funnier, or wealthier appears. It is up to you to keep thinking of your spouse as the best, because the total person is the best for you. Sandra may no longer be the prettiest, but she understands and cares for Jerry more than anyone else can. Morey may not provide Claire with unlimited finances, but he is the best at providing Claire with a warm, loving home.

Grandma is sitting on the beach watching her little grandson Shimmy build castles in the sand with his shovel and pail. He looks adorable with his little baseball cap perched atop his blond curls. Suddenly a great wave rolls in and washes Shimmy into the darkness of the ocean.

From the depths of her soul the grandmother cries out, "Please G-d! Help me! Please bring back my precious little Shimmy!" With that, the tide rolls in and carries back her little grandson. Again Grandma looks lovingly at Shimmy playing in the sand. Then she looks up toward the heavens and says, "So what happened to his baseball cap?"

We want it all. We want perfection rather than appreciating what we have.

A man who has imperfections is just about as perfect as anyone can be.

Be realistic about your relationship. Nobody's perfect – and that includes you too!

Larry said, "I'm looking for the kind of wife who can sew. The kind you can give a handful of buttons to and say, "Here, sew some shirts on these."

People want it all without realizing that "all" is in your mind and your assessment of the person's worth. It is wonderful if you can find a person you believe to be perfect, but in truth, perfection is in the eyes of the beholder. And does a person really need perfection? What if Mr./Mrs. Right does not exist? Maybe there's a Mrs. All Right or a Mr. Nice Guy who can make you unbelievably happy.

American women expect to find in their husbands a perfection that English women only hope to find in their butlers.

—*W. Somerset Maugham*

No one is perfect. We all come with our challenges and our different expectations, objectives, opinions, beliefs, and dreams. A person who is perfect in one aspect will have flaws in another aspect. We must accept and choose to love a person with all his or her positive and negative characteristics. The trick is to make sure the positive traits outweigh the negative traits, and that you can live with the negative traits.

Before marriage, analyze the person and be sure you

are happy with what you are getting. After marriage, accept the person and stop looking for better.

"I miss Al so much."

"Why?"

"Because I married his widow."

8: The Dating Period

I was on a date recently, and the guy took me horseback riding. That was kind of fun until we ran out of quarters.
—*Susie Loucks*

Use the dating period to get to know your date well, and have your date get to know you.

Time is important for anyone truly ready for a commitment. You do not want to date someone for an extended period of time only to discover that s/he is really not for you, or is unable to commit and has taken up precious time for no reason.

Author Shaya Ostrov, L.C.S.W., suggests that, because you are dating in order to find your life partner, each date should have an agenda and direction (*The Inner Circle: Seven Gates to Marriage*). Prepare for it psychologically and emotionally, thinking: *What do I hope to learn on this date? What do I want to convey? What do I want to experience?*

The first date or first few dates create a comfort zone; you want to get a feel for one another, becoming relaxed in each other's presence. Going forward, some dates will be more serious and intense while others may be more fun and carefree, but every date should help couples get to know each other better. By seeing each other under different circumstances, each person will move toward a better understanding of the other, and the relationship can grow.

A woman dated a man who said that he didn't want to get too seriously involved. In fact, when they were playing tennis, he wouldn't say, "Fifteen-love." He would say, "Fifteen-I really like you, but I'm not ready to get married."

"Life has taught us that love does not consist of gazing at each other, but in looking outward together in the same direction" (Antoine De Saint-Exupery). Creating a realistic picture of what you wish your life to be like in the future is a great way to determine what you are looking for and how you can get there. Explore your friendships, connections, and experiences to find out what has made you reach different emotional levels. What made you feel happiest or saddest? What made you feel fulfilled or frustrated? Whom do you most admire? Whose marriage would you most like to emulate? The mental images of these experiences are the pictures that you will attach to the wall in the recesses of your mind. Many different pictures can be portrayed together to create a beautiful gallery. If one of your ideals is a strong, wonderful family, that's a picture to hang up and reference as a road map for you to follow in your quest for your life partner. If you are searching for a sensitive spouse who will be your best friend, hang up that picture as well. Check your pictures often, making sure that the person you are dating and investing time and energy in has the same vision or is willing to readjust his/her vision to make it work with yours. If your experiences with and your emotions about this person echo the experiences and emotions in your ideal picture gallery, it is worthwhile investing in that person.

Life partners should share the same goals. The more disparate your values and beliefs are, the more challenging the marriage will be. Even two wonderful individuals will have a difficult time creating a happy marriage if their dreams, goals, and beliefs differ. That is why you want to make sure your date has a picture gallery similar to yours, or is willing to hang additional pictures to make it work with yours.

Find out as much as you can about your date prior to a first meeting. This will make the date more comfortable because you can prepare in advance for issues that may arise. For example, if your date holds down a job that makes you uncomfortable, you can examine your own attitude, trying to become comfortable with it ahead of time, rather than being surprised and unable to deal with it on the date.

Give me my golf clubs, fresh air, and a beautiful partner, and you can keep my golf clubs and the fresh air.

Many dates feel like superficial meetings, since people tend to keep an emotional distance. By opening up and revealing your thoughts and feelings you create trust, giving your date a sense of security that strengthens the emotional bond.

Giving emotionally constructs a bridge that can bring two people closer together. We can give in many ways: by communicating our feelings, understanding the other person's viewpoint, validating another person's feelings, and encouraging him/her. Constructive criticism, given with care and sensitivity, is also a form of emotional giving. Spending money is not always necessary, but it reminds the giver that the recipient is worth the gift, and the receiver realizes that the person is willing to invest in him/her.

Giving of yourself opens a door to your soul, allowing the other person to enter. When you share your emotions and receive positive feedback, a connection is built and a mutual path of entry is opened. Responses to emotional sharing include reciprocal sharing, smiling, a nod of agreement, or any other positive reaction that touches a chord in the other person.

Chana was very close to her grandmother and appreciated when Aaron praised her for their beautiful relationship. Chana felt more comfortable with and appreciative of Aaron because of his approval.

Barry, hearing that Carol was artistic, took her to a pottery shop where they spent the evening painting earthenware. This small act showed Carol that Barry cared about her interests.

A patient says to the psychologist, "I have a problem. I think I am an umbrella."

The psychologist says, "Don't worry. We'll talk. We'll get to the source of the problem. All you have to do is open up."

The patient asks, "Why? Is it raining?"

If there are issues you want to discuss with your date, you must feel comfortable enough to bring up those topics. Don't consider marrying a person when you have questions that are unanswered. Likewise, you should not marry someone if you have not revealed things about yourself that s/he should know.

"Congratulations, my boy!" said the groom's uncle. "I'm sure you'll look back and remember this as the happiest day of your life."

"But, I'm not getting married until tomorrow," protested his nephew.

"I know," replied the uncle. "That's exactly what I mean."

Discuss personal issues. Is she open and honest? Do you think he is erecting walls and keeping you out of places in his life? A shut-out feeling that persists even though you have dated long enough for trust to be established may remain a challenge even after marriage, requiring a therapist's intervention.

Don't marry someone until there is an open and honest environment between the two of you, with nothing intentionally hidden. Of course people can keep certain things to themselves, but secrets that will affect your well-being and the ability to have a healthy relationship must be discussed.

Any illnesses or medications that may adversely affect the relationship must be revealed. One should seek proper guidance from your rabbi as to when and how to divulge such delicate information. Sometimes people in the *shidduch* system avoid taking necessary medications because they are afraid of word getting out that they are on medication. Most psychologists will tell you that a person who properly medicates is healthier than a person who requires medication but avoids taking it.

Of course, many people have something they would rather other people did not know about or focus on, but it is hard to establish a real relationship unless you know that your partner is aware and accepting of your foibles. Someone who is nervous about making a living must be allowed to express his fear. In turn, he needs his date to say, "I am sure it is overwhelming, but it is very common for young people to feel this way." A woman who is insecure about her housekeeping abilities will be afraid of a relationship unless she can express her fear and hear her date answer, "I wouldn't worry about it. It takes time to feel comfortable taking on tasks that seem like monumental jobs, but over time most people learn to handle it."

When a person experiences validation, s/he feels better about him-/herself and better about the person who gave the approval, and in turn, more hopeful about the relationship. Of course, you must be certain that the level of insecurity is within normal range.

As in all things in life, timing is essential. Although it is important to reveal your fears and reservations, you must do so at the appropriate time. Since you are letting down your defenses and disclosing a sensitive part of your being, you cannot open up too soon. First you need to feel confident that you are making these revelations to someone whom you believe is worth investing in, someone who cares about you and is trustworthy.

Taking a person into your confidence creates closeness. By confiding their deepest feelings to each other, people are naturally reassured and validated, and a bond is established. After gaining a deeper insight into each other's feelings, a couple is able to move toward a more serious commitment.

Why can't nations solve their problems like husbands and wives? Just get mad, pout, and don't talk to each other for a couple of weeks.

Date conversations must progress from the mundane to the deep, from the obvious to the private. Each time you help your date understand who you are, who your circle of relatives, friends, and confidants are, what you stand for, what you believe in, what motivates you, what made you develop into who you are, what you live for and what you would die for, you are inviting him/her to view the inner you. Each time you strip away one of the protective layers you usually wear, you are giving a piece of yourself to your date.

How are these confessions received? Hopefully, you will gain the other person's respect and trust, and s/he will incorporate this piece into his/her heart, reciprocating in kind. When each person lets down his/her barriers and allows the other entrance, two hearts eventually become one.

Jerry told Rona that his father had been abusive toward his mother, which is why he eventually moved out and sought help. Rona sympathized with Jerry's situation, commending him on the strength he showed by leaving his parents' home to seek a better type of life. Sharing these private experiences with Rona was difficult, but if she were to become part of his life, Jerry needed her to understand and accept who he was. For Jerry, Rona's acceptance made her an insider. If before she had lived outside his heart, now she was a part of it.

A man who says marriage is a fifty-fifty proposition doesn't understand two things: 1. women 2. fractions.

Sometimes people feel they are not getting any closer to each other even after they have been dating for a while. Complimenting one another helps tear down that barrier. Many people are afraid of complimenting one another too soon, thinking this makes them seem vulnerable, desperate, or too forward. But because self-esteem is a vital ingredient in a healthy marriage, someone who fosters that self-esteem is cherished. An individual on a date is usually nervous, so strengthening your date's self-esteem will only make him/her appreciate you more.

There are appropriate ways to compliment someone that will make him/her feel comfortable, while still retaining modesty. You can say something like: "You have a pleasant smile" or "You have a good sense of humor" or "Thank you for planning such a lovely date." Bolstering your date's confidence makes him/her less uptight, affording you the opportunity to get to know the real person.

Compliments that remark on specific personal qualities you noticed can deepen your connection to your date. If a man says to a woman, "I had a nice time," and she answers," So did I," that's okay. But if she answers, "I also had a nice time, because you are fun to be with," she has put a positive spin on the date. If your date says, "The evening was very pleasant," answering "Yes, I thought so too," is fine, but saying, "It was pleasant because of your warmth," adds a new dimension to the relationship. A kind statement is not a commitment and it should not be taken as such. However, the nice feeling it creates is a catalyst for positive emotion. It goes without saying that you should never say something you don't believe, but you can usually find something positive to say to someone. You can always start with, "You seem to be a very good driver."

My wife has frequent accidents while driving, but they're not really her fault. Just the other day she was driving down the street, minding her own business, when a telephone pole cut right in front of her.

Some individuals need a challenge; they want a date that plays it cool. Others want someone open and ready to commit. Evaluate the person you are seeing and act accordingly. If someone is not psychologically ready, they may feel pressured and unable to commit. Don't get too far ahead of the other person. It may scare him/her off. Hopefully, if you are in the *shidduch* system, both of you are in the mind-set to make a serious commitment.

Girl to fiancé: "When we're married I want to share all your troubles and worries."

Fiancé: "But I don't have any troubles and worries."

Girl: "I know, but we're not married yet."

9: Recognizing the Right and Wrong Person

The longest sentence anyone can make with two words is "I do."

—*H. L. Mencken*

Many people think a good marriage partner is one with whom you have fun, feel chemistry, and enjoy romance. These ingredients are wonderful and should be present in a marriage, but they don't make a marriage. These ingredients keep a person interested enough to find out if there is substance while dating; however, they do not help you truly evaluate whether your date is a suitable life partner. In order for love to last, one's choice of whom to marry must be grounded in reality. We cannot allow our chemical impulses to control our rational thinking, blinding us to another's shortcomings. Be sure to distinguish between love and infatuation.

Webster wrote the dictionary because of his wife. Every time he opened his mouth, she said, "Now what's that supposed to mean?"

It is a mistake to be lured by outward trappings such as beauty or money. Although attraction is necessary, infatuation wears off and then the work begins. Therefore, besides chemistry, which is the mysterious ingredient of personal attraction, there is a practical side to choosing a mate that requires thoughtful consideration.

The right spouse will help you navigate your way through life while someone you may be infatuated with can deter you, sending you down a path that you never intended to travel. Too often, people forget to take the long-term picture into account. You need to decide if this person will help you grow. When you choose a mate for the right reasons, you will respect each other, develop an appreciation for one another, and be dedicated to each other's dreams and goals.

Nothing's more expensive than a girl who's free for the evening.

Love at first sight sounds great, but it is rarely real love. A psychologist's rule is: "If it seems too good to be true, it usually is." Get to know a person. Be wary if s/he is rushing you to commit before you truly get to know one another. If someone wants to marry you without knowing you, it's superficial. S/he either wants a commitment before you discover something about him/her or s/he is interested in you for your looks, money, status, or what you can do for him/her.

When we look for a life partner we usually are concerned about personality, intelligence, financial standing, religious conviction, family background, mutual goals and interests, and looks. These all have some effect on the course of a marriage, but how we act, because of or in response to each of these characteristics, is more important than the characteristic itself.

I've had bad luck with both my wives. The first one left me and the second one didn't.
—*Patrick Murray*

A marriage can fail because people are unable to judge a prospective marriage partner with objectivity. Most men and women are unaware of their subconscious inclinations, which either drive them toward or away from marrying a certain individual. People should be attracted to a potential spouse, but it is difficult to think clearly in areas as sensitive as love and human relations. Is your attraction toward your date based on an objective appraisal of his/her qualities, or are you subconsciously projecting virtues where there are none, and ignoring disturbing character flaws?

Your date comes to the door. Her slip is showing, her lipstick is crooked, and her left shoe has toilet paper stuck to it. Diplomacy is the art of explaining the surprise recurrence of your malaria a minute ago!

People often close their eyes, unwilling to see what they don't want to see. If you are looking for someone cultured and refined, don't settle for a narrow-minded and crude person. If you are you searching for spirituality, don't tolerate a materialistic personality. If you want a warm, happy, and accepting spouse, don't settle for one who is indifferent, depressed, self-centered, or judgmental. Loving a person won't magically erase his/her bad traits.

Being cognizant of a person's flaws does not mean rejecting him/her. We all have faults. Look at this person's flaws in relation to his/her positive traits. Assess the flaws, deciding whether you can, or indeed should, tolerate the shortcomings. Try to get a realistic picture of your date.

While waiting their turn in a drugstore, Gittel spotted a scale next to the register. Gittel got on and a moment later a card came out. It read, "You are warmhearted, lovable, understanding, and an excellent cook." Peeking over his wife's shoulder, Moishe said, "It didn't get your weight right either."

Search for a friend, someone you can talk to and confide in; who listens, tries to understand you, and values your opinion; someone whom you can trust and whose character you admire; someone with a healthy self-esteem, who knows how to define boundaries (see chapter 26, "Boundaries"); a person who understands the value of compromise and has grown up with good role models and admirable morals.

Experience has taught me that looking into an individual's family and upbringing is one of the best ways to judge a person. My grandmother often said, "The apple doesn't fall far from the tree." People are a product of their parents and the experiences they provide. Although there are no guarantees, good, healthy homes usually produce good, healthy, well-adjusted children. Sensitive, honest, and respectful interaction between generations of grandparents, parents, and children, between husband and wife and among siblings, are the seeds that produce fine people.

It is wise to find someone whose background and beliefs are similar to yours. Although people can weather their differences, it often brings extra conflicts and challenges. Common backgrounds result in common expectations.

Look for someone who is committed to work on him-/herself and wishes to do his/her part to develop a solid and mutual relationship.

G-d made Adam and then He rested. He made Eve, and since then nobody's rested.

Is his/her personality what you truly want? Everyone is entitled to his/her personal preferences. Where someone shy and demure may feel right to one person, another may be more comfortable with someone talkative and outgoing. One may prefer organized and scheduled, while someone else is happier with easygoing and unpredictable. Only you can decide what feels right for you.

Someone may possess qualities you enjoy, but can you live with those qualities for a lifetime? You may find a comedian pleasurable when you are dining out but prefer marriage to a serious guy. You may have fun with an outspoken fellow but feel more comfortable with a quiet one. A boy may be impressed with sophistication but feel at ease with a low-key girl. He may find a woman who is intellectually challenging to be interesting but discover he has an easier time relating to a simpler woman who appreciates his intellect. She may have thought she wanted someone confident and aggressive but find that this stifles her personality. Look for someone who brings out the best in you and makes you feel most comfortable with yourself.

Beware of incongruent behavior, such as if your date tells you one thing but you are seeing something else. If s/he says s/he respects you but treats you with disrespect or if s/he claims to care for you but never answers your phone calls, these are red flags.

Dating is like fishing. You may have to go through lots of worms until you get a good catch.

Is she extremely sensitive and overly dependent? Will this get on your nerves, or do you appreciate someone who makes you feel needed? Is he lovable and loving? Is she complimentary or does she frequently criticize you? Is he inflexible? Is she domineering? Is he happy and easygoing or serious and intense? Is she positive or cynical? Watch out for a person who believes s/he is never wrong, blames you for everything, and never apologizes for any deed. Examine every aspect of a person's personality and ego to decide how this will affect you, and if this will enhance or hurt your potential for enjoying a satisfying life.

Do you enjoy each other's company? Is s/he pleasant to be with? Do you have common interests? If you say, "Let's go bowling," does she look at you as if you are from another planet? When she says she wants to go to the museum, do you think, *She can't subject me to that.* You may still be compatible if you find a friend to bowl with while she goes to the museum with her friend, provided there are other interests the two of you share.

Look for maturity and responsibility. Mature people are committed to working at a marriage. They are willing to give and share without constantly measuring or worrying that everything is tit for tat.

Does s/he communicate well with you? Does he "get" what you are saying? Is she tuned in to your needs and feelings? Is he easily upset or angered? Does she seem to have a good sense of self? Does he turn small issues into major offenses?

Does she consider how many hours you have been driving before she asks you to take another long drive? Is s/he angry or merely disappointed that you had an exam this morning, and are too tired to stay out late? His/her reactions to these situations tell you if s/he can be empathetic and understanding. Is this person someone who will be there for you and try to meet your emotional needs?

Watch out for avoidant behavior. If after dating for a while s/he refuses to discuss family, to reveal personal information, or to meet your friends, this is a sign that a person has something to hide. If a person shuts down and doesn't listen to you but rather is so self-absorbed as to only want to hear him-/herself, be careful.

He never got married. He said he didn't want to make the same mistake once.

When I asked my cousin what made him decide his *kallah*, fiancée, was the right girl for him, he beautifully replied, "I saw that she is *simchadik* and *tochendik* — She is happy and has substance."

Don't spend the date continually assessing your partner or you won't relax enough to get to know him/her, but do be cognizant of his/her behavior. If a guy indifferently arrives late, if a girl intentionally keeps you waiting, if he is antsy in a traffic jam, if she can't wait peacefully for a table in a restaurant, if he fights with the maître d' over seating, if she complains that the restaurant isn't nice enough, if he is more concerned about his car than his date, notice and assess these traits. If the waiter makes a mistake with the order, the driver in front of you nastily cuts in front of your car, or your plans get messed up, your date's reaction reveals a wealth of well-kept secrets. Does s/he scream or use inappropriate language, or accept it with calm and sensitivity? Does s/he retain the anger for a long while or is s/he able to forget about it and move on? Is s/he understanding and forgiving? Does s/he easily bounce back, think straight, readjust, and move forward? These reactions are excellent indicators, helping you decide if this person is rigid and difficult to live with, or well-balanced and flexible.

Always be aware that any person you marry will have some issues or behaviors that are not exactly to your liking. This does not mean you should reject that individual. It means you should understand which issues you can or cannot accept.

The little sensitivities and details can tell a bigger story. If you are seated under an air-conditioning vent in a restaurant, is s/he concerned about your comfort? Does he offer to switch seats with you or give you his jacket? Does she worry that you feel cold or uncomfortable? Does he ask for another table or does he just expect you to adjust? These kindnesses are what make marriage feel nurturing and safe.

This is the time to notice whether s/he is caring and considerate. Does s/he seem to notice only what you can do for him/her, rather than consider what s/he can do for you? You need to know that s/he is capable of giving as well as receiving love.

A man asks his wife, "Darling, how did you get the car into the living room?"
She sweetly replies, "I turned left at the kitchen."

How does s/he drive a car? Is he cautious or aggressive? Is s/he polite, letting other cars join the lane, or nasty? Of course you shouldn't judge someone based on one experience or a single observation.

Pay close attention to the stories s/he tells you about him-/herself. This is how s/he is representing him-/herself, giving you information about who s/he is when s/he is not with you. Do not dismiss anything that makes you cringe. This is the time to explore any disturbing elements, checking them out to get a complete picture of your date.

Notice how your date acts when s/he thinks no one is watching or judging him/her. Everything is observable, because most people are external beings. They can put on an act for a while, but given time, the real personality usually emerges. It's your job to take time to get insight into the total person.

As soon as Susie left for the ladies' room, Jack unabashedly berated the waiter in front of her friends. Later, when her friends told Susie how Jack had embarrassed the poor waiter, she assumed they were exaggerating. She found herself married to a guy who was critical and domineering. Listen to all the information without brushing anything off.

Be careful of an individual who has a terrible temper, who abuses or bashes others, or who speaks *lashon hara* (bad-mouths others). How a person treats others is a direct reflection of how s/he will treat you.

Wife to husband: "I need a new dress."

Husband: "What's wrong with the dress you've got?"

Wife: "It's too long and the veil keeps getting in my eyes."

Be on guard for anyone who is cheap with money, time,

or attention. If you are at the bottom of your date's to do list, don't accept this.

It's not hard to meet expenses...they're everywhere.

Watch how a person tips or how s/he gives charity when approached by someone on the street. Even if s/he is uncomfortable giving money to a beggar on the street, there are those who respectfully decline, while others treat this type of person with contempt.

A woman had plastic surgery the other day. Her husband cut up her credit cards!

Watch how a person shops. It is most informative. Is he tight or generous? Is she a smart shopper or does she buy everything she sees despite your budget? Is he critical of the service? Does she complain that everything is overpriced? Is shopping together fun or difficult?

Does she seem oblivious about spending lots of someone else's money? Is he so tight that he is unwilling to pay for even a Coke? Does she enjoy only high-end products?

My wife makes the budget work. We go without a lot of things I don't need.

Young couples are often naive about money matters, unaware of the budgeting that must accompany buying power. To be aware of your own financial outlook, discuss your feelings and expectations in this domain with each other. Are you both responsible about money? Do you have a similar philosophy about spending and saving? Are you conscious of your income and spending without being uptight? Is s/he generous or frugal? Is s/he practical and reasonable? Are you realistic about what's appropriate to spend? You may have different philosophies, but can the two of you calmly and rationally discuss and compromise on a budget?

I always just hoped that I'd meet some nice, friendly girl, like the look of her, hope the look of me didn't make her physically sick, then pop the question and, um, settle down and be happy. It worked for my parents. Well, apart from the divorce and all that.
—*Actor Tom Fleet, Four Weddings and a Funeral*

The way a person is brought up shapes his/her attitude and behavior. People's personalities, actions, and reactions are heavily influenced by what they saw in their home. You will have a better idea of who a person truly is if you can find out about any traumas or significant occurrences in that person's life. Usually, the children in a well-adjusted family have been exposed to good values and behavioral patterns.

Background checks involving divorcés/divorcées or children of divorced parents can be cause for concern. However, although divorce carries with it significant issues, if someone has processed his/her own or parents' divorce in a healthy way and has grown from the experience, developing a solid understanding of what marriage truly requires, there is no reason to presume that this issue is different from any other marital challenge people face.

The trouble with some women is that they get all excited about nothing – and then they marry him.
—*Cher*

Try to learn all you can about a person's social life. Friends are a major influence on a person's thoughts and behavior. You can tell a lot about a person by observing whom they choose as their friends, how they interact, and how and where they socialize. Before becoming engaged, observe him/her in various settings and interactions with other people.

Why don't Jews drink? It interferes with their suffering!

Marriage is a lifelong commitment, so it is important to know the challenges a person faces, especially regarding his/her physical and mental well-being. Are there any signs of addictive or emotional issues such as depression, obsessive-compulsive disorder, or bipolar or borderline personality disorders that haven't been properly managed? Are there eating disorders such as anorexia or bulimia that should be considered?

In his lecture "Mind over Matter," Rabbi Dr. Abraham Twerski encourages people to look out for these problems while dating. Unfortunately, although these problems are prevalent, they often remain undetected until after marriage.

All of these problems can affect the quality of your future with this person. Honestly assess the extent of these issues and whether you can reasonably handle them.

Some people don't realize that the Ten Commandments aren't multiple choice!

Religious and spiritual beliefs are another important arena to explore, in order to assess compatibility. Does s/he preach one thing but do another? Does he study *Pirkei Avos* — Ethics of our Fathers — yet act unkind? Is she lax about religious practices that are important to you? Do you want more religion in your day-to-day life than s/he has in mind? Religious differences are too important to be overlooked. Make sure you have a rabbi or mentor whom you trust that you both feel comfortable talking to about this as well as other marital issues.

He was a responsible worker. If anything went wrong, they said he was responsible for it.

You should know something about your potential spouse's education and job history. Does s/he have a steady job? Do you have the same standard of living in mind? Does he plan to learn, work, or combine both of these activities? Can you respect his/her level of education? Does s/he plan to continue her education? Does s/he work well with others? Is s/he willing to work hard? Some people research even more, finding out if the person is in debt, owns property, or will come into an inheritance.

Richard applied for work but was told that the company had more employees than it needed.

"Don't worry," said Richard, "The little work I do won't be noticed."

Is this man bright enough for you? Is this woman intuitive enough? Is he sharp enough? Does she understand your humor? Does he have street smarts? Does she read a newspaper; does he read books? Your IQs don't have to match to a tee, but you need to be intellectually compatible.

Someone stole all my credit cards, but I won't be reporting it. The thief spends less than my wife does.

Are you comfortable with each other's lifestyle? Do you feel that you both want the same things in life? Lifestyles differ dramatically, depending on who is responsible for supporting the family. If both of you plan to work, you will need to discuss child-rearing and housekeeping responsibilities. If a woman expects her husband to provide for her, she'd better make sure he is willing and able to do so. If she wants to work, her husband must be someone who respects a woman who works. Conversely, a man who wants his wife to get a job outside the home has to be sure his wife is willing to work. Discuss these issues to make sure you both have the same vision for your future.

My wife is so neat she has slipcovers for everything. I can understand the couch and the chairs, but the refrigerator?

Cleanliness, or lack thereof, is another significant character trait to assess. Is this person a neat freak or a slovenly mess? Is s/he organized or is his/her life in disarray? Can this person run a home? How does this person dress? Do you feel proud or embarrassed to be seen with her/him? Some people become more responsible once they are married; some don't. Kids who never dreamed of cleaning up after themselves suddenly become model homemakers because now it is their responsibility; others continue to drop their clothing on the floor even after marriage. You have to make sure you can live with these idiosyncrasies if s/he doesn't seem to have the potential to change. No one is flawless, but every individual can accept and cope with different flaws. Determine your own tolerance level.

When my husband comes home at night, if my children are still alive, hey, I've done my job!

—Roseanne Barr

Of course, part of seeking a suitable spouse includes assessing his/her potential as a future parent. Will s/he be a devoted father or mother? People tend to either imitate their parents or do the opposite of what they saw in their parents' home, so you can make some educated guesses by observing the person in the framework of his/her family. How does he treat his siblings? Does she have patience for children? Are his parents disciplinarians? Are her parents close with their kids? Would you be happy if your children took after this person? Discuss your views on disciplinary measures and child-rearing techniques. If you have different points of view, are you both willing to explore different child-rearing methods?

Once you are dating someone for a while, introduce him/her to your family and friends, so you can see how s/he deals with and adjusts to different circumstances and settings.

When the Home for the Aged asked him for a donation, he gave them his mother and father.

Observe your date's parents. Do they speak politely to one another? Do they respect each other's opinions? Do they seem to share common values, interests, and disciplinary methods? How do the parents treat their children? Are the children respected, allowed to express themselves, and allowed to make mistakes? Are the kids scared or comfortable with their parents? Is the family rigid and opinionated, or easygoing and cooperative? Does the home seem like a happy one where laughter pervades, or is there an air of anger, jealousy, or distrust? Do either of the parents have traits that you would not want your spouse to inherit?

How does your date treat his/her parents? How does s/he speak about them? Does she refuse to make any decisions without consulting her mother? Does he speak disparagingly about his father?

Unfortunately, there are people who are products of dysfunctional families or adverse circumstances. Be aware of significant family dynamics; be wary if there is a dysfunctional relationship between siblings or between a child and a parent. When communication between close family members has been severed for an extended period of time, there is major cause for concern.

I stopped going to the psychiatrist because he kept asking me the same question my wife asks: "Who do you think you are?"

Does your date get along with your relatives and friends? Does your family have bad vibes from him/her? Does everyone tell you to stay away from her? Does he make everyone feel uncomfortable? Don't ignore warning signs. Even if s/he acts the perfect gentleman around you, s/he might let down his/her guard when you are not around.

"Last night my wife had a dream in which she was married to a millionaire."

"You're a lucky guy. My wife dreams that during the day!"

Two people may enjoy each other's company while dating, yet their goals may not be compatible because they have different visions about family and recreation. She may be content with a simple life, while he hopes for a lavish lifestyle. He may enjoy the job he has, but she is much more ambitious. She may love to travel, while he refuses to leave his little village. He may love to party, and she only feels comfortable in the privacy of her own home.

She may enjoy loads of company, but he feels that's an invasion of his privacy. He may be dreaming of moving to a foreign country one day and she won't even entertain the possibility. Don't ignore these differences, assuming they will just work themselves out after marriage.

"Honey, I had a dream last night in which you bought me a new mink coat."

"In tonight's dream see if you can come up with the money."

It is much easier to discuss these dreams and goals while you are dating. The differences only become more glaring once you are married, so take the time to work them through now, and know what you are both planning.

About the only time a woman really succeeds in changing a male is when he's a baby.

Don't assume you will change the other one's attitude. A common misconception is: *If he really loves me, he will do it for me.* The other person is probably thinking the same thing, and that can lead to the creation of two disillusioned individuals.

It is best to have an open relationship in which you are honest with yourself and one another. Assess your compatibility, because marriage is not about each one's individual qualities; it's whether the combination of these qualities makes sense. Discuss your strengths and weaknesses as a couple so you can strategize from this point forward. If both of you believe you are good at supporting a family but neither feels comfortable organizing a home, consider how to handle this aspect of your lives. If each of you feels you will be great at child care but neither of you feels capable of earning a solid living, examine whether your combination makes for a successful marriage. You can consult experts, find role models, or get advice from couples just a few years ahead of yourselves.

Talk about marriage and the unique relationship it offers before you commit to each other, to get a sense of how each of you feels about matrimony. This is a good way to find out whether someone is really interested in you and in marriage itself. Is the discussion a positive, uplifting experience, or is he contemplating it with dread? Is she forced into this discussion? Is it one she'd rather not have? Does she tell warm, funny stories about married people she knows, or does every tale finish on a depressing note? Do his stories always defend the husband, hinting that any problems were the wife's fault? Does he emphasize the ideals of compromise and working together, or does he seem to encourage divorce? Does she stress the freedom and independence she insists on retaining? Is he more focused on his nights with you or on his nights out with his friends? Does his/her Torah learning translate into *middos tovos*, pleasing character traits?

"Marriage certificate" is just another term for a work permit.

Make sure you can love this person the way s/he is. Of course, even while committing to accept your differences, you can grow together in order to make each other happy.

Realize that some differences are irreconcilable, while others can be worked out. It is important to understand what can't or likely won't be altered. Most people will not, and should not, compromise on their health, religion, family relationships, lifelong friendships, and self-respect.

At the end of a party a guest said to Chico Marx, "I would like to say good-bye to your wife."

"Who wouldn't?" Marx replied.

Don't marry someone who will never meet your expectations or live up to your ideals. If you only respect someone who works, don't marry someone who doesn't believe in working. If you only respect someone who is learning, don't even date someone who does not share the same conviction. A person must respect his own non-negotiable needs and principles. This is not to encourage someone to be inflexible. A smart woman who is looking for a Torah learner who is aware of life's financial demands, might do well to consider a man who would love to devote his time exclusively to Torah study, but knows it is his job to support a family.

Marriage is a wonderful institution, but who wants to live in an institution?

—Groucho Marx

Life will not be perfect once you marry; life's ups and downs will be there just as they were there when you were single. Marriage is the challenge of creating a comfortable existence with another person, with the benefit of a partner to share the vicissitudes of life. Choose carefully.

When you come to a fork in the road, take it.

—Yogi Berra

Keep examining. If you think you are on the same path, yet each time you come to a fork in the road each of you chooses a different direction, this may be a red flag. You may have a fabulous connection if the two of you share a common interest in the arts, dreaming of becoming great painters. But if one of you wants to live in Paris spending your days and nights painting, while the other wants to paint in addition to having a home in the suburbs and raising a bunch of children, are you compatible? The grand, idealistic part of your dream and your needs seems perfect, but you must also examine the total picture, making sure it appeals to you. The frame comes with a whole picture. Be sure you see it and like it in its entirety.

Most importantly, never accept someone with an abusive personality. Choose someone who admires you and treats you respectfully, and after that, there is no wrong or right in determining who is right for you. Only you can determine that you have heard the "click" that says: "Yes, this is right!"

My wife says I have only two faults – everything I say and everything I do.

Size up the person you are dating and determine whether you are comfortable with his/her character, personality, religious standards, maturity level, values, attitude, disposition, outlook, and future plans. If all seems well, move forward.

A man and his friend are playing golf one day at their local golf course. One of the guys is about to chip onto the green when he sees a long funeral procession on the road next to the course. He stops in mid-swing, takes off his golf cap, closes his eyes, and bows in prayer.

His friend says, "Wow! That is the most thoughtful gesture I have ever seen. You truly are a kind man."

The man replies, "Yeah, well, it's the least I can do considering that we were married for thirty-five years."

10: Signs of Abusive Behavior

Once I got into a fight with a really big guy, and he said, "I'm going to mop the floor with your face."

"You'll be sorry," I said.

"Oh, yeah? Why?"

"Well, you won't be able to get into corners very well."
—*Emo Phillips*

It says in *Tehillim* (34:15), "Keep away from evil and do good." This certainly applies to one's spouse. Do not hurt your spouse, either with words or deeds.

Does this person make you feel insecure, guilty, controlled, or defensive? Does s/he act superior, excessively angry, sulky, or withdrawn? Does s/he exhibit extreme mood swings? Does s/he act kind one minute and cruel the next? Does s/he exhibit anger that seems so threatening, you change your behavior because of it, or feel forced to do things that contradict your principles or better judgment? Is s/he manipulative, insulting, belittling, or overly insecure? Is s/he unable to handle frustration without becoming angry, sulky, or withdrawn? Is s/he jealous or accusatory? Does s/he always blame, curse, or ignore you? Does s/he exhibit a low tolerance for frustration or anxiety? Is s/he overly sensitive to criticism, whether real or perceived? Is his/her personality suspicious, fearful, distrustful, or paranoid? Is this someone who wants immediate gratification, with little or no consideration for the consequences? Is s/he moody and quick-tempered? Does s/he threaten violence against him-/herself or others? Does s/he always view him-/herself as a victim rather than victimizer? These are telling characteristics, red flags of emotional abuse. It is vital to recognize these and all other abusive traits and take them as warning signs.

Although each characteristic mentioned above does not necessarily make one an abusive person, each is worth watching. In some cases, an abuser may exhibit only one behavior in an exaggerated fashion. Someone exhibiting a few of these behaviors should trigger a flashing red light in your brain.

Both men and women can be abusive. By learning to identify these patterns and signals, you can stop unhealthy relationships as soon as the abuse begins. Abusers are skilled at acting, so you probably won't experience abuse until the abuser is sure you are under his/her control. This type of person often excuses the behavior by claiming that you are overreacting or overly sensitive and that everyone talks or acts this way. But that is not true. Everyone has the right to be spoken to and treated with respect.

Controlling behaviors are not the result of stress, anger,

drugs, or alcohol. They are learned behaviors that one person uses to dominate, intimidate, and manipulate another person.

Jealousy is a form of abuse in which your partner tries to control your life and relationships; this includes controlling which friends you see, what relationships you keep, and even how you dress. This is often done under the guise of caring; the abuser claims that his actions are a sign of love and concern. Jealousy has nothing to do with love and everything to do with possessiveness and lack of trust. As this behavior becomes more severe, it is more easily recognizable as abuse. It includes checking your phone or Internet to monitor your activities there, or checking your mileage to see where you drove.

Anyone who uses physical coercion to attain your compliance and invades your personal space by sitting too close to you, or who touches you when you have asked him/her not to, is being physically violent with you.

Both emotional and physical abuse are extremely painful, and the abused partner requires major help.

There was a study done in Maine that found that if you marry someone who doesn't appreciate you, tries to control you, and always has to be right, you may be unhappy. They also discovered that going without water for long periods of time makes you thirsty.

—*Caroline Rhea*

An abuser typically comes on like a whirlwind, claiming, "You are the only person I could ever talk to" or "I've never felt like this for anyone before." With phrases like "If you love me, I am all you need and you are all I need," an abuser attempts to isolate you from your friends and family and pressure you to commit to the relationship. Generally, s/he is chronically unemployed and always feeling as if someone is out to get him/her. S/he blames you for anything that goes wrong and then says "You make me mad," or "You are hurting me by not doing what I want you to do," using your feelings to manipulate you. This type of person is easily insulted, claiming s/he is hurt when s/he is actually angry. Every setback is taken as a personal attack. Being called in to work overtime, receiving a traffic ticket, or being asked to help others with chores can generate a rant.

Someone who is preoccupied with violence; or who has pathological issues such as fighting, setting fires, and rejecting authority; or who has battered someone before; or who threatens violence, breaks objects, or physically restrains you, is prone to being physically abusive. Indeed, such behavior usually escalates over time.

Why don't you leave and let live?

Be extremely careful if you suspect that the person you are seeing may have abusive character traits. Don't allow excuses to cloud your vision. See a person for what s/he truly is. Marry a person who will treat you with the love and respect that every human being deserves.

Husband at a performance: "Can you see, dear?"
Wife: "Yes."
Hubby: "Is there a draft on you?"
Wife: "No."
Husband: "Is your seat comfortable?"
Wife: "Yes."
Husband: "Let's change seats."

11: Research

To err is human. To admit it isn't!

A car that was driving at night crashed into a speeding train. The family of the deceased auto driver sued the railroad company. The lawyer for the plaintiff questioned the stationmaster, who testified on behalf of the insurance company. He claimed that the barrier post, which should have come down, was broken that night, and therefore he himself went out with a lantern, waving it to warn cars of the approaching train. When he saw the car approaching at high speed he waved the lantern frantically, but the car never slowed down, and therefore it crashed into the train. The jury felt the auto driver was at fault for not heeding the warning and ruled in favor of the insurance company.

After the verdict, a lawyer on the defense team who represented the insurance company asked the stationmaster,

"You seemed so calm and confident during your testimony. Was there any time during the cross-examination when you were nervous?"

"Yes," responded the stationmaster. "I was petrified when I thought the plaintiff's lawyer might ask me if the bulb in the lantern had been working that night!" In this famous legal case, the lantern had been waved although the bulb in the lantern was not working. But because the question was never asked, the jury was misled.

When researching for marriage, it is nearly impossible to know if you are asking the right questions and getting all the facts. For different reasons, much of the information you receive will be one-sided. People who want the date to occur will dwell only on the person's positive qualities, without mentioning any faults. Others may have personal motives to block the date, such as wanting that person for their own child, or resenting that she seems to date all the good guys. Still others don't want to mention negative things about the person in question, afraid to take responsibility for harming a match. Sometimes they worry that their words will get back to the person in question. They may tell you a person is wonderful without mentioning their suspicions that s/he is manic depressive, abusive, a miser, or exhibits other problematic behaviors.

Rabbi Weiss was shaking hands with his congregants when he saw Gideon. Pulling him aside, he said, "I think you have to join Hashem's army."

"But I'm already in Hashem's army," replied Gideon.

"So *nu*, how come I don't see you in shul except on Rosh Hashanah and Yom Kippur?" asked Rabbi Weiss.

Gideon whispered, "I'm in the secret service."

People who have something to hide often know how to hide it. People who are deceptive are able to deceive. Individuals with negative traits are careful to conceal them. Even knowing a person very well does not guarantee that you will not be fooled. The entire truth about the person and his/her family is often revealed only after marriage.

"Did you tell everybody?"

"No. I didn't know it was supposed to be a secret!"

It is up to you to get to know your date as best as possible by getting feedback from others, familiarizing yourself with those in his/her life, including family, peers, rabbi, boss, and so forth, and doing some basic research. After this, only prayer can help.

Be certain to consult reliable people who are well intentioned and well informed, who possess good insight, and who have your best interests at heart.

We had to fire our maid because she spilled things. She told the other maids what went on in our house.

Shira found out the inside story about a girl she was looking into for her son from the girl's housekeeper. Shira had her housekeeper ask the girl's parents' housekeeper to describe the family.

The housekeeper said, "It is a very nice family but watch out when the father gets mad."

"Why?" asked Shira. "What does he do?"

"When he gets angry at the table he throws dishes. But he doesn't hit with a belt, only with his hands."

Obviously Shira was not interested in pursuing this match.

Someone asked Gladys if she thought Sharon would be a good match for Gary. Gladys, who knew Gary well, suddenly realized that Gary was a terrific boy who would make a great husband for her own daughter. She quickly said, "Gary's nice but he is too quiet and introverted for Sharon." Gladys nixed the match for her own selfish reasons. Even people who consider themselves truthful individuals can do things like this, rationalizing that they are honestly being helpful.

As part of a diet, I took up exercising by riding horses. It worked. In three weeks the horse lost eighteen pounds!

After Ralph agreed to date Lisa, someone pointed out to him that Lisa had once been heavy, so she could potentially regain that weight. Ralph reneged, refusing to date Lisa. Lisa remained thin her whole life, while Ralph's wife was never able to lose the weight she gained with her first pregnancy.

Brenda asked me about Shawn, who had been married to Molly, one of my closest friends. I knew that he had physically and mentally abused her and was divorced from his second wife as well. When Brenda called, I felt it was my duty to tell her what I knew. Brenda's response was, "Well, he is dating my cousin. I'll tell her, but I am sure she will marry him anyway. She is alone and her husband ran off with one of her kids."

At this point I asked, "What could I tell you that would dissuade her?"

"Nothing, I guess," she answered.

"Then why are you bothering to do research?"

"My cousin just wanted to know."

Research is important, but don't bother researching if you will totally disregard your findings.

When Michelle was asked about her ex-boyfriend Alex, she angrily stated that he was as cheap as they come. In truth he was quite generous, but she was furious that he had dropped her, and this was her revenge. You can't believe everything you hear, but that doesn't mean you should ignore something you hear from a reliable source, especially if the facts point to its accuracy.

In the final analysis, the best type of research is the kind you conduct yourself by getting to know a person well.

I discuss some of the *halachos*, Jewish laws, of disclosing or not disclosing *shidduch* information in the chapter "Problems with Research" in my book *The Art of the Date*. According to the Chofetz Chaim, although *lashon hara* is forbidden, for *shidduch* purposes, under the right circumstances, as long as one makes it perfectly clear whether s/he is certain of the information being revealed, one is permitted to tell someone what s/he knows about the person in question. The rule of thumb is: When unsure, consult your rabbi.

Waiting on the platform at the train station, Samuel asks a man standing nearby for the time. The man ignores him. Samuel asks again, and the man continues to ignore him. Frustrated, Samuel asks, "Excuse me, but I've twice asked you for the time. Why are you ignoring me?"

The man looks up and says, "Look, we're both waiting for the same train. If I answer you, when we board the train you will probably sit next to me, we will start talking, and I'll invite you to my house for a meal. There, you will meet my daughter, you will probably like her, and eventually you'll want to marry her. Now, let me be honest with you from the start: Why would I want a son-in-law who can't even afford a watch?"

12: The Right Person Is Not a Perfect Person

The right person to marry is someone who meets your needs. Any combination of looks, personality, disposition, intellect, warmth, potential, shared dreams, common goals, and so forth, that works for you is right.

Find the combination that makes you happy. You will need to compromise in some areas and you will get a better deal in other ways. People's positive attributes are often the flip side of their negative traits. An easygoing fellow may not be aggressive in business. A real go-getter may not have the patience to stay home.

The most important ingredient in a relationship is a good, caring individual who wants to make you happy. A selfish, self-centered person who thinks marriage is only about him-/herself makes an inflexible spouse.

12: The Right Person Is Not a Perfect Person • 77

He found it impossible to make a date. When he'd try talking to a girl, his tongue would twist up like a pretzel. On impulse, he went to a bookstore, looking for something that might help him overcome his timidity. A book entitled *Ways to Women*, displayed on the non-fiction rack, caught his eye. Blowing his whole allowance, he bought the book, rushed home, and discovered that he had purchased volume 10 of the encyclopedia.

Here are some basic don'ts. Don't make unrealistic demands. Don't make snap judgments. Don't reject someone without giving him/her the same chance you would want for yourself. Don't ask silly questions like: "Do you put ketchup bottles directly on your elegant table or do you transfer the ketchup to a pretty dish?" Don't make ridiculous remarks like: "I can't date him because I heard he started walking a bit late."

Be friendly and receptive when you meet someone, giving him/her time to loosen up, feel comfortable, and make a proper impression. Be open-minded. It is unrealistic to make lists of demands etched in stone. Keep refining your list, asking yourself: Do I really need someone gorgeous? Do I need the most popular or funniest person? Do I need someone who is brilliant? Do I need someone with a top career, or one with an outstanding family? Is someone who loves to travel important?

Isn't it more important to find someone who loves and appreciates you, sharing your dreams, goals, and beliefs? Isn't it more important to find someone whom you can respect and enjoy spending time with, while being your real self? There is a major difference between what you want and what you really need. No one gets everything he wants or needs, but most people are smart enough to recognize that what they have found can fulfill their needs, and become what they want and appreciate.

When the window of opportunity appears, don't pull down the shade.

You may need someone who is exceptional in a particular area. A brilliant scientist may find a person with a normal IQ an unacceptable choice, but ordinary looks will be something s/he can accept. Once you realize which of your demands are necessities and which are non-essential luxuries, you will have an easier time finding your life partner.

My husband said he needed more space so I locked him outside.

—*Roseanne Barr*

Mature adults don't expect one person to fulfill all their needs. Friends or relatives can meet some needs, while personal introspection and achievements will fulfill others. Be certain your potential spouse has the desire to make you the center of his/her existence (or at the very least an integral part of it) and that his/her priorities are in sync with your own. Then the small needs can be supplemented with other people and outside activities. If your spouse is not funny enough, you can call a friend for a few good laughs. If your spouse doesn't spend all your leisure time with you, occupy yourself with activities like reading, painting, shopping, or working.

A man inserted an ad in the classifieds: Wife wanted. Next day he received a hundred letters. They all said

the same thing: **You can have mine.**

Opposites often attract, but people who are alike are drawn to one another just as often. No matter which type of couple you are, you and your spouse will not be carbon copies; you will have many differences that make sharing a life interesting. Just make sure you respect those differences while sharing many common interests and goals.

A marriage is finalized at the wedding ceremony, when the *chassan*, groom, says, "*Harei at mekudeshes li*, You are designated and consecrated to me according to the laws of Moses and Israel." The choice of the word *mekudeshes*, consecrated, signifies that marriage is infused with sanctity. The marriage is set apart for G-d and apart from the rest of the world. Therefore, a couple separates from the rest of the world in order to have this *kedushah*, holiness, penetrate and elevate them. For a marriage to be holy, this sanctity must be pervasive. Hashem wants these two individuals to create their own world. To do so, each spouse must make his/her spouse the focus of his/her life, so together they may be elevated to the heights of *kedushah* (Marcus, Rav Yaakov, essay in *Sason Vesimcha: An Anthology of Divrei Torah for Sheva Brachos*, p. 88).

"Will you please tell me what a wife really is? Some of my friends say their wife is an angel and others say theirs is a she-devil."

"Well, a wife is a woman who will stick by you in all the trouble you would never have gotten into had you not married her in the first place."

13: Rejection

Be discerning but don't be overly critical.

You meet a woman and put her on a pedestal. Ten years later you put her on a diet.

Many people misconstrue reality, finding fault with everyone. Indeed, if you look for faults in people, you can always find them. The trick is to look for the positive aspects in people while recognizing their negative traits. As long as those negative traits are within the realm of normal behavior, you may be able to live with them.

Myra fixed up Shmuel with Ellen. Shmuel didn't like the shoes Ellen wore, so after the date he told Myra, "She's not for me."

"Wasn't Ellen very pretty?" Sharon asked.

"Yes," answered Shmuel.

"Wasn't Ellen outgoing and fun to be with?"

"Yes," answered Shmuel.

"And wasn't Ellen exceptionally nice?"

"Yes," answered Shmuel.

"So," said Myra, "what's the big deal? Shoes can be changed."

Shmuel answered, "The thing is, I don't like the fact that Ellen chose those shoes."

Myra could not convince Shmuel to give Ellen another chance. Perhaps she could not tell Shmuel to his face how juvenile he was behaving, but I would have loved to tell him, "If the shoe fits…wear it."

People tend to be overly critical. Mrs. Stein told a matchmaker, "You set my daughter up with half a guy." The matchmaker answered, "What are you talking about? Didn't he have legs?" The matchmaker believed that a silly statement deserved a silly answer.

"You look like my first husband."

"How many times have you been married?"

"None."

A boy's mother inquired about a prospective date for her son, asking, "When was the girl toilet trained?" I guess it's better than asking whether she was toilet trained or not. The mother explained that if the girl was trained at an early age, she believed her son would wind up with a domineering mother-in-law. Maybe he would wind up with a domineering mother-in-law; he certainly already had a ridiculous mother.

My grandfather often said, "Don't overestimate yourself and don't underestimate the other person."

Mrs. Young told the matchmaker, "You don't understand how great my son is. He's a blue chip." The matchmaker answered, "I don't know if you've heard, but the stock market has been going down."

Of course, don't underestimate yourself either. If someone suggests a match, you need not accept it immediately; just make sure to say no in a kind and sensitive manner. An appropriate response might be an enthusiastic, "Thank you so much for the suggestion. I will be in touch." Or you can say, "Thank you but I am presently busy." Later on, if you are not interested, you can say, "Forgive me, I feel s/he is not right for me, but thanks so much for trying."

People are rejected for many different reasons. Some people are rejected for not being pretty enough and others are rejected because they are too pretty. There are those who are afraid that very attractive individuals will be egocentric. Some people are rejected for not being smart enough, while others are rejected for being too smart, which can be intimidating. You can be rejected for being too tall or too short, too poor or too wealthy, too quiet or too loud, too funny or too dry, too popular or not popular enough. No one wants anybody who is "too" anything, yet no one wants mediocre. Bright, beautiful, personable people get rejected as well.

People often reject one another based on inaccurate information, or because they are not willing to give a person a chance to present a total picture of him-/herself. After one look at a résumé or at a person, they decide, "Not for me," whereas had they taken time to know the total person, they might be crazy about him/her.

13: Rejection • 83

If your boyfriend or girlfriend wants to leave you, it should be like leaving a job. They should give you two weeks' notice, there should be severance pay, and the day before they leave you, they should have to find you a temp.

—*Bob Ettinger*

Breaking up is hard to do, but if someone is not for you, don't drag him/her along. A breakup can be a painful, devastating blow to your ego, and it's also depressing to think of beginning again, but it's something most people experience at one time or another. Time heals all wounds, and each person will move on to the next chapter. If a breakup is inevitable, it is much better that it happens before a couple marries and has children.

Before you reject someone, remember that your spouse doesn't have to be everything to you. You must be able to respect your spouse, communicate well, enjoy being together, and share the same goals and dreams. If s/he is supportive and a good provider but can't play tennis, play tennis with a friend. If you love visiting museums but your spouse refuses to go, go with a friend.

If you want to find out what life is like without a man around…just get married.

14: Go Out

I've been on so many blind dates I should get a free dog.

People can be overly rigid about whom they are willing to date, refusing to broaden their outlook. Although you must have guidelines, it is important to be more open, less critical, and sometimes, even if everything doesn't sound ideal, realize you never know.

Morris was an exceptionally good-looking fellow who boarded in Renee and Itsik's home. Renee often fixed up Morris, but only with exceptionally pretty girls, since Morris insisted that great looks were essential for him. One day, Renee was asked by her neighbor to fix up Morris with her daughter, Sharon. Sharon was plain looking, certainly not up to Morris's standards, but Renee was too uncomfortable to say no to her neighbor. This was despite the fact that Itsik was a naysayer to the idea, certain that

Morris would resent being fixed up with Sharon. Morris agreed to the date, never even inquiring about Sharon's looks, since Renee had always set him up with beautiful girls. Morris and Sharon went out, and at midnight Morris were still not back from the date. Both Renee and Itsik were sure he was furious with them. When he was still not home at one o'clock they were convinced he would never return. At two o'clock in the morning Morris banged on their bedroom door. "In your entire life did you ever see such a beautiful girl?" he said. Renee and Itsik were in absolute shock, but they were certainly thrilled to dance at the couple's wedding. It just shows you never know who will appeal to whom.

Beauty is truly in the eyes of the beholder. Two people can look at the same thing and each will see something different. Most people don't know what they are looking for until they find it.

Rabbi Akiva Tatz tells of his friend, who had only one real eye. He set him up with a girl without telling her about this defect, thinking to himself: *What are the chances she will agree to the date if I say that I have a great guy with one eye?* Sure enough, she liked him so much that she didn't even notice his problem. You need not tell a date everything about a person you are setting him/her up with.

A blonde calls her friend Jake and says, "Please come over here and help me. I have a killer jigsaw puzzle, and I can't figure out how to get started."

Jake asks, "What is it supposed to be when it's finished?"

The blonde says, "According to the picture on the box, it's a rooster."

Jake goes over to help with the puzzle. She lets him in and shows him where she has the puzzle spread all over the table.

He studies the pieces for a moment, looks at the box, then turns to her and says, "First of all, no matter what we do, we're not going to be able to assemble these pieces into anything resembling a rooster."

He then says, "Second, I want you to relax. Let's have a nice cup of tea, and then," he says with a deep sigh, "let's put all the cornflakes back in the box."

You never know what aspect of a person will attract someone. For some, the great personality is the appeal. Others are drawn to the person's warmth. Still others like the sweetness or the smarts. Like a puzzle, you never know which piece will pull it together to create the beautiful whole. It is the complete person that should be viewed and appreciated.

One groom wore a sign to his wedding, "You are everything I never knew I always wanted."

I'm standing on line at the bakery, and this really cute guy asked for my number. So I had to get another one.
—*Wendy Liebman*

15: Your Family's Attitude

I think; therefore, I'm single.

Bentzi was dating a lovely girl but he couldn't get himself to propose. He finally went to a rabbi for help, explaining that he was forty-one and still lived at home with his widowed mother. Speaking to Bentzi's mother, the rabbi was shocked to find that both Bentzi's mother and sister felt there was no reason for Bentzi to disrupt his life by getting married. Obviously, it was to their benefit to keep him single and living at home in order to keep his mother company. It was hard to get Bentzi to move on in life when his closest relatives were making him believe he was doing the wrong thing.

Zevi's mother bought him two new ties. He went into his bedroom, immediately put on one of them, and hurried back. "Look, Mama. Isn't it gorgeous?"

88 • The Art of Marriage

His mother said, "What's the matter? You don't like the other one?"

When it comes to love, the rabbis agree that you do not have to obey your parents' wishes. Nevertheless, it is smart to listen to and hear their opinion. Mr. Morgan wanted a wealthy son-in-law and objected to Fred, who was presently unemployed, as a husband for his daughter Susan. But Susan had gotten to know Fred well and was confident he would find a job. She followed her instincts, and today Fred has a good job, Susan and Fred have a good marriage, and Mr. Morgan is very proud of them.

Renee's mother felt uncomfortable with Jerry, whom Renee was dating, explaining that she felt he created competition between himself and the family. Renee claimed that he was just working hard to make a good impression. Renee's mother begged her to get to know Jerry better before making a commitment, but Jerry pressured her to stand up to her parents. Finally, she agreed to marry him despite her mother's feelings. After the wedding, Jerry's possessive attitude became obvious. He felt threatened by her family and friends, refusing to visit them, and was also jealous of the time Renee spent with them. He resented even their slightest involvement in Renee's life, questioning every phone call she made. She had to sneak out of the house to visit her family, and when Jerry found out about her visits, he demanded she break off communication with them. He wanted to be the only important one in her life. He refused help, and eventually Renee divorced him.

Ira's mother discouraged him from dating young. Then, as he got older, she discouraged him from dating seriously. "Why settle now?" she would ask. Now he is close to forty and unmarried, and his mother is begging for grandchildren.

Sometimes it is your friends who are critical of the person you are dating. Listen to what they say, because their criticism may be legitimate. At the same time, realize that other emotions can be at play. A friend may unwittingly be jealous, afraid the new person in your life will take you away. Or s/he may worry about being the only one left of the old crowd who is still single. Ultimately, you must respect your brain and follow your heart.

At a weekly husbands' marriage seminar, the instructor asked Giuseppe, who said he was approaching his fiftieth wedding anniversary, to share some insight into how he had managed to stay married to the same woman all these years.

Giuseppe replied to the assembled husbands, "Wella, I'va tried to treat her nice, spenda da money on her, but besta of all is, I tooka her to Italy for the twenty-fifth anniversary!"

The instructor responded, "Giuseppe, you are an amazing inspiration to all the husbands here! Please tell us what you are planning for your wife for your fiftieth anniversary."

Giuseppe proudly replied, "I gonna go picka her up."

16: Older/Younger Dating

Dating may be an exciting experience at first, but it can become tiring and frustrating. Many individuals who begin the process with a great attitude have a tough time staying optimistic.

"To what do you contribute your old age, Wilbur?"

"I was born a long time ago!"

Younger people have an easier time making a commitment. Their friends are getting married and they are caught up in the excitement, rather than entangled in the complicated questions that marriage can conjure.

Older, more experienced individuals who have already dated a lot may have a terrible sense of despair that what they want may never actually happen. Sometimes they will refuse the opportunity to meet another person because they don't believe they can find the right one anymore. Or, afraid of being hurt, they rebuff dates as a defense mechanism. They will reject the other person before they are rejected.

Additionally, older singles have invested a lot in establishing their lifestyles, working hard to have this lifestyle accepted by themselves and others. Therefore, rather than becoming more flexible, they become more rigid and demanding, feeling they have much more to give up. If this relationship fails it will upset the stability and balance they have worked so hard to achieve.

There comes a moment when you have to stop revving up the car and shove it into gear.

Some people feel that since they waited so long and have passed up so many other candidates, it's not smart to settle on this one now. They question, "Why is this person better for me than all the others I dismissed?" This perception must be changed. People must channel their efforts in positive ways to change their outlook.

"How does an eighty-year-old man like you get a gorgeous twenty-year-old bride?"
"I told her I was ninety!"

Older singles have established a home, a job, friends, and even an attitude that is in their comfort zone. They also have independence. They don't have to answer to a spouse and can come and go as they please. In order to give this up, they must believe the gain is worth it. A woman who lives alone and makes a good living may not want to commit to someone who will not contribute much to her present income. A man who has a full social life with no strings may feel: *Why should I take on the care and support of someone else?* People who do not see marriage as improving their lifestyle will not move forward in a relationship.

Life still offers fun and excitement when you're old. It just offers them to younger people.

Singles need to focus on the positive contributions a spouse makes to a person's well-being. Rather than focus on financial considerations, they can learn to appreciate the emotional connection, the friendship, the companionship, and the security a spouse can add to their life. In his book *The Inner Circle: Seven Gates to Marriage*, Dr. Shaya Ostrov says that it is the shared experiences of trust, understanding, and mutual nurturance that combine to result in emerging feelings of certainty that love can occur in one's life.

An old man finds a frog and puts it in his pocket. Suddenly he hears a tiny voice, "Mister! Mister! I am not really a frog. I am a beautiful princess, but a mean witch put a curse on me. Please take me out of your pocket and give me a kiss so I can turn back into a princess."

The old man thought about it as he continued walking and again he heard the frog cry, "Mister, please take me out of your pocket and give me a little kiss."

The man kept walking and the frog cried even louder, "Mister, I'm a beautiful princess! Please take me out of your pocket and give me a little kiss."

The old man took the frog out of his pocket, looked at it, and said, "Sorry. At my age I think I would rather have a talking frog than a beautiful princess."

17: Should I Settle?

List of Demands – Age: Twenty-Two
1. **Handsome**
2. **Charming**
3. **Financially successful**
4. **A caring listener**
5. **Witty**
6. **In good shape**
7. **Dresses with style**
8. **Appreciates finer things**
9. **Full of thoughtful surprises**
10. **Romantic**

Revised List – Age: Thirty-Two
1. Nice looking (prefer hair on his head)
2. Opens car door, holds chairs
3. Has enough money for a nice dinner
4. Listens more than talks
5. Laughs at my jokes
6. Carries bags of groceries with ease
7. Owns at least one tie
8. Appreciates a good, home-cooked meal
9. Remembers birthdays and anniversaries
10. Is attentive

Revised List – Age: Forty-Two
1. Not too ugly (bald head okay)
2. Doesn't drive off until I'm in the car
3. Works steady – splurges on dinner out occasionally
4. Nods head when I'm talking
5. Usually remembers punch lines of jokes
6. Is in good enough shape to rearrange the furniture
7. Wears a shirt that covers his stomach
8. Knows not to buy champagne with screw-top lids
9. Remembers to put the toilet seat down
10. Shaves most weekends

Revised List – Age: Fifty-Two
1. Looks presentable
2. Doesn't belch in public
3. Doesn't borrow money too often
4. Doesn't nod off to sleep when I'm venting
5. Doesn't retell the same joke too many times
6. Is in good enough shape to get off couch on weekends
7. Usually wears matching socks and fresh underwear
8. Appreciates a good TV dinner
9. Remembers my name on occasion
10. Shaves some weekends

Revised List – Age: Sixty-Two
1. Doesn't scare small children
2. Remembers where bathroom is
3. Doesn't require much money for upkeep
4. Only snores lightly when asleep
5. Remembers why he's laughing
6. Is in good enough shape to stand up by himself
7. Remembers how to get dressed himself
8. Likes soft foods
9. Remembers where he left his teeth
10. Remembers that it's the weekend

Revised List – Age: Seventy-Two
1. Breathing

—Anonymous

Although this section may seem discouraging or depressing at first glance, it contains advice to help you marry and raise a family, leading to a happy and rewarding life.

An old man was sitting on a park bench, crying.

"What's wrong?" asked a concerned passerby.

The old man explained, "This afternoon I married a gorgeous twenty-one-year-old woman who is not only personable but also wealthy. She is waiting for me at this very moment."

"So why are you crying?" asked the passerby.

The old man sniffled and said, "I can't remember where we live!"

The younger you are, the more time you have to look for your ideal spouse. This does not mean you will always find him/her, as evidenced by the fact that there are many older singles still searching for their mate. If you are an older single and truly want to get married, you must figure out where the problem lies. Very often it is not your fault. I resent when people ask an older single, "Why aren't you married?" For reasons unbeknownst to us, G-d has not yet blessed this individual with his/her partner. Some of the most amazing, bright, well-rounded, great-looking, personable, successful individuals are not married. Most go on to carve out a fulfilling life for themselves.

Despite this, it's important to examine all the possibilities to help yourself. Perhaps you are finding potential mates but they do not display a mutual interest. How can you make yourself more appealing? Do you need to improve your physical appearance, your intelligence, your personality, or your strategy?

What is the difference between a wife and a girlfriend?

Forty-five pounds.

Examine your expectations. Are they unrealistic? You may want someone great looking, but perhaps you are overweight or unattractive. Or maybe, despite your fabulous looks, you are destined for someone who is mediocre looking but has a great disposition. You may want someone exceptionally bright, but perhaps such people don't find you stimulating enough. Or perhaps, even though you are an intellectual, you are destined for someone who possesses normal intelligence but an exceptional personality. Open your horizons. Don't box yourself in, deciding that you know what you are looking for and what you need. People often create fantasies in their childhood that, with maturity and understanding, can be modified.

Maybe you are actually unsure if you are ready for marriage. Are you afraid of the responsibilities of marriage? Are you worried that you may not be a good spouse? Are you unable to make a commitment to one person? Are you afraid to be tied down? Are you afraid to give up your independence? Are you worried that you will no longer be in control of your life? Are you scared of a failed marriage? Do you trust the sincerity of other people? Are you afraid you may have a disillusioning marriage like your parents have? Some people are unsure if they are capable of taking care of themselves, let alone another person's psychological, emotional, and financial needs. Some people just don't want to grow up. These individuals should seek help from a marriage specialist.

An older man states his intention to marry a girl of twenty.

A friend says, "Such a marriage can be fatal."

The man answers, "So she'll die!"

Once in a while a sixty-year-old man marries a twenty-year-old woman, an older girl gets a much younger man, or a funny-looking girl gets a gorgeous guy. These things happen, but they are rarities. A man who can hardly support himself will not be attractive to someone who wants a comfortable lifestyle. Someone who is severely overweight or terribly anorexic will have a difficult time attracting most people. Divorcées, widows, widowers, or individuals with children appeal to different people. Different circumstances determine our prospects. One should reach for the stars, but if the stars are unrealistically unreachable, don't waste precious time. A young single mother of three children might be compelled to marry a man a few years older than she would have originally wanted, yet she may find herself married to a mature, sensitive husband.

Sharon, a forty-year-old woman, said, "I'm sorry I didn't marry the last man I dated."

Her friends asked her, "You went out with so many men. Why do you only regret not marrying the last one?"

"Because," she answered, "I didn't know he would be the last one."

Don't keep waiting, thinking that someone better will come along. There are people who think: *This girl is really pretty, but if I meet a prettier one after I am married, I will be frustrated.* Or: *He makes a nice living, but what if I commit to him and then I meet someone who makes a really great living? Will I be happy?* They ask, "Should I settle?" You should not "settle," but you should be able to continually evolve and grow. This process is not called "settling"; rather, it is reevaluating your goals with a maturity that is grounded in reality. Sometimes, by giving up one thing, you gain more in the long run.

One ninety-year-old man married a woman of the same age. They spent their honeymoon trying to get out of the car!

Some people do not readjust their thinking as they get older. Sixty-year-old bachelors are still looking for thirty-year-old women who can have three or four children. A bachelorette in her forties might still want a man who will take a year off after the wedding to live and study abroad. What is feasible for a twenty-year-old couple is not always realistic for a forty-year-old couple. An older couple can often afford to buy a home when they get married, while young couples dream of the day they can afford it. It is unrealistic to expect your twenty-three-year-old husband to afford the luxuries a fifty-year-old husband can buy.

I asked a mediocre-looking woman in her late thirties what type of man she wanted. She wanted someone with green eyes and blond hair, although if his hair were dirty blond she would adjust. Here, I realized, is a woman who is not being realistic about her situation or her expectations.

I dialed a number and got the following recording: "I am not available right now, but thank you for caring enough to call. I am making some changes in my life. Please leave a message after the beep. If I do not return your call, you are one of the changes."

Sometimes people have to reevaluate what they are looking for and change their attitude.

It is wonderful and rare to fall in love, get married, and live "happily ever after." Young women in their early twenties may be concerned about finding a spouse, but women in their thirties are panic-stricken, wondering if they will ever find their life partner. By age forty, a single, mature woman will not tell you that what she wants is love, romance, understanding, or an intense connection. Rather, her most fervent desire is for a husband and a child.

Although we are brought up on literature and media that try to convince us that a level of passionate intensity in a marriage will make us happy, it is actually a nice, stable, and reliable spouse that makes life pleasant.

What makes a romantic relationship great is not what makes a marriage great. Marriage is not about with whom you want to dine, or with whom you want to ski; rather, it is about with whom you want to run a household. Lori Gottlieb, in her article "The Case for Settling for Mr. Good Enough," which appeared in *The Atlantic*, writes: "Marriage isn't a passion fest; it's more like a partnership formed to run a very small, mundane, and often boring non-profit business."

Once you reach a certain age, certainly by the time you are in your thirties, it is important to focus on the big picture. This is a family of your own. You may have to compromise on some of your dreams to achieve this. Often, this compromise or "settling" will make you happier in the long run, since if you marry with great expectations you can be disappointed, while if you have lower expectations you are often pleasantly surprised. While there are women who have a long list of complaints against their husbands, and who secretly wonder if they should have held out for that perfect spouse, most would never trade places with an unmarried woman. As Lori Gottlieb puts it: "They would rather feel alone in a marriage than actually be alone, because they realize that marriage ultimately isn't about cosmic connection – it's about having a teammate; even if he's not the love of your life, it's better than not having one at all."

Between work and child care, many women do not spend that much time with their husbands anyway. Therefore, Lori Gottlieb argues: "If you don't see that much of your husband anyway, but he is a decent guy who takes out the trash and sets up the baby gear and provides a second income that allows you to spend time with your child, how much does it matter that the guy you marry is 'The One'?"

As you get older and your priorities change from romance to family, your perspective and the type of person you look for and are willing to accept changes as well. Some older single women claim that they grew up idealizing marriage. Had they had a more realistic understanding of its cold, hard benefits when they were younger, they might have been married. Lori Gottlieb says, "We grew up thinking that marriage meant feeling some kind of divine spark, and so we walked away from uninspiring relationships that might have made us happy in the context of family."

Shulamit, a young lady in her thirties, got engaged to Joseph, a young man who followed a *rav* whose customs differed from her own. Joseph doesn't hold that *Tehillim* has any special powers, nor does he believe in singing at the Shabbos table. For Shulamit, who recited *Tehillim* every day for years in the hope of finding her *bashert* (intended), this was very hard. When asked how she could marry Joseph, she smartly answered, "I thought about my children not being able to sing at the Shabbos table, and that bothered me. But then I thought, if I don't marry Joseph, I may never have any children."

The goal is to have a partner with whom to share your life, to raise children together, and to create a spiritually uplifting home where the Shechinah, the Divine Presence, can reside. This is true for older single men as well, who realize too late that they have missed the boat because they were searching for that ultimate Hollywood movie star.

How old are you and how long have you been that age?

When do you decide to settle? Lori compares this to musical chairs: "When do you take a seat, any seat, just so you're not left standing alone?" Decide to settle before settling is no longer an option! As you get older there are fewer choices, and the concessions you have to make are even greater. You might hear a nagging voice in your mind: *Why are you settling now when you have held out this long? Haven't you earned the right to find your Mr. Right? Why not look a bit longer?* But often, by the time someone is ready to settle, s/he is settling for someone who is settling for him/her. The idea is to get smart earlier, settling while you can still make intelligent compromises, rather than later, when there are far fewer options and you are forced to compromise on much more.

Marrying someone who doesn't share all your interests may feel as if you are settling when you are thirty, but at thirty-five it is a sensible, realistic move. If you enjoy being with someone, and you can build a life together even without romantic sparks flying, deciding to marry him/her is making a mature adult decision, not settling. Observing some friends who have not married their dream husband and others who have not married at all, I see that my married friends are happier. Compromising on looks, personality, financial standing, or social status was the smart thing for them to do.

I am a marvelous housekeeper. Every time I leave a man I keep his house.

—*Zsa Zsa Gabor*

Even women who marry yet eventually get divorced can be better off than someone who never married, because they hopefully have children, and perhaps even someone to help with child support.

A Frenchman, an Italian, and a Pole are stranded on an island. Suddenly, a genie appears and agrees to grant each of them one wish. The Italian is lonely and wishes to return to his family in Italy. He says good-bye to his two friends, and the genie snaps her fingers and sends him back to Italy.

The Frenchman says, "I too am lonely. I'd like to be back in France." He says good-bye to his friend, and the genie snaps her fingers and sends him back to France.

The genie then asks the Polish man what he wishes for. He says, "I'm so lonely. I wish I had my two friends back…"

When all your friends find their spouses, you might feel like the last man standing. The specter of loneliness and the fear of your biological time clock running out can make some people accept a spouse who is harmful. An intelligent choice of compromising in some areas does *not* include marrying a spouse who is verbally or physically abusive. You must be careful that you are compromising on appropriate things. If a person is less handsome, outgoing, or humorous than you had originally hoped for, that is okay. But it is not okay if the person is uncaring or unable to give love or attention.

The Bible tells us: *Ve'ahavta lere'acha kamocha*, Love your neighbor as you love yourself. The rabbis interpret this to mean: Overlook people's bad qualities and focus on their good ones. But this does not mean that a person should overlook bad character traits in a potential spouse. G-d wants us in a marriage that promotes harmony and unity.

Let your intellect guide your heart.

After dating someone a few times it should be legal to stamp their foreheads with their faults; otherwise, the next person has to start figuring out what's wrong with them from scratch.

—Rita Rudman

18: Committing

Why is marriage like the splitting of the Red Sea? Pursuing the Israelites, the first group of Egyptian soldiers rushed into the sea and drowned. The second group of Egyptian soldiers witnessed this, and yet followed them into the water and also drowned. Still a third group, after seeing the first two groups go under, rushed in. Similarly, even after seeing other individuals marry and go under, people still forge forward.

Baruch Hashem, thank G-d, most people are successful and do make it across.

Although every bride and groom marches down the aisle wearing a big smile, looking calm, comfortable, and secure, that is often a façade. Certainly there are people who feel secure, confident, and madly in love on their wedding day, but there are many others who feel uncertain. Their decision to walk down the aisle is based more on logic than on love. They have decided this is the best spouse for them now, although s/he is not like their original dream. Many people get married because they are getting older and do not want to be alone. Some brides and grooms have been known to cry, throw up, or threaten to run away, suddenly overwhelmed and petrified that they are making a terrible mistake. Yet you can walk down the aisle with great trepidation and have an amazing marriage, or walk down feeling totally secure and wind up in divorce courts. Walking down the aisle is the time to decide that no matter what the circumstances, reason for marrying, or intensity of feelings of love or doubt, the strength of commitment to this marriage is what counts.

As long as you marry someone whom you respect, you can make the marriage work and grow into love, with time, shared goals and experiences, and intimacy.

A wealthy man threw a dinner party and said to his guests, "Whoever swims across my river, which is full of crocodiles, can ask me for anything he desires." Everyone looked at the water and looked at the crocodiles, but no one moved. Suddenly Duvidal, a little man, jumped into the water and swam like a madman across the river. Everyone cheered as he safely came ashore. The wealthy man strode over to Duvidal and said, "Tell me what you want and I will grant it."

Panting and gasping for breath, Duvidal said, "What do I want? I want you to tell me who pushed me in so I can kill him!"

No matter how much you analyze your feelings, you

may not be ready to commit to marrying someone until you are pushed a bit. Sometimes you just have to say a prayer and jump in, and sometimes people have to push you to make a commitment.

At the conclusion of his lecture to a group of young recruits, the legendary paratrooper asked for questions. A hand shot up. "What made you decide to make the first jump, sir?"

Without hesitation, the paratrooper replied, "An airplane at eighteen thousand feet with three dead engines."

Alan was an eligible bachelor with a choice of many different women. One day he accompanied his friend to a nursing home to visit his friend's grandmother. Seeing all the lonely people there made him realize he didn't want to grow old and die alone. Suddenly he was ready to make a commitment.

Because of their biological time clock, women often feel at a disadvantage, plagued by the pressure to find a spouse while they are still young enough to have children. Women approaching their forties should consult both their rabbis and doctors to explore available, permissible medical advances, which could extend the possibility of their having children for many more years and eliminate some of the pressure.

My decision is maybe and that's final.

Eventually one has to make a decision and take the leap.

We were married for better or worse. I couldn't have done better and she couldn't have done worse.

—*Henny Youngman*

Usually, once someone stops analyzing and does make that commitment, s/he is often much happier and more sure of his/her feelings. However, if you proposed or accepted a proposal of marriage, and then realize you have made a terrible mistake, apologize and walk away. A broken engagement is far better than a broken marriage, both for you and for your intended.

One way to decide whether or not to marry someone is to imagine being engaged to him/her. Without proposing or accepting a proposal, and without involving the other person, act and think as if you were already engaged. Do you feel excited or do you feel trapped? Picture yourself on a deserted beach with this individual. Is it pleasant or do you want to start swimming away? Or worse yet, do you want to drown him/her or yourself?

How do you save a man from drowning? Take your foot off his head!

Picture yourself being married to this individual and explore your emotions. Are you glad or sad when you think this way? Is s/he saying and doing things that make you feel elated or deflated? When you think that this is the person you will spend your life with, are you happy? If you feel even calmly happy, take the step. If you are worried, proceed with utmost caution.

I used to have a handle on life, but it broke.

Part Two
Marriage

19: Let the Marriage Begin...

A woman finds an unusual bottle on the beach. A genie pops out and says, "Due to inflation, I can grant you only one wish. What will it be?"

The woman pulls out a map and says, "I live in New York, but my daughter lives in Australia, and I hate flying. Please construct a bridge from Manhattan across the ocean to Australia."

The genie says, "I'm good, but I'm not that good. Is there something else you want?"

Thinking for a moment, the woman says, "Okay, I want a good man. One who is considerate and fun, caring and helpful, willing to lend a hand with the household chores, has good values, gets along with my family, and doesn't watch sports all the time."

Sighing, the genie says, "Let me have another look at that map."

Finding the right spouse and developing a good marriage is harder than one might have expected. It is a great blessing to quickly and easily find and marry the perfect spouse and go on to establish a happy, problem-free marriage. It usually is a bit more complicated.

G-d said to Adam, "I am going to give you a woman who will be perfect, who will always help you, who will love you, respect you, look up to you, and admire you."

Adam asked, "What will it cost me?"

G-d answered, "An arm and a leg."

Adam said, "What can I get for a rib?"

G-d created woman saying, "*Lo tov heyos adam levado*, It is not good for man to be alone" (*Bereishis* 2:18). A spouse completes us by giving us someone to give to, share with, provide for, work with, build a home and family with, and make us whole. But these things do not come easily, even though we all want marriage to be easy. We must invest in our marriage. It is an adjustment, and it takes work to be successful at it.

The most difficult years of marriage are those following the wedding.

Although the first year of marriage is beautiful – full of magical, memorable, and intimate moments – it is also a time of many adjustments. This is what you waited for, with a whole life together ahead of you and all your dreams waiting to be realized. Yet for many newlyweds this period is full of tears, misunderstandings, fears, and disappointments. Each of you is struggling in unfamiliar territory. As much as you may know one another and have mapped out your future together, the present is unclear and confusing. Now you must incorporate another person into the life you had before you met.

"Do I have to share all my thoughts with him?"

"Do I have to spend all my free time with her?"

"Is she always so slow to get ready?"

"Is he always going to race out after breakfast without even noticing me?"

"I can't believe she knows nothing about housework."

"I don't understand how he can drop his clothes all over the floor."

"It seems he is more concerned about his friends than about me."

"It seems she would rather talk to her mother than to me."

"Is he ignoring me?"

"Is she just insensitive to my needs?"

Millions of worrisome questions enter your mind, and you wonder:

"Why didn't I realize he was so self-centered when we were dating?"

"Why didn't I realize during our courtship how mad she can get?"

"Why did I ignore all the times he made excuses for coming late?"

"How did I close my eyes to so many of her faults?"

Every year Morris and his wife Esther went to the state fair, and every year Morris would say, "Esther, I'd like to ride in that helicopter."

Esther always replied, "I know, Morris, but that helicopter ride is fifty dollars! And fifty dollars is fifty dollars."

One year Esther and Morris went to the fair, and Morris said, "Esther, I'm eighty-five years old. If I don't ride that helicopter today, I might never get another chance."

Esther replied, "Morris, that helicopter ride is fifty dollars! And fifty dollars is fifty dollars."

The pilot overheard the couple and said, "Folks, I'll make you a deal. I'll take both of you for a ride. If you can stay quiet for the entire ride, not saying a word, I won't charge you! But if you say one word, it's fifty dollars."

Morris and Esther agreed, and up they went. The pilot did all kinds of fancy maneuvers, but not a word was heard. He did his daredevil tricks over and over again, but still not a word. When they landed, the pilot turned to Morris and said, "By golly! I did everything I could to get you to yell out, but you didn't. I'm impressed!"

Morris replied, "Well, to tell you the truth, I almost said something when Esther fell out, but you know – fifty dollars is fifty dollars."

During the first year of marriage, you learn many unexpected things. Some are wonderful, but some things are disappointing and can make you feel apprehensive.

You had always decided where and when to go out, but now she seems to be taking control.

He used to love when you spoke up, but now he seems to hate it.

He's sloppy and you must always pick up after him.

Her wardrobe may be gorgeous, but there is no room for your clothing.

He's warm and gentle, but his tossing and turning all night hurts you.

She was on time for every date, but now she is constantly late.

He used to laugh at all your jokes, but suddenly he's questioning whether they may be inappropriate.

Both of you used to enjoy eating out in nice restaurants, but now he insists that eating out is squandering money.

She used to make you feel special, but now she acts like you are there to serve her.

He always brought out the best in you, but now you find him irritating.

These situations increase the tension between couples.

"Mushka, I wish you'd learn how to make the bread my mother makes."

"Sure, if you learn to make the dough my father makes!"

Most married couples will tell you that marriage is work. Although people may want to work on changing their spouse's behavior, they really need to work on changing their own behavior, learning to accept and adjust to their spouse's needs and expectations. Behavior modification requires much effort and time, but the reward for this is growth in the relationship leading to even greater understanding, care, and intimacy. If you enter marriage cognizant of its difficulties as well as its potential reward, you will deal calmly with the struggles, enjoy the bonding, and find that your relationship is continually on the ascent. Of course, this must be true of both partners. If one partner is unwilling to do any of the work that a marriage requires, the effort for the other partner may be too great and non-productive.

My ex-husband always said he could be anything he wanted to be. Apparently, he wanted to be an idiot.

The Maharal of Prague explains that man was named Adam after the word *adama*, ground. Land represents potential, the ability to grow things, bringing them to fruition. Like the land, Adam is unique in that he also represents pure potential, with the ability to bring forth a distinct type of growth, the growth of his own perfection. Man is pure potential waiting to be realized. The challenge of marriage is to create a mighty arena in which our potential for growth is limitless.

One is never too young to learn skills that will prepare you for a good marriage. If parents and educators can teach children the importance of being caring, showing sensitivity and appreciation, learning good communication skills, and approaching life with flexibility, then adjusting to marriage will be much smoother.

Rebecca and Sam had just had yet another of their fights. At the end of this one, she said to him, "You'll be sorry; I'm going to leave you."

To this Sam replied, "Make up your mind, dear, which one is it going to be? It can't be both!"

20: First Disagreement

Marriage is very difficult. It is like a five-thousand-piece puzzle, all sky.

— *Cathy Ladman*

Because many newlyweds are totally naive about marriage, they think something is catastrophically wrong when they experience their first disagreement. They immediately obsess: *I shouldn't have married him/her.* They need to learn that a lifetime of marriage consists of loads of disagreements and loads of making up.

Little by little your lives begin to meld. You discover more wonderful things about one another as you teach each other your needs, likes, and dislikes. Together you learn how to express your expectations and disappointments. By cooperating with each other and working together with a positive outlook, and with the realization that an adjustment period is status quo, newlyweds can grow together and form a great marriage.

All marriages are happy. It's the living together afterward that's rough.

Simple, silly issues that were never discussed before can evolve into big fights if they are mishandled. The key to a good marriage is not a relationship without any disagreements; it is the strength of the bond you create when you are not arguing. Let the quarrels be a minor part of the marriage, overshadowed by the love and admiration you share.

After just one year of marriage, Shani filed for divorce. A friend, Miriam, trying to console her, said that you never know what a man's like until you live with him.
"Awwww Miriam... I shoulda left him right after the honeymoon," Shani said. "Not only did he NOT take me to Niagara Falls like he promised – all we did was drive through a car wash a couple of times, real slow."

Before marriage, most couples don't discuss marital basics like whether each prefers to sleep with the lights off or dimmed, if they are late or early risers, or if the bedroom temperature should be cold or hot. After marriage, newlyweds can spend an entire night opening and closing windows, raising and lowering the air conditioner, or turning the radio on and off. When you were young you may have shared a room with a sibling, but your parents refereed the disagreements, telling you to keep quiet and go to bed. Now the couple shares the room and has to work through any issues.

Decorating the apartment can also become an issue to

resolve. Marriage does not necessarily mean sharing tastes and preferences. Joan may like the dainty little chair, while Sidney wants the plush, comfortable one. Joan loves the eclectic look, while Sidney likes modern and can't understand what eclectic is. A couple that has made it through the decorating process has achieved a milestone in their marriage!

A guy knows he's in love when he loses interest in his car for a couple of days.
—Tim Allen

When they first get married, many young couples have only one car and they must decide how to share it. Before they were married, Dina usually used her mother's car, but her new home isn't close enough to her parents' house to make borrowing the car feasible. Will Dina drop off Dov at the train station so she can have the car to go to school, or will Dov drop off Dina at school so he can have the car to drive to work? Will Dov do the shopping if he has the car? Will he pick up Dina so they can shop together? Perhaps they'll split the week. These are the type of issues that need to be discussed.

Questions like whose relatives to visit for Shabbos, arguments over how to run a house, disagreements over coordinating schedules, and balancing the budget are all part of a newlywed's agenda.

Husband: "Another new dress? Where do you think we'll get the money to pay for it?"

Wife: "Darling, you know I'm not inquisitive."

There are couples that adjust easily to marriage. These couples usually were prepared beforehand with knowledge of what marriage entails. There are wives who love cooking, cleaning, and doing things for their new husbands. There are men who are not afraid of the new responsibility of caring for another person. There are people who naturally enjoy the special feeling of being two together, and they instinctively know how to incorporate their jobs, relatives, and routines into their shared life. However, most people need some molding and adjusting to acclimate to marriage.

Young people have spent their life until now gathering lots of things they value: their collections of books, pictures, CDs, DVDs, memorabilia, computer software, sports equipment, instruments, games, and clothing. Moving out of the comfort of their home, they are somewhat disoriented to live in a small apartment, forced to leave much of their stuff behind. They can feel apprehensive about separating from so many things they considered to be part of home. Additionally, many individuals lived in a home full of people and action. With only two people in the house now, they may be pressured by the responsibility to entertain their spouse, or be worried that there is no one but their spouse to entertain them.

Partners must be solution oriented, understanding each other's perspective and working together to resolve the issue. You have chosen to be a couple, two individuals who act and decide as one, with each other and for each other. You are no longer the only one involved in decisions that affect both of you. Any change that a couple decides to implement must therefore be discussed and worked out together. Neither partner can look at life anymore thinking: *What makes me happy? What makes me unhappy? What bothers me?* Now s/he must think: *What makes us happy, unhappy, or bothered?*

The Rambam states that a husband and wife are considered as one (*Bereishis* 2:24) since they become the closest of relatives through the sanctification of marriage. A couple who view themselves as one unit will be sensitive to the needs and wishes of each other, willing to meet each other's needs and avoid causing each other unhappiness.

I think the bottom line difference between being single and being married is this: When you're single, you're as happy as you are. When you're married, you can only be as happy as the least happy person in the apartment.
—*Tom Hertz*

21: Dealing with Differences

I've been trying to save my marriage for the last thirty-five years.

Expect to have differences. Couples must agree to disagree. "The goal of marriage is not to think alike but to think together" (Robert C. Dodds).

Research has shown that every happy, successful couple has approximately ten areas of incompatibility, or disagreements that will never be resolved (www.smartmarriages.com/divorcepredictor.html).

Disagreements in a marriage should be viewed as a challenge, to welcome and embrace change. Successful couples learn to deal with their disagreements, living life around them. They love one another in spite of their areas of difference, developing an understanding and empathy for their partner's positions. Indeed, they gain comfort in the knowledge that they know their partner and know which issues they disagree on and must learn to manage. These couples also understand that if they switch partners they'll just get ten new areas of disagreement, and sadly, the most destructive will be about the children from their earlier relationships.

A husband comes home and finds his wife crying.

"Honey, why are you crying?" he asks.

"Because, darling, the dog ate one of the chicken pot pies I made."

Her husband comforts her, saying, "Honey, stop crying. I'll buy you another dog."

Dr. Sue Johnson, creator of Emotionally Focused Therapy for Couples, believes that most arguments are actually protests against disconnection. Underneath all the frustration and anger, partners are asking one another, "Can I count on you? Will you respond to me when I need you? Do you value me? Do you accept me?" The anger, attacks, criticism, and demands are cries to a loved one: "Please be here emotionally for me, care and respond to me, help me reestablish a sense of safe connection."

According to the attachment theory, when our loved one is emotionally unavailable or unresponsive, we feel alone and helpless, and therefore react with anger, sadness, hurt, and most of all, fear. This reaction, a cry that says, "I need you to notice me and be with me," causes one to attack, blame, and hurt the other, or to put up defenses to protect him-/herself from being hurt, including tuning out or walking out on the other spouse.

Smaller differences and even harmful disagreements can be managed when you are able to recognize your and your spouse's need for connection. Because connection comes from being there physically and emotionally for one another, when a disagreement is brewing, remember that marriage is an agreement to validate one another and allow your spouse to depend on you. Understanding, caring, accepting, and being supportive of one another is part of being connected in marriage.

Each spouse commits to give the other a feeling of security and comfort by attributing a positive intent to all that his/her partner does, controlling his/her actions and reactions, and expressing anger in a careful, less hurtful, less negative manner. Each spouse should be able to reach out to the other, confident that s/he will be there, supportive of his/her feelings, concerns, and goals (see chapter 42, "Anger").

Terrance Reel, developer of Relational Life Therapy, examined disagreements under the lens of "relational mindfulness." He explains that one's initial, knee-jerk reaction when faced with a disagreement is to fight, take flight, or fix. A fight reaction includes screaming back, hurting, or attacking. With flight, one either physically leaves, mentally tunes out, or turns to blocking substances like drink or drugs. Individuals in a fixing mode think, "I can't tolerate the tension of arguing so I will do whatever I must to fix it." None of these reactions stem from a mature place; they are all accompanied by frustration and resentment.

Be aware that partners act in response to one another. For example, the angrier one partner becomes, the more the other withdraws; and then, the more the other withdraws, the angrier the first partner becomes, causing a vicious cycle. Couples must remember that their goal is to remain connected. To do this, each partner must control his/

her first instinct to fight or flee, and work out the best path to restore a calm, cooperative, communicative relationship.

Everyone should examine his/her disagreements to determine if the issue over which s/he is fighting is really the crux of the argument, or whether s/he feels attacked or wounded, and therefore unconnected.

Marriage is nature's way of keeping people from fighting with strangers.

Couples must be willing to work together, realizing that neither one is always right or always wrong. Couples must compromise, although you can't ask a spouse to compromise on everything. Try to see the other person's point of view without needing to win *every* argument, because you can win many fights and lose your spouse. No one wants to be overruled all the time. The answer to "Who is right?" is "Who cares?" For the sake of the relationship, each person must understand that who is right or wrong is not important. If one partner says, "This doesn't work for me," then adjustments have to be made. A technique to help you determine whether you are right or wrong about what you are saying or doing is to ask yourself, "How would I react if my child said or did this?"

Each person must hear and validate what the other is saying. Validation does not mean you agree with your spouse, but it does mean that his/her opinion is heard, respected, and processed.

My husband needs glasses. He still doesn't see things my way.

Even when you disagree, discuss issues as equals and respect your spouse's point of view. Listen and try to understand where s/he is coming from, and his/her state of mind. Is s/he operating out of logic or frustration? Is his/her attitude due to overwork or stress? Is his/her attitude due to fear? Is s/he just trying to be heard? Is s/he trying to punish you, retaliate, or trying to equal the score?

In a marriage, each person should have the self-esteem to formulate his/her own opinion. Each one must be able to say, "I will not be coerced or threatened into making decisions that I am not comfortable with." It is fine and admirable if a person is willing to be swayed, but it is wrong for a person to be manipulated, controlled, criticized, or showered with guilt in order to change his/her stance. A person's free choice, as long as it is not at the expense of harming another, should be exercised. A person must be in touch with his/her own beliefs and needs in order to pursue them. Each one has to empower him-/herself so that together a couple can reach healthy decisions.

Each spouse's ability to retain self-esteem is based on the feeling of being secure in his/her partner's steadfast acceptance of him/her. Dr. Sue Johnson's Emotionally Focused Therapy for Couples is based on A.R.E.:

Accessibility

Responsiveness

Engagement

Accessibility means: "Can I reach you?" Despite your own emotional feeling of disconnection, you must be able to step back and hear your partner's concerns and fear of disconnection.

Responsiveness is defined as: "Can I rely on you to respond to me emotionally? Can you tune in and show me that my attachment needs and fears have an impact on you?"

Engagement asks: "Will you stay emotionally connected to me? Will you value me with the kind of attention one gives only to a loved one?"

My wife and I made a rule: If we quarreled, the one who was wrong would walk around the block. My wife hasn't been out of the house in thirty years.

Some people won't compromise because they feel hurt by their spouse's suggestion. Ira and Linda lived near Linda's parents, who visited the couple almost every day. Finally, Ira told Linda that he did not want her parents to visit more than twice a week. Linda was taken aback and felt there was no way she could tell this to her parents. She refused to discuss the issue at all, although she could have floated the idea of going by herself to her parents' house more often, so they would not feel the need to come every day. Eventually she walked out on her marriage.

Marriage is when a man and woman become as one. The trouble starts when they try to decide which one.

What makes a happy marriage is not how compatible you are, but how you deal with incompatibility. Couples deal with their differences in different ways. Some couples talk out their differences, while others argue a lot. In some marriages a couple who is upset will take a time-out; she might strum a guitar, and he might take a walk until they calm down enough to deal with their differences. During a time-out, a wise couple can put their differences in perspective, realizing that the problem is small compared to the "big marriage" they enjoy. As long as the style of arguing works for both husband and wife, and ultimately they are able to come to an agreement, that style is fine. However, if one partner wants to talk but the other partner wants to walk out, the couple has a problem that they must address. The great secret of a successful marriage is to treat all disasters as incidents and none of the incidents as disasters.

Just as you require a strategy when you go to war, you need to find the proper strategy for your marriage to run smoothly. People must learn to have a smart marriage. If one approach does not work, try another.

Remember, a quarrel is ended as soon as one party deserts the battlefront.

Love and care often work better than fighting. Rather than arguing and attempting to talk your spouse out of his/her opinion, acknowledge his viewpoint. When appropriate and permissible, hug him/her or stroke his/her face. If your spouse shows warm concern when you are stressed or worried, even if s/he is the cause of that worry, you feel that you are not alone.

Most of the time, the issues in an argument are not important in and of themselves. Their significance lies in the emotional distress they evoke, including feeling exploited, misunderstood, unloved, or disrespected. These feelings cause frustration and resentment because people need their spouse's respect. People do not like having their spouse dispute what they say, and that is why one should be particularly careful not to contradict his/her spouse in public. Some people find it especially difficult if their spouse questions or disagrees with them.

Many disagreements can be resolved easily, using common sense and logic. If a wife wants her husband to take her out every once in a while, a calm discussion might encourage her husband to think, "Okay, what's the big deal? If that makes her happy, I'll do it." Unfortunately, many husbands say, "How often is once in a while?" or, "You know we are trying to save up for a house. We really can't spend any money right now."

Choose your battles. Decide what is really important to you and therefore worth a disagreement.

Compromise! If a wife wants to go out three times a week, but her husband demurs, either because he has too much work, or because he likes to relax at home, an understanding wife says, "I understand. Maybe we can go out once a week, and perhaps twice a week sometimes." This works because the husband feels less pressured and his wife realizes he is making time for her.

Social issues are a common problem. Which wedding shall we attend? Whose parents shall we go to for the holiday? Some issues are spiritual. Which school offers enough religious values for our children? These kinds of issues can become emotionally charged. You must determine for yourself which issues are major and worth an argument. Often, each partner thinks a different issue is important. A woman may be overly emotional if she is discussing having a child, while her husband may be very logical. She wants her husband to understand the depth of her emotions, while he wants her to understand the issues of timing and the financial burden. Each must acknowledge and consider the other's point of view, dealing with it with the utmost sensitivity.

My wife and I were sitting at a table at my high school reunion, and I kept staring at a drunken woman swigging her drink as she sat alone at a nearby table.

My wife asked, "Do you know her?"

"Yes," I sighed. "I once dated her. I understand she started drinking right after we stopped seeing each other those many years ago, and I hear she hasn't been sober since."

"For heavens sake!" said my wife. "Who would think a person could go on celebrating that long?"

So you see, there really are two ways to look at everything...

Donna had just given birth to her first baby and was totally overwhelmed caring for her child and the apartment. She hoped her husband Dave would take notice and call in a cleaning woman to help her out. As her tiredness increased, her frustration with Dave continued to mount. Unable to hold back any longer, she finally burst into tears, accusing Dave of not caring about how hard she worked. Dave had noticed and truly did care! He said he wished Donna had asked for help. He had been too afraid to suggest it because Donna might have felt put down and hurt, as if he thought she weren't capable enough. Differences are often due to misunderstandings.

A man who compromises when he's wrong is wise. A man who compromises when he's right is married.

Men and women can fight over things as simple as the toilet seat. Women think men are inconsiderate because they never remember to put down the seat after they use the bathroom. Men think, "Why can't a woman put the seat down herself? We don't ask them to lift it up for us; why should we put it down for them?" Both have to adjust and be considerate. The good news is that a marriage can survive even if the man leaves the seat up and the wife leaves the seat down. Although an extra-considerate partner will do what the other wants, sooner or later everyone comes to an understanding and adjusts to a properly or improperly adjusted seat.

Following a holiday of watching marathon football games on television, a husband heard his wife attempting to wake him. "Honey, it's ten to seven," she said.

"Who's ahead?" he asked.

Many women never adjust to their husband's sports mania, which can cause perpetual arguments. They can't understand why, if there are only three minutes left to a game, it can still take forty minutes to end due to overtime and time-outs. But Sunday sports and Monday night football are here to stay. Women should learn not to fight that.

My wife will buy anything marked down. Last year she bought an escalator.

—*Henny Youngman*

On the other hand, many men are never reconciled to their wives' shopping. But shopping is in a woman's genes, even if most men don't want to accept that. Of course this too must be in moderation. Men feel about sports the way women think about shopping, so husbands and wives must learn to deal with these issues. The amount of time and money spent on sports and shopping must be negotiated by each husband and wife, although of course both these things must be in moderation.

Don't make ridiculous demands. Carol said, "If I gain five pounds my husband will divorce me." A husband can't expect his wife of twenty years to compete with twenty-one-year-old girls. Kate said, "If you can't make enough money for us to live in Manhattan, I am moving back in with my parents." Arguments and threats like that poison a relationship.

Although it is not the relationship of choice, some couples actually relate to each other through bickering, and they quite enjoy the arguing. For them it symbolizes real involvement and connection. Happily married couples can and do argue with each other, often raising their voices. Just because two people quarrel does not mean they don't love each other. It may be their way of communication. On the flip side, never arguing is not necessarily a sign of love between two people; it could be a sign of indifference or lack of communication. A relationship works because two people have things in common with each other, but the differences between two people can make a relationship passionate. Working through those differences and learning to live with them or change them are what make us grow.

My wife and I had a rather interesting fight last night. She said it was five days since our last fight – and I said it was four.

Influence one another for the better. If you truly dislike something in your spouse, don't adopt his/her bad habit in order to please him/her.

Be aware that domestic violence, whether it is emotional or physical abuse, is not a disagreement. It is abuse. It is a whole pattern of behaviors used by one partner to establish and maintain power and control over the other (refer to chapter 10, "Signs of Abusive Behavior").

It is advisable for a couple to agree on one individual, be it a marriage counselor, a rabbi, or a trusted friend, whom they can turn to for help with argument resolution.

A man was telling of his power at home, saying, "I'm the boss at home. Just this morning there was no hot water. I blew up. I demanded hot water and got hot water. I can't wash dishes in cold water!"

22: First Year

"I have discovered that the hardest years of marriage are the first ten," a man tells his psychologist.

"And how long have you been married?" the psychologist asks.

The man answers, "Ten years."

There is a road to discovery. My grandfather was fond of saying, "You know 1 percent about a person before marriage and you learn 99 percent after you are married." I can't swear by these statistics, but it is certainly true that you learn a lot about your spouse after marriage.

The only real argument for marriage is that it remains the best way to get acquainted. No matter how long or how often you date someone, there are certain things you learn only after marriage. Does your spouse wake at the drop of a pin or does it take an explosion to get his/her head off the pillow? Does s/he wake up cheery or grouchy? Does she look great without her makeup or are you in for a rude awakening? Does she even let you see her without makeup? Does he wet the entire floor when he showers or is he careful not to drip? Do we share hairbrushes and toothbrushes? Life is made up of millions of little details. You can question one another about lots of them prior to marriage, but it takes a lifetime of living together to get all the answers.

What is the difference between polygamy and monogamy? Polygamy is having one wife too many. Monogamy is the same.

During the first year of marriage couples learn about the person they are married to, and about the state of marriage as well.

My wife asked me to take her somewhere she had never been. I took her to the kitchen.

—*Henny Youngman*

The first year of marriage is like wet cement: the impressions made in it are hard to change. Start your marriage by being realistic and optimistic, ready for the challenge and armed with the conviction that no matter what happens, the two of you will make the marriage a success. Even in a marriage that's a week old, you can find grounds for divorce. The trick is to continually find reasons to stay together. Happily marrieds are not perfect marrieds; they are couples who have learned what it takes to be happy in a marriage.

Marriage is like twirling a baton, turning handsprings, or eating with chopsticks…it looks easy until you try it.

Marriage does not solve all your problems. It only solves the problem of whom to marry and with whom to create a life together. After you find the right person, you realize that marriage is not easy.

Shaindel, a newlywed, said, "I never realized how much work my mother must have put into preparing for Shabbos. I always thought the food just magically appears." Things that seemed simple when your parents were doing it seem overwhelming when the responsibility falls directly on you.

It takes time to grow into being a couple. Making a marriage successful takes two people working together and dealing constructively with day-to-day responsibilities to resolve tensions and problems.

Marriage is like a tea bag. When you first open the box, the aroma is sweet. Then you notice there are strings attached. And before you know it, you are in hot water!

Couples are exhausted after the wedding. The pressure and tension preceding the wedding takes a toll. The dancing and socializing at the wedding itself leaves a couple worn out. The week of *sheva brachos* may be exciting but it is also exhausting. Moving into a new apartment, decorating it, going through wedding gifts, writing thank-you cards, and returning gifts is overwhelming. Learning to cook, cleaning your own apartment, and doing laundry are all new and problematic experiences. Figuring out his responsibilities is a challenge for a new husband. He might analyze every move. Should he take out the garbage, or is he setting a precedent that he does not want to continue? Likewise, a new wife is also unsure of herself. Should she help carry the luggage? Does he want a helpless or a helpful wife? Is she threatening his manliness with her offers of help?

Marriages may be made in heaven, but the details are worked out here on earth.

Young couples often worry that only they are incompetent. Everyone else seems to know what to do and how to make his/her spouse perfectly happy. This is not true. Marriage is a new experience for everyone. No matter how proficient you are at doing new things, no matter your level of competency, everyone makes mistakes throughout his/her marriage, and this is especially true in the beginning.

When she gets through with burning a roast, it can only be identified through dental records.

No woman can forget the first time she did the laundry, and her husband's underwear turned a bright pink. With luck, the second time she does the wash she only turns it a nice shade of blue. This usually teaches the husband that you have to keep laughing and not sweat the little things. In a few months, when his wife gets the wash figured out, the husband will once again be wearing white underwear (how dull) while his newlywed friends are experimenting with designer colors.

He found a great way to eat his wife's soup. He pretends it is mud.

My first dinner with company was a disaster. My mother always called paprika "red pepper," so rather than buying paprika, I bought hot red pepper to spice the London broil I planned to serve for dinner. Luckily, my husband tasted it before his friends arrived. It was so hot that his eyes bulged out of their sockets. Still, I didn't realize my mistake.

I thought the meat must have spoiled, so I quickly ran out and bought another London broil and repeated my recipe. This time I tasted it. My heart was racing as I turned bright red and began choking. Now I knew I was doing something wrong. By this time the company had arrived, and I was without dinner. Bravely, I confessed that there was no food, and one of my husband's friends wondered aloud why I put red pepper on the meat. We all had a great laugh as I broiled a batch of minute steaks for dinner.

Eating my wife's cooking is like playing Russian roulette. I never know which meal is going to kill me.
—Harvey Stone

One of the first times I made *challah* I quadrupled the recipe, figuring I would give out *challas* to all my friends. I covered the dough to let it rise before I left for work in the morning. Because I knew that heat makes dough rise, I thought it would be smart to put the dough near the oven. I turned the oven on low, opened the oven door and left the bowl of dough sitting on the oven door. Returning from work in the afternoon, I felt like I had stumbled onto an *I Love Lucy* set. The dough had risen, spread all over the oven, and fallen down, covering the entire kitchen floor. Gathering the dough was an experience I will never forget. Globs of dough became bits of air as I tried to grab hold of them. Pieces stuck to the floor like glue. I couldn't stop laughing as my husband and I spent hours trying to clean up the mess.

My wife says that my problem is that I judge food too much by its taste.

I used to make a fabulous trifle of custard, whipped

cream, nuts, bananas, strawberries, coconut, and cherries. One Friday I bought the ingredients for the trifle but never found the time to assemble it. On Shabbos, my husband and I were walking home from shul with friends, and when we reached our apartment, I felt obligated to invite them in from the cold, despite having nothing to serve. Opening the refrigerator, I pulled out bowls of whipped cream and strawberries, a bowl of vanilla pudding, a bowl of bananas and walnuts, and a bowl of cherries, thinking that at least I had some food to serve them, even if it was an interesting assortment. My friend said, "What fun! Are we going to be making our own trifles?"

I bought my wife a foreign cookbook. Now she complains she can't get parts for our dinners.

Young wives are often intense about their cooking. They are eager to please; yet they have very little experience in the kitchen. Even girls who always helped their mothers in the kitchen have a hard time when shopping and preparing for a meal is solely their responsibility. It looks so easy when Mom does the cooking, because moms have had years of experience. But they also went through the nerve-wracking newlywed stage where ingredients are missing, new recipes flop, and overcooked or burned food is the norm. Just laugh through this period. You too will master cooking, along with the other skills of marriage. It just takes a little time.

I said, "Let's eat out tonight and give the smoke detector a rest."

Women soon discover that most men aren't really prepared for marriage.

Summer Classes for Men at
THE ADULT LEARNING CENTER
DEADLINE FOR REGISTRATION
Friday, August 22nd

NOTE: DUE TO THE LEVEL OF COMPLEXITY AND DIFFICULTY, CLASSES WILL BE LIMITED TO 8 PARTICIPANTS MAXIMUM

Class 1: How to Fill the Ice Cube Trays, Step by Step, with Slide Presentation. Meets 4 weeks, Monday and Wednesday, 7 to 9 PM.

Class 2: The Toilet Paper Roll: Does It Change Itself? Roundtable Discussion. Meets 2 weeks, Sundays, 12 to 2 PM.

Class 3: Fundamental Differences between the Laundry Hamper and the Floor, with Pictures and Explanatory Graphics. Meets Thursdays at 2 PM for 3 weeks.

Class 4: Dinner Dishes: Can They Levitate and Fly into the Kitchen Sink?
Examples on Video. Meets 4 weeks, Tuesdays and Thursdays, 7 to 9 PM.

Class 5: Learning How to Find Things, Starting with Looking in the Right Places and Not Turning the House Upside Down while Screaming.
Open Forum, Monday, 8 to 10 PM.

Class 6: Health Watch: Bringing Her Flowers Is Not Harmful to Your Health. Graphics and Audio Tapes. Three nights: Monday, Wednesday, Friday, 7 to 9 PM.

Class 7: Real Men Ask for Directions When Lost. Real-Life Testimonials. Tuesdays at 6 PM, location to be determined.

Class 8: Is It Genetically Impossible to Sit Quietly While She Parallel Parks?

Driving Simulations. 4 weeks, Sundays, 12 to 2 PM.

Class 9: How to Be the Ideal Shopping Companion: Relaxation Exercises, Meditation, and Breathing Techniques. Meets 4 weeks, Tuesdays and Thursdays, 7 to 9 PM.

Class 10: How to Fight Cerebral Atrophy: Remembering Birthdays, Anniversaries, and Other Important Dates and Calling When You're Going to Be Late. Cerebral Shock Therapy Sessions and Full Lobotomies Offered. Three nights, Monday, Wednesday, Thursday, 7 to 9 PM.

Class 11: The Stove/Oven: What It Is and How It Is Used. Live Demonstration. Tuesdays at 6 PM, location to be determined.

Upon completion of any of the above courses, diplomas will be issued to the survivors.

—Anonymous

23: Ingredients for a Successful Marriage

You always know when the relationship is over. Little things start grating on your nerves. "Would you please stop that? That breathing in and out, it's so repetitive!"
—*E.D.*

Too many people go into marriage totally unprepared – unprepared to work at it; unprepared to commit; unprepared to sacrifice; unwilling to bend, compromise, and respect one another; and unwilling to devote themselves to making the other one happy. Rather, they think of *me*: make *me* happy, see it *my* way, do it *my* way. And they need more – more attention, more money, more understanding, and more excitement.

Marriage is about learning to give, share, care, and think

about your spouse's needs and desires. When both people work at a marriage, the marriage can work. Everyone wants to be happy when they marry. You will be happy when you make your spouse happy, and in turn, your spouse is working to make you happy. A marriage works when two people work at making each other happy.

Standing under the *chuppah*, marriage canopy, Rav Dessler says, the *chassan* and *kallah* both want to give. Each dreams of making his/her new spouse happy. But suddenly, after the wedding, too many individuals think, "What about my happiness? '*Im ein ani li mi li*, If I am not for myself, who is?' If I don't look out for my rights and my wishes, who will?" Each half of the young couple begins to focus on him-/herself rather than on his/her partner.

But, Rav Dessler continues, one must remember the rest of the verse, "*Im ani la'atzmi mah ani*, If I am only for myself, what am I?" A narcissist is one who thinks only about himself and his own needs. He focuses on the thought "*Bishvili nivra haolam*, The world was created for me." Although it is true that Hashem created this world for each individual to enjoy, one must also remember "*Lo l'atzmo nivra haolam*, Not for him alone was the world created." This world is not just about me and my needs. I was created to do for others, to convert my enjoyment into the opportunity to do good deeds.

Rav Dessler explains that a person's greatness is defined by the size of one's *ani*, one's "I." An individual whose "I" means I alone, is a small person. The individual who incorporates his wife and children and their wants and needs into his "I" is a greater person; and the individual who can encompass his community and all of *Klal Yisrael*, the Jewish nation, into his "I" is an even greater person.

One should continually strive to recreate the feeling one experienced at the inception of the marriage, giving to your spouse and incorporating your spouse's wishes into your every thought. The more you give, the more you love.

At a cocktail party, one woman said to another, "Aren't you wearing your wedding ring on the wrong finger?"

The other replied, "Yes I am. I married the wrong man."

A successful marriage depends more on being the right person than finding the right person. Assuming both individuals are mentally and intellectually competent, if you treat the wrong person like the right person, s/he'll turn into the right person. You can bring out the best in his/her attitude and personality; likewise, s/he will bring out the best in you. If you treat the right person the wrong way, you can turn your spouse into the wrong person, and you will bring out the worst in each other. By deciding to be the right or wrong person, you determine whether you married the right or wrong person.

My mom had good advice about staying married for a long time. She said, "Always remember, honesty is very important. It must be avoided. And the most important thing is, you have to let your husband be himself, and you have to pretend he's someone else."

—*Rita Rudner*

Some say if a wife treats her husband like a king he will treat her like a queen and vice versa. In an ideal world this holds true. But sometimes he may feel smothered or pressured, and she may feel talked down to or inadequate. A wife who does not want to upset her husband and therefore does not complain when he says hurtful things is giving her husband a false sense of security. A husband who sleeps on the sofa because he is angry with his wife, yet he tells her it's because he doesn't want his alarm to wake her, is likewise giving her a false message. Although you should not make a fuss over little things, disagreements that are ignored can lead to resentment that eventually builds up a lot of anger.

It is important to learn about and fill each other's needs at the same time that you communicate your own needs with sensitivity. Caring about your spouse and working to discover what makes him/her happy and fulfilled while considering your own needs as well helps promote a better marriage.

Of course, marriage is not about keeping score, reckoning who gives more or who receives more. Mature adults are able to give and receive without tallying points. A person should be able to give love without adding it to the debit column. A person should be able to receive love without feeling a sense of debt.

I want my husband to come home and whisper those three little words that all women long to hear: "You were right."

—*Kelly Smith*

It is great to marry someone you love, but it is more important to love the person you marry. The idea is to choose your love, then love your choice.

Richard thought he'd married a quiet, demure girl. During the dating period she had been reserved, agreeable, and almost subservient. After the wedding he found she was actually loud and opinionated with a tendency to be disagreeable. At first Richard was stunned. Then he reevaluated the situation, especially because he knew that Rita had loads of great qualities. She was a thoughtful, compassionate, giving person with a good heart and fine intentions. Her loudness stemmed from insecurity and a need for attention. When Rita was loud, Richard laughed at her jokes. When Rita was opinionated and demanding, Richard would acknowledge the merit of her opinion and then suggest another way of looking at things. When her opinion was right, as it often was, he confirmed it with a big smile. If the issue was not an important one, he often just kept quiet if he didn't agree with her. Rita learned that his silence was a private sign of disapproval. She began to reevaluate her way of communicating in an effort to be rewarded with that wonderful smile of approval.

The secret of a happy marriage remains a secret.
—Henny Youngman

Marriage doesn't automatically make you happy and satisfied. It is up to you to make your marriage happy and satisfying. A good relationship is more a process of learning the dance than of choosing the right dance partner. "Sometimes you make the right decision. Sometimes you have to make the wrong decision right" (Phillip C. McGraw).

If you are married and now wonder if you made a mistake, do not panic. Everyone has to put effort into his/her marriage. Some people have to put in more effort, and sometimes you must seek help. Marriages that start off on shaky ground can become very stable when the spouses work together, investing time and energy to understand each other and establish a powerful foundation for a good marriage. It takes two to tango, and two to invest in a marriage and make it work.

I love being married. I was single for a long time, and I just got so sick of finishing my own sentences.
—Brian Kiley

Even those who marry each other because they are compatible rather than being in love with each other will find that love grows with a little nurturing. Sharing, communicating, and having a physical connection make love flourish.

The first part of our marriage was very happy. But then, on the way back from the ceremony...
—Henny Youngman

Even when people marry for love, they are not usually in love every moment of every day throughout their marriage. They may feel a comfortable feeling of love but not feel "in love." Over a lifetime marriages will run the gamut of feeling madly in love, devastated, totally connected, numb, indifferent, angry, thrilled, ecstatic, frustrated, turned on, turned off, enlightened, and just comfortable. We work through the tough times because we know that the relationship is right or because we want to make it right.

I was once kidnapped and my wife didn't want to pay the ransom. She said she didn't want to break a ten.

Love is a feeling, marriage is a contract, and a relationship is work. Keep your eye on your goal line. Your goal is to make your marriage a strong and loving one. Do what you must in order to achieve that goal. If you look and listen with a positive eye and ear, you will appreciate what you have. If you look at everything with a critical eye and ear, it will all seem negative. Your life becomes a self-fulfilling prophecy, and you create your own reality. View and hear what your spouse says with optimism.

A sign reads: Lost dog, scar across face, missing one ear, limps, blind in one eye, answers to the name "Lucky."

The best way to make a marriage work is to concentrate on your spouse's positive qualities and on the positive side of your relationship, so the negative aspects can remain in perspective. In a good marriage a wife can say, "He may drive me nuts sometimes, but I still find him adorable." Or a husband can say, "She may have gained a lot of weight, but I still find her attractive." When the focus is on the whole rather than the parts, the negative parts don't overshadow the positive ones. The friendship, the sharing of memories and dreams, the looking back and forward, the opening up and confiding, the reaching out and pulling in, the respect, the need for one another, the dependence, the sharing inside jokes and private thoughts, the understanding of each others' moods and feelings and even predicting them, all form a bond that overrides the disagreements and weaves an unbreakable connection, binding a couple together.

I have learned that it is important to compliment your wife's cooking. For example: "I suppose it's a matter of taste, but I like the burnt part better than the frozen part."

Spouses in a good marriage care for each other. They are willing to be unselfish and see someone else's view, and they are secure enough to appreciate each other's differences. They are able to run a home emotionally, negotiating compromises, managing feelings of anger and frustration, communicating their dreams and goals, and working together to fulfill them.

Marriage is about two people feeling they each have someone to turn to and count on who will give them emotional security. Psychologist J. Bowlby describes the benefit of "effective dependency," which is the positive affect of being able to turn to others for emotional support. Of course, this too must be in moderation. Dr. Sue Johnson concludes that "a sense of secure connection between partners is key in positive, loving relationships and a huge source of strength for the individuals in those relationships" (Johnson, Dr. Sue, *Hold Me Tight* [New York: Hatchette Book Group, 2008]).

Ever since we got married, my wife has tried to change me. She got me to stop drinking, smoking, and running around until all hours of the night. She taught me how to dress well, enjoy the fine arts, like gourmet cooking, enjoy classical music, even how to invest in the stock market," said the man.

"Sounds like you may be bitter because she changed you so drastically," remarked his friend.

"I'm not bitter. Now that I'm so improved, she just isn't good enough for me."

24: Men and Women Are Different

Men and women are a lot alike in some situations. Like when they're both on fire, they're exactly alike.
—*Dave Attell*

In 1992, Dr. John Gray wrote *Men are from Mars; Women are from Venus*, reiterating something that many of us already knew: Men and women are different! Studies show that men and women act, react, interact, think, speak, and even experience life differently. In order to make a marriage work, husbands and wives have to be cognizant of this fact.

Every person is searching for a unique mate, yet studies show that all men are alike in many ways, as are women, and they are both different from each other.

Husbands never think they have a headache; they think they have a brain tumor. My husband always says, "What should I take for a brain tumor?" I give him baking soda.

—*Rita Rudner*

Although a woman's brain is approximately 10 percent smaller than that of a man, it has more neural connections. Dr. Marianne Legato, founder of the Partnership for Gender-Specific Medicine at Columbia University, writes, "Women get more brain bang for the buck."

Men like cars. Women like to shop. Women like cars only because they take them to the store to shop.

Men hardly ever shop and always have what to wear. Women shop all the time and never have a thing to wear.

A man's life is less stressful. For one thing, whatever he is wearing now will be in style for the rest of his life. A man never went to a party and said "Quick! Get me out of here. Someone is wearing the same black tuxedo!"

The reason women don't play football is because eleven of them would never wear the same outfit in public.

—*Phyllis Diller*

Men are happy if they all look alike because it means they haven't made a mistake.

Men are afraid that if they make a wrong turn, we'll never get back to our lives. I never panic when we get lost. I just change where I want to go.

—*Rita Rudner*

Men are better at map reading. They may not have the gene to ask for directions but they are more adept at getting to their destination. The male brain focuses on real facts such as miles and direction, whereas women focus on recognizable things like landmarks.

I have a bad memory. So far this month, I forgot my wife's birthday, our wedding anniversary, and who's the boss.

Because they have higher levels of estrogen, which aids in memory, women remember things better, including remembering things that happened a long time ago. A man may be having a simple argument with his wife and she will throw in all the times that he forgot her birthday.

Marriage is the alliance of two people, one who never remembers birthdays and one who never forgets.

—Ogden Nash

Most men maintain that anything said six months ago is inadmissible in an argument. In fact, they all *seem* to agree that comments become null and void in seven days. You will not find many women agreeing to this.

Women's stress hormones remain elevated longer. That is why women remain angrier for longer. Men are content to let an argument go unresolved, while a woman wants to discuss it.

I haven't spoken to my wife in years. I didn't want to interrupt her.

Women have a greater need to communicate with their husbands than vice versa because they have a larger capacity for communication and body language. Studies show that a man's brain and a woman's brain process language differently. In "How Genders Think" (*New York Post*, November 1, 2006), author Sara Stewart cites the results of a study showing an inverse correlation between testosterone and verbal ability in males. The higher the testosterone level, the lower the verbal ability. The study also indicated that while women have better developed speech centers, men communicate more concisely and efficiently. A woman might discuss their relationship ad nauseam while her spouse tersely responds, "Uh-huh." Many women talk themselves into exhaustion, yet men are happy to avoid confrontation and keep quiet.

The Sages teach that ten measures of speech came down to this world, nine of which were given to women. Properly used, speech is an arena of achievement. "*Hakol min ha'isha*, Everything comes from the woman" (*Bereishis Rabbah* 17:12). A good woman and worthy wife makes her husband righteous, and the opposite is also true. Used correctly, women can influence, encourage, and empower their husbands and children through their power of speech. With calm words and a serene tone of voice, women can create a beautiful and harmonious atmosphere in the home.

A husband read an article to his wife about how many words women use each day: 30,000 to a man's 15,000. The wife replied, "That is because women have to repeat everything to men."

The husband turned to his wife and asked, "What?"

For one marriage exercise, a therapist divided a group of ten couples by gender. Placing the men in one room and the women in a second room, he instructed each group to write down ten things that bothered them about their spouse. When the allotted time span was over, he asked one of the men, "Before we begin, tell me the names of the other men." The man didn't know. He then asked, "Tell me what the other men do for a living." Neither that man nor any of the other men could answer him. When the therapist asked one woman the same questions, she knew four of the women's names and was also able to tell him about most of their work involvements. "This," the therapist said, "is the difference between men and women. Women are relationship oriented." It is therefore up to a wife to help her husband form a relationship. She is the one to encourage conversation and the sharing of confidences.

Men and women have always had problems relating. As children, men were told, "Be a man. Don't cry!" Women were told, "Let it out. Cry and you will feel better!" And that's why as adults, women become very emotional and men become snipers.

—Pam Stone

When a woman speaks to a man, she should cut her planned introductory remarks by 90 percent! This is what Sylvia wants to tell Barry: "Mom went to the doctor, who suggested that she see a back specialist. Now she is considering back surgery, which will cause her to be out of commission for weeks. She will have a long recuperation period, and after the operation she will have to exercise quite a bit to get herself back into shape. She has no one to take care of her, although a nurse or a friend might drop by once or twice."

This is too much detail for Barry. Sylvia will likely find him dozing off rather than really paying attention. Sylvia should limit her remarks to: "Mom may need a back operation. Do you mind if she stays with us after the surgery so I can help her?"

It has been biologically proven that men are more easily overwhelmed by marital arguments than women. In 85 percent of marriages the husband is the one who tunes out during a marital confrontation. Many men keep their thoughts and feelings to themselves, not realizing that women feel shut out.

Some people go through life hoping their spouse will figure out what is bothering them. But you must speak up and tell your spouse what you are feeling, even if you have to force yourself to do so. It will help you and your marriage. Eighty percent of men withdraw from any conflict, since they feel attacked. Because they don't know how to deal with that type of stress they shut off. On the flip side, 80 percent of women become louder and more aggressive as they try to force their husbands to communicate. As the women become shriller, the men become less communicative. Obviously, this scenario does not promote understanding.

If a woman has to choose between catching a fly ball and saving an infant's life, she will choose to save the infant's life without even considering if there is a man on base.

—Dave Barry

Women talk in order to feel close, to share feelings, and to elicit understanding. They speak to build a relationship and to establish a connection.

I had some words with my wife, and she had some paragraphs with me.

Men speak to exhibit strength, knowledge, and power. They enjoy stating their opinions and willingly show their grasp of business, news, or sports. They do not take criticism well. They do not like to be told that they are insensitive or do not understand. They don't want to discuss their problems, preferring to keep those things to themselves. Their usual response is, "Don't worry. I have it under control." Most men help their wives deal with problems by saying, "I'm sure it will be fine." But some women are offended by this attitude, which can be perceived as aloof.

Whereas most women are uncomfortable and feel threatened arguing with someone they love, some men feel quite comfortable showing their authority in this way.

It is better to keep one's mouth shut and be thought a fool than to open it and resolve all doubt.

—Abe Lincoln

Most men do not have the patience to sit and listen to women talk about their emotions, preferring substance instead. They feel it is not manly to discuss sentiment. In fact, men and women are usually bored with the other's topics of discussion.

Women have a greater need to speak and they are often hurt when a man doesn't express his feelings. A man who has nothing he feels like saying will say nothing, whereas a woman will feel the need to keep the conversation flowing.

Most women are introspective. "Am I in love? Am I emotionally and creatively fulfilled?"

Most men are "extrospective." "Did my team win? How's my car?"

—Rita Rudner

A man must be trained to tune in to his wife's feelings. Although he may require time to think and organize his thoughts, a husband must realize he can't shut his wife out for an extended period of time because she will be hurt.

Both men and women are sensitive to their spouses' reactions. When a relationship is in crisis, men typically say they feel rejected, inadequate, and like a failure, while women usually say they feel abandoned and disconnected. Women also respond by reaching out to their partner. Researchers call this a "tend and befriend" reaction, attributing it to the presence of more oxytocin, the "cuddle hormone," in their blood, which comes into play when a woman feels this disconnect.

A group of men are waiting to enter heaven. The angel says, "All men who are henpecked by their wives line up on the right. All men who are not henpecked by their wives line up on the left."

All the men stand on the right side, except for Sruli. The angel says to him, "Sruli, you are the only husband who stood on the line for those men who were not henpecked by their wives. Why is that?"

Sruli shrugs, "I don't know. My wife told me to go on this line."

Many men are ready to give advice, but they do not want to be told what they ought to do. Because they are insecure about this, they want to be in the driver's seat, rather than feel their wife is the boss. Some men will refuse to do what their wife asks in order to show her who is in charge. Others are worried that helping their spouse will set a precedent that they don't want to continue.

Yussel buys a horse and feeds it three times a day, but finds it very expensive. Because the horse is strong, Yussel decides it can probably survive on two meals a day. The horse continues to thrive so that Yussel cuts down to one meal a day. Still the horse does well enough for Yussel to think, "Why not save money? I'll just give it water without feeding it at all." The horse lives for a week and then drops dead. Yussel is totally frustrated, "Just when I finally teach my horse to live without food, he goes and dies on me."

If there's no communication between spouses concerning each other's needs, just when one spouse thinks his/her partner is acting the way s/he wants, the partner will get up and walk out on the marriage.

What's the difference between apathy and ignorance?

I don't know and I don't care!

Most women naturally include their families in their lives. They automatically share their company, their thoughts, their belongings, and their food. Although Jewish men are better than most, men often have to be reminded to include their wives in their calculations.

Ah, children. A woman knows all about her children. She knows about dentist appointments and romances, best friends, favorite foods, secret fears, and hopes and dreams. A man is vaguely aware of some short people living in the house.

Most men are not as naturally interested in and worried about their children as women are.

Most men want to be respected for their accomplishments. They do not want to be told what to do or how to do it. They want to prove they can earn a living, find their way, read a map, fix the broken door, and change a lightbulb. (Of course, a woman must find the bulb for him, hold the chair, and switch the light off.) They don't need anyone's help. They are competitive in business, sports, even in predicting the weather. They have a need to be taken seriously and admired for their successes. This can cause many men to put their wives and families after their business, creating a great deal of marital strife.

In order to retain their self-respect and reinforce their image of being in control, men like to resolve issues without any help. Women would rather have their emotions validated. Understanding your own psychological needs as well as your partner's psychological needs helps a husband and wife feel fulfilled.

Because men need to feel capable, they do not like it if their wives are better at sports than they are. The adage "Win at tennis, lose at love" has a lot of truth to it. They do not want their abilities challenged, their business acumen questioned, or their opinions analyzed. They do not even like being second-guessed about directions. They want appreciation and acceptance.

Arriving at the hotel, the new bride asked her husband, "What can we do to hide the fact that we just got married?"

He said, "You carry the luggage."

That's why men should carry suitcases for their wives, grab packages from their arms, and open doors for women. It makes the women feel good and the husband feel manly.

If a man is alone in the forest and he makes a statement but no one is around to hear it, is he still wrong?

Women thrive on talking and spending time in groups, whereas men like to do things on their own.

Women are better at multitasking than men, while men are better at focusing on and completing a single task. When a man is concentrating on one subject or a single task, a woman should not distract him with another task, or by starting a conversation.

To be happy with a man you must understand him a lot and love him a little. To be happy with a woman you must love her a lot and not try to understand her at all.
—Helen Rowland

Men want love but are usually quickly satisfied and happy to return to their independent state of doing work, learning, doing their hobby, or being with the fellows. This is normal behavior for men, and they resent it if their wife does not understand, but is instead critical of this behavior.

Women need to like the job of the guy they're dating. If men are physically attracted to a woman, they are not that concerned with her job.

"Slaughterhouse? You're just lopping their heads off? Great! Why don't you shower, and we'll get some burgers."
—Jerry Seinfeld

Men and women must feel that their spouse respects what they do for a living, although most men feel that their wife's job and salary is not that important of an issue.

The Rambam identifies respect as the primary male need. This translates into his being seen as the authority figure, the man of the house, looked up to and even revered. Supplying this affect nourishes and supports the male ego. Right or wrong, easy or difficult, like it or not, the reality is that this constitutes the hard drive of the male persona. It is part and parcel of the way he is constructed.

Most husbands like to believe that only he can fill his wife's needs. To satisfy his ego he wants to be acknowledged as dependable, yet he will feel smothered if he feels she is totally reliant on him.

On the other hand, women just want to be loved. Although they also want respect, their basic need is to love and be loved in return. They want their husbands to be available to them without any barriers. This difference has to be worked out between couples. A man who works non-stop and does not make sufficient time for his wife must know that she will feel lonely and emotionally drained. He may wonder: *What does she want from me? I love her. I give her a beautiful home and everything she asks for; if I work less, I won't be able to give her this magnificent lifestyle.* He is filling his own need, not hers. She would gladly have fewer presents and have his presence.

My wife says she doesn't understand football. Why would seventy thousand people gather in one place for anything, except dollar days at Kmart?

Men and women have different interests. From an early age boys are playing and watching sports while girls are talking and playing house. This difference is biological and makes women better prepared for relationships, interaction, and communication. Of course, because of their orientation for sports, men are far better than woman at yelling, "Go! Go! Go!"

Men are sensitive in strange ways. If a man has built a fire and the last log does not burn, he takes it personally.
—*Rita Rudner*

Women are usually more sensitive and more emotional than men.

The great question, which I have not been able to answer, is, "What does she want?"
—*Sigmund Freud*

I have been told that a man really wants to make his wife happy. I believe it starts that way, but after a while all a man wants is not to be in trouble with his wife.

You know what I did before I got married? Anything I wanted to do.
—*Henny Youngman*

Most people are under the misconception that men make the first move. Studies show that men fear failure and rejection and do not want to waste their time. Therefore, it is only after a woman returns a man's glance and signals that she is approachable that he will make a move.

Most men and women do not truly understand one another; however, a smart husband will understand that a woman is less hormonal and stressed at different times of the month. If he is sensitive to this, he will discuss important issues during a woman's most energetic, least emotional times.

We don't know much about women. We know when they're happy, we know when they're crying, we know

when they're mad. We just don't know what order those moods are going to come at us.

—*Evan Davis*

Educating men and women about their differences, as Dr. John Gray did, and teaching them how to deal with the emotions of the opposite sex helps couples cope with marriage. Men and women will be in a better position to accept their spouses, please them, and be happy with them and their marriage. Learning these skills can help each spouse strengthen his/her relationship.

After marriage a guy often wonders how he ever even managed to get dressed by himself.

No matter the differences, both men and women want to marry someone who will be a good friend to them and who will respect them. If there is a strong friendship and a powerful bond between the couple, their differences will be a small, inconsequential part of their feelings for one another. This invaluable friendship will cause romance, passion, and love to carry the couple through life.

The city council decided to build a new tunnel from Manhattan to Queens and gave the plan out to contractors for bids. Browns Construction Company gave a bid of thirty million dollars. Grace Construction came in at twenty-seven million. Green Brothers bid two thousand. *Impossible*, **thought each member of the council when they saw the Green Brothers' bid, but they agreed to give the contract to the brothers since their bid was the lowest.**

The council invited the brothers in and said, "All the other bids were in the high millions, and yours was

very low. Can you tell us how you plan to construct the tunnel for that price?"

"Very simple," said Abe. "I take a shovel and go to the Manhattan side and begin digging. My brother Isaac goes to the Queens side and starts digging. When we meet, you have your tunnel."

"Okay," said the council, "but what happens if you don't meet?"

"In that case," said Abe, "for the same price you get two tunnels."

If a husband and wife can't find a way to meet, they will each create separate lives. Men and women are different and husbands and wives are different, but you can accept and bridge your differences by caring about each other. With some compromising you can meet somewhere in the middle and tunnel your way into each other's lives.

25: The Need for Self-Esteem

My father said I wouldn't amount to anything. Lucky guess.

—David Cousins

Each partner in a marriage must have a healthy self-esteem in order to understand and accept the things his/her spouse says or does without misconstruing its meaning. A self-confident person is able to overlook other people's words and actions, not taking them personally and reacting inappropriately to them. Furthermore, a person with a healthy self-esteem does not allow another person to define him/her, or manipulate him/her into being someone s/he is not.

Of course a self-confident person is not someone who holds him-/herself above others, looking down on them, or one who thinks s/he is always right and others are always wrong. A person should be secure enough to understand him-/herself, as well as to be sensitive to others. In a good marriage the partners are neither selfish nor selfless. Value yourself so your feelings and opinions never cease to matter. Value your spouse so his/her feelings and opinions are always heard and considered.

You need not be perfect to have self-esteem. No one is. Possessing self-esteem means having a generally positive feeling about yourself, your abilities, and your opinions. Someone with self-esteem does not belittle him-/herself just because s/he has some flaws. S/he knows that no one is perfect and all people have some flaws. Self-esteem is about forgiving yourself for your imperfections.

A woman worries about the future until she gets a husband. A man never worries about the future until he gets a wife.

Making yourself feel whole is your responsibility. Recognize your own insecurities, jealousies, sensitivities, faults, and frustrations and work to conquer them.

I'd marry the right girl – someone beautiful, successful, and independent who only wants to talk about me.
—*Richard Jeni*

Self-validation is crucial in every aspect of a person's life, whether it is how one behaves, speaks, appears, or conducts business. Your spouse's validation should be an extra bonus, not a necessity. Needing a spouse to validate you makes you too dependent and vulnerable.

Before one can be part of a pair s/he must be an individual. S/he must enrich his/her own life; develop his/her own thoughts, abilities, and talents; and expand his/her own outlook.

Although each of the pair must give to one another and depend on one another, each must independently be whole. A man must cultivate his ability to support a wife and family, financially and emotionally. A woman must develop her intelligence and personality. Each must develop his/her social and verbal skills, since communication is the key to a relationship. Together a husband and wife become part of a greater whole.

Michael would return from work to find Sarah still in her pajamas, begging for conversation. She had no life of her own because she had not cultivated any friendships and did not work out of the house. Because she was desperate for attention, she resented it if Michael called his friends or brought home any work. By being so emotionally dependent on Michael, she drained him, depriving him of his own emotional space and energy. Sarah needed to be a person in her own right in order to have self-esteem without suffocating Michael. She needed her own thoughts, ideas, and outside interests to contribute to their relationship.

Neither a husband nor a wife should dominate the other. Rather, each should make the other feel important and needed. Both partners need to feel that their accomplishments are respected, their opinions matter, and their decisions carry weight. Both spouses can give their partners this feeling by showing appreciation and by complimenting each other. Be helpful, compassionate, and non-judgmental so your spouse will turn to you, seeking your involvement and advice.

A woman was bemoaning the fact that her husband

had left her for the sixth time.

"Don't worry," consoled the neighbor, "he'll be back."

"Not this time," sobbed the wife. "This time he took his golf clubs."

If you feel insecure, do whatever it takes to feel better about yourself. If you think you are not a good provider, find a way to get a better education or a better job. If you feel unaccomplished, find some area in which you can shine. Take up singing, art, a sport, or exercise. Get involved in charity work, which is mentally rewarding, or take a parenting or marriage relationship course. Become better at something so you are proud of yourself. Once you respect yourself, you will not be so desperate for the respect of others.

People are insecure for different reasons and to varying degrees. Insecurity is usually present in people who were raised in a chaotic, unpredictable, volatile, or abusive environment. People who were subjected to unrealistic rules and expectations can feel inadequate, lacking belief in their personal goodness, skills, or abilities.

Insecurity can develop in individuals who never received positive reinforcement, in those who received too much criticism, in people whose opinion was considered unimportant, and in a person who believes s/he was a continuous disappointment or source of embarrassment to his/her parents. These people can develop a self-defeatist attitude, a lack of trust in others, and the belief that they will never amount to anything.

Insecurity can also develop in people who were given everything without ever proving to themselves that they could earn it, or who were given very little discipline, leaving them unable to cope with pressures. Additionally, people who felt overshadowed or overlooked, thinking they had to vie for a parent's attention can be insecure. Unfortunately, in today's society insecurity is quite common.

My father's not a warm and fuzzy guy. He can't bring himself to ask about my feelings or emotions. All he ever asks is, "How's the car doing?"

Finally, I said, "The car is experiencing low self-esteem and financial distress. The car could use a new computer, and probably a new car."

—Dana Eagle

How you feel about yourself will define your relationships, moral values, education, ethics, career choices, and finances. Children who are raised feeling insecure, belittled, and controlled tend to become controlling, demanding, and rigid in their rules and views. They often refuse to do or agree to anything their spouse asks for, believing their spouse is trying to control them. They may be starved for love, envious, fearful, easily frustrated, insensitive, manipulative, needy, demanding, depressed, or easily angered. A person like this can't hear his/her spouse, and thus can't work to create a beautiful family unit.

Married life is frustrating. The first year of marriage, the man speaks and the woman listens. In the second year, the woman speaks and the man listens. In the third year, they both speak and the neighbors listen.

An insecure person can resent a spouse who manages the family finances, taking charge and making decisions; s/he can also resent a spouse who is afraid to make these decisions. His/her treatment of the children may be too strict or overly lenient. S/he may often operate on the extreme of the behavioral spectrum.

A few days ago I was working on the roof and fell off. Torn and bloody, I managed to make it back into the house. My son asked, "What did you bring me?"

Someone who received everything s/he always asked for when s/he was a child may interpret a spouse's refusal of anything – even a legitimate refusal – as a rejection.

Having kids is like eating half a grapefruit. No matter what you try, you end up with a little squirt.

Parents are challenged with making their children feel protected, secure, capable, valued, happy, and unconditionally loved, without overly indulging them. Mature, caring parents will consider the needs and feelings of their children, allowing them to express a dissenting opinion. They will protect their children. They will not deliberately hurt, berate, or embarrass them. They will help their children thrive by directing them, yet allow them to make their own mistakes and learn from them. They know that trust builds character. Healthy parents foster a relationship that is not self-serving. Rather, it is based on what is best for one's child. Loving parents instill positive self-esteem and good values.

However, try as we will, most parents cannot control everything life throws at their children. Most people, therefore, are insecure in some way, and they can develop some negative habits that affect their married life.

My dad asked me, "Stuie, have I been a good father?"

I answered, "Dad, you're the best. Why do you ask?"

He said, "I wanted to make sure the way you turned out is your own fault."
—Stu Trivax

Insecure people are often envious of the relationship between their spouse and his/her family or friends, almost as if there were a competition. Often, a husband or wife will marry a spouse who is close to his/her family or friends, and then embark on a campaign to rip the spouse away from family and friends in order to become the center of his/her life. But a certain amount of family enmeshment is beneficial. It creates a feeling of belonging.

A spouse who allows you to hold on to the people you love, albeit with a newly developed degree of separation, is someone you learn to love more and will eventually be cherished and appreciated more than anyone else.

A good family empowers you, giving you people to trust, rely on, and mutually love and appreciate. It also helps you foster positive feelings about yourself. Because most people do not leave home emotionally, a good family is a good influence and is beneficial to a marriage.

This marriage was made in heaven, but so was thunder and lightning.

Of course, people from a good family can still bring issues into the marriage. It is not only your upbringing but also how you react to that upbringing that shapes your ideas and attitudes about your marriage. An eldest child who was given a lot of responsibility and may have mastered taking responsibility may now resent all responsibility or may resent not being given full responsibility. A middle child may be well adjusted and content to be in the background, or s/he may insist that his/her opinions always be heard. A youngest child may have always had his/her needs catered to and may expect a spouse to continue catering to every whim, or s/he may resent a spouse who tells her/him what to do since s/he does not want to feel like the baby in the family. An only child may want to be in the spotlight or may have learned independence. A child from a large family may demand attention, or he may have learned to share and compromise because of the family dynamics. Sibling rivalry for a parent's affection also has a major affect on how one reacts to his/her spouse.

Each person must consider if the issues s/he is experiencing stem from his/her own insecurity, and if so, how s/he can understand and deal with the problem. A loving, encouraging, and reassuring partner can help a spouse conquer his/her insecurities, while a bad spouse can take a secure person and destroy his/her self-esteem through negativism, indifference, and rejection. When individuals complain that their spouse is verbally abusing them, they usually believe their spouse is mentally playing into their insecurities, making them feel incapable, inadequate, and unneeded.

I was set up with a woman. On our date her hair caught fire. And all she talked about was herself.

"I'm on fire!" **You know the type.**

"Oh, G-d, help me! Put it out!"

Come on, can't we talk about me a little bit?

—Gary Shandling

Insecure people often have a desperate need for attention and approval. Their approach to problems is not rational. They may believe that everything that goes wrong is their fault, or they may never take responsibility for anything that goes wrong. Some become depressed and can't function. Others become self-absorbed; they try to be noticed and gain respect by turning into control freaks, hurting themselves and their marriage.

Insecure individuals may be quiet and subservient, or they may be loud and confrontational. People who are insecure are often anxious and intimidated by differences. An insecure person feels inadequate and may worry that his/her spouse will stop loving him/her and find someone else.

It can be hard to identify insecure individuals, because some insecure people overcompensate by acting overly confident and secure.

A neurotic is a person who worries about things that didn't happen in the past, instead of worrying about things that won't happen in the future, like normal people do.

—Henny Youngman

Insecure individuals tend to interpret everything as a put-down. Weak self-esteem causes a person to be easily insulted; s/he feels slighted by statements that they take the wrong way. A husband offers help with the dishes and his wife interprets it as: *Are you suggesting that I am incapable of doing this chore myself?* A wife wants to finish the crossword puzzle before going to bed and her husband decides: *She would rather do the puzzle than go to bed when I go to sleep.* Unfortunately, insecurity takes control of one's thought processes, so anything a spouse, relative, or friend says is heard with a negative twist. Once someone accepts the presence of the insecurity, s/he can realize that s/he may be hearing something that is not being said. When s/he understands this about him-/herself, s/he can more easily and honestly understand the other person. A person who is not realistic about him-/herself is incapable of dealing with or changing the situation.

"That's a beautiful mink you bought your wife. Does it keep her warm?"

"I didn't buy it to keep her warm. I bought it to keep her quiet."

Max was an accountant. When Tammy noticed that her husband's job seemed never ending, she suggested taking some accounting courses to help him. Max was hurt and angered, thinking that Tammy didn't have confidence in his abilities to support them. He refused to even consider the possibility. He did not allow Tammy to explain that she was sure he could succeed and that she only wanted to ease his work schedule so they could spend more time together. Additionally, because they had no children yet, Tammy was a little bored and looking for something productive to occupy her time. Tammy was not suggesting that Max was incapable and he should not have taken it that way.

If both spouses are insecure, with neither being healthy enough to provide the other with the assurances s/he needs, their marriage will be unstable. They will either attack one another or retreat from each other, and both partners will feel unfulfilled.

What is the difference between your spouse saying, "I told you so" and saying, "I'm not going to tell you, I told you so!"

Self-esteem is tricky. A woman married to a successful

man may feel she is thought of only as Mr. X's wife, despite her own great qualities. She might need her husband to build her self-esteem, acknowledging and thanking her for all she does. On the other hand, although all his friends constantly sing his praises, Mr. X might think: *Everyone else praises and admires me, while my wife doesn't appreciate me.*

Just as a woman never tires of hearing how attractive and wonderful she is, a man also wants praise and appreciation. Everyone needs and deserves to have someone, especially his/her spouse, build up his/her self-esteem. A wife can destroy her marriage if she pounces on her husband when he returns from work, complaining that he is too involved in work and not helpful with the children, rather than making him feel good about his job. Likewise, a husband can compliment his wife on her mothering skills, or destroy their marriage by boasting about his work while criticizing how she is raising the kids. Each one needs to make the other feel secure in his/her position.

I tell you, when I was a kid all I knew was rejection. My yo-yo, it never came back.

—*Rodney Dangerfield*

Insecure individuals can become overly possessive, smothering their spouses. They might check their spouse's whereabouts, e-mails, text messages, and phone calls. They may examine credit cards and memos. Some will question their spouse's words, where they were, what they were doing, what they meant, and even what they were thinking. When that happens, suspicion rather than trust becomes the tone of the marriage. A spouse should not feel s/he lives on the witness stand.

He was in a position to marry anyone he pleased. Unfortunately he didn't please anyone.

Some insecure individuals need constant reassurance that they are loved and appreciated. Although it is important to compliment your spouse and avoid being critical, the need for constant praise without voicing even the slightest disapproval puts a great strain on a marriage.

Other insecure individuals are too frightened to state their opinions or wishes. They believe their views don't matter, and therefore they feel dejected and abused. They are afraid to take on new challenges or experience new situations. Since marriage continually presents new circumstances and different issues with which one must cope, this inability puts a strain on the marriage.

Many insecure individuals fear that differences in opinion indicate incompatibility. A major ingredient in a solid marriage is to be outwardly directed, but the focus of these people is self-directed. Because they are so worried and concerned about themselves, they can't become a team.

If at first you don't succeed, try it your wife's way.

Insecure people often refuse to hear advice, considering it to be criticism rather than help. They feel doubted and controlled, rather than realizing that a mentor is someone whose hindsight can be your foresight. Be secure enough to hear advice and take it if it works for you. You can always ignore it if you're not comfortable with it.

I received a letter saying that poor, starving people need my clothing. If they fit into my clothing, they are not starving!

An insecure woman usually worries about every ounce

she gains, fearing her husband will not see her inner being but will judge her superficially. If her husband speaks to or helps another woman she may be jealous, believing him to be more concerned about the other person.

As far as women in the workplace are concerned, we still have a long way to go. A girlfriend of mine just got a new job. The first question the boss asked her was if she could make a good cup of coffee. She stormed right out of that Starbucks!

—Carol Leifer

Wives who have their own careers intimidate insecure men, who feel unneeded or threatened by the competition. These men often try to take back control by telling their wives what to wear, whom to talk to, and where they are allowed to go.

Where there's smoke – she's cooking.

A wife who is insecure about her cooking will probably not be happy if her husband buys her a cookbook as a present. Although he may think she'll enjoy it, she may interpret it as: *He thinks I need more instruction in cooking.* He would be better off saying, "Darling, I love your cooking. Would you like me to buy you a new cookbook so you can experiment with new dishes?"

Man said to G-d: "G-d ,why did you make woman so beautiful?"

G-d replied, "So you would love her."

"But G-d," the man asked, "why did you make her so dumb?"

G-d said, "So she would love you."

Samuel was feeling great. Having just won a big case, he was offered a partnership in his law firm. Iris wanted to be happy for him but she secretly worried about the long hours he would be spending with his attractive secretary. Iris's insecurity surfaced and everything Samuel said or did suddenly upset her. She began nagging Samuel, insisting he come home early for one reason or another. Of course, this affected his work, and Samuel finally insisted that Iris change her attitude before he lost his job and she lost her husband! Iris spoke to her mother, who told her to get a new hairstyle to feel more attractive. She also encouraged her to use her physical therapy degree and go back to work for a few hours a week. On her own, Iris joined a volunteer cancer organization. Before long, Iris was feeling great about herself and therefore could feel good about Samuel's accomplishments as well.

Mike was a star at work, breaking all the firm's records. He loved being in the limelight and felt great. His wife Miriam was home playing with the kids and changing diapers. No one made a fuss over how terrific she was. She was sure she had broken the record for changing more diapers than anyone in the USA, yet no one cared. Her insecurities kicked in and she became moody and depressed. Mike told her to pull herself together or get help. Each one thought he was right, so both refused to go for help. Eventually they wound up in the divorce courts.

A therapist could have taught Mike to take notice of his wife and appreciate the job she was doing. A therapist could have taught Miriam to appreciate herself and self-validate the good job she was doing in raising her children. A therapist might also have taught Miriam not to be jealous of her husband's accomplishments. Your partner's achievements should be a reflection of you, not a competition for you. Don't pull your partner down or expect him/her to be less. Rather, build yourself up and learn to feel good about yourself. Ask yourself if your own insecurities are causing your difficulties.

Some spouses intentionally attack each other's personalities, accomplishments, or relationships. Sometimes this is because they are insecure, and putting their partner down makes them feel more important. Sometimes they are insensitive or mean and enjoy disturbing their spouse by pressing his/her buttons.

The goal is to feel secure about yourself and to feel secure in your marriage. But when a spouse boosts his/her own self-esteem by constantly criticizing his/her partner, or by belittling or attacking the things his/her spouse is proudest of, s/he is being abusive (see chapter 10, "Signs of Abusive Behavior").

Mitch is about to fall off a cliff into the icy river. He desperately calls out to G-d for help. Suddenly a helicopter comes along and the pilot throws him a rope to grab on to.

"It's okay," shouts Mitch. "G-d will help." Then a man in an air balloon passes by and calls out to Mitch to grab on.

"No thanks," cries Mitch, "G-d will help."

Along comes a boat. "Jump," says the captain. "I will catch you."

"No, thanks," shouts Mitch, "G-d will help."

At that point, Mitch can no longer hold on and he

plunges to his death. Mitch goes up to heaven and confronts G-d.

"How," he asks, "can You have ignored me when I had such faith in You? I was so sure You would save me."

"What more could I have done?" answered G-d, "I sent a helicopter, a balloon, and a boat."

To feel in control, an insecure spouse may try to control you. Don't ignore the messages. Notice if your spouse is using your vulnerability to manipulate and control you. Don't lose yourself. Take back control. Your spouse will respect you only if you are secure within yourself. You will respect yourself only if you hold on to yourself and what you deeply believe. Marriage is two individuals who work together to build one another. Each should become more secure and more empowered from the relationship.

We've been happily married for ten years. Ten out of thirty are not bad!

Continually work on building each other's self-esteem.

You are your spouse's mirror. No matter how everyone else may view you, most individuals view themselves through the eyes of their spouse. If everyone tells you that you are terrific but your spouse tells you that you are good for nothing, your self-esteem will eventually diminish. However, if the whole world doesn't see your worth but your spouse makes you feel good about yourself, you will develop confidence and go around shining.

In one town, it was customary for a man to give a girl's father a dowry of three or four cows in order to marry her. One young man chose a very simple girl, yet offered her father eight cows for her hand. Everyone thought the man was crazy. For a plain, quiet girl like her, they all agreed, he could have gotten away with paying only three cows. Why did he insist on giving the father eight cows? A year after the wedding, one of the groom's friends visited the newlyweds and was shocked to find his friend married to a beautiful and charming girl.

"How," he asked, "did this come about? What transformed the plain woman you married into this lovely creature?"

The husband responded, "I wanted an eight-cow woman. When I paid eight cows for her and treated her in that fashion, she began to believe that she was indeed an eight-cow woman. She knew that I thought she was special, and so she became special."

Each spouse should make the other feel good, instill in the other a sense of security, and make the other feel that s/he is loved for him-/herself. Each should feel s/he is accepted for who s/he is, rather than feel s/he is perpetually on trial and being judged. Every person should feel comfortable and good being him-/herself. Don't put each other down; rather, raise each other's self-esteem. A happy spouse will make you happy.

A man goes to a rabbi and says, "Rabbi, rabbi, I don't know what to do. My wife is trying to poison me."

The rabbi says, "Don't worry. Bring your wife to me, I'll talk to her."

So the man brings his wife to the rabbi. The rabbi takes the wife into his study and talks to her for one hour, then two hours, and then three hours. The husband is waiting anxiously, pacing outside the

office. **Finally, after six hours, the exhausted rabbi walks out.**

"So," says the nervous husband, "what should I do?"

The rabbi thinks a moment, looks at him and says, "Take the poison!"

Gloria Steinem, the leader of the women's liberation movement in the sixties, married for the first time at age sixty-six. She said, "Being married is like having somebody permanently in your corner. It feels limitless, not limited."

Encourage one another to grow. Don't compete. Don't let the other one's success make you feel inferior or insecure. You are a team. You have someone in your corner. Each one's individual success belongs to both partners.

A husband and wife must help each other emotionally, with encouragement and compliments. In order to succeed in business, a man needs his wife to take care of the children and the home. Conversely, for his wife to do a good job caring for the home, a husband must be a good provider. Or, if a woman chooses to work, her husband must be supportive, helping to run the home.

At the marriage counselor's office the wife complained, "What's-his-name here doesn't give me enough attention."

Making your spouse feel secure and good about him-/herself and about the relationship makes a stronger marriage. If both spouses make each other feel good, they will like each other, and the relationship will flourish.

Freda is walking down Hendon Road when she hears

a voice shout in her ear, "Stop at once! Don't take another step!"

She stops immediately and a brick smashes into the pavement just in front of her. A few minutes later, Freda is about to cross the street when the same voice shouts in her ear, "Stay where you are. Don't cross the street."

She stays where she is and a bus speeds against a red light. Freda, shaken by this second narrow escape, says aloud, "Who are you? Why are you helping me?"

"I'm your guardian angel," is the reply, "and I'm just doing my job looking after you. Is there any other question you would like to ask me?"

"Yes," replied Freda. "Where were you on my wedding day?"

26: Boundaries

A couple is in their home, relaxing, when the door suddenly crashes open to reveal a thief. Pushing the husband off the sofa, the thief stands him on the floor and draws a circle around him with some chalk he takes from his pocket, while shouting, "If you so much as put one foot out of that circle, I will shoot you."

The thief then forces the wife to open and hand over the contents of their safe, along with the silver in the silver cabinet and all her precious jewelry. When the thief finally leaves, the husband bursts out in hysterical laughter. "What in heaven's name are you laughing about?" she cries.

"I showed him," replies her husband. "When the thief wasn't looking, I put my foot outside the circle."

Healthy boundaries are essential to a good marriage because they are an integral part of each person's self-esteem.

Boundaries preserve one's sense of self since they serve as a protective wall. By defining your boundaries you make it clear to others that you deserve and expect respect, because that is your right as a human being. Every person is entitled to this respect, despite his/her imperfections.

With clearly established boundaries, you take responsibility for how you allow others to treat you. Setting these boundaries is self-empowering, because you determine the boundaries that are comfortable for you.

Clearly defined boundaries proclaim: "You must respect my wants and needs. My mind, body, and space are my own. You can't abuse me or take advantage of me. You can't humiliate, hurt, embarrass, or belittle me. You have no right to curse at me, ignore me, or fling insults at me. You can't touch my personal belongings or me unless I give you permission. Neither have you any right to check my e-mails, listen to my phone messages, read my personal mail, or examine my medications. You are not allowed to lay a hand on me against my will."

Marriage does not give a husband or wife the right to violate his/her spouse's boundaries. On the contrary, a marriage thrives if each spouse respects all of his/her partner's boundaries. Although a healthy marriage can't exist without bodily contact, you are allowed to say, "Right now, I do not feel like being touched." Indeed, one cannot have a healthy relationship with a person who does not set proper boundaries for him-/herself.

Many individuals are afraid to set up boundaries for fear of hurting others or causing them to be angry. They may also worry about losing a relationship, fearful that boundaries will cause their partner to abandon them. Adults who do not feel worthy, who feel defective and shameful, can be terrified of setting boundaries. Often, these feelings stem from a childhood filled with blame. Some children who constantly hear "You let me down, you hurt me, you make me so angry" can react by becoming invisible in order to feel safe. Other individuals, in order to protect the wounded child within, put up huge walls to try to keep people from getting too close to them and thereby sabotage any relationship that starts getting too intimate.

When you are in a healthy relationship, you realize that the people unwilling to accept your boundaries are those who abuse, embarrass, abandon, and betray you, while those who can work out boundaries with you are those who hear you, treat you respectfully, and value you enough to change their behavior when necessary.

Change starts with awareness. If someone constantly insults or hurts you, you must remind yourself that you deserve to be treated with dignity. You must then communicate those feelings directly and honestly to the other person. You must express your feelings by saying the words, "I feel…" thereby acknowledging your right to have these feelings.

If your spouse shouts at you, answer, "I'd like to hear what you have to say, but please speak to me with consideration, in a tone that is not heard by the entire neighborhood. If you do not lower your voice I am leaving the room." If your spouse continues to shout, you are entitled to walk out of the room.

Learn to communicate your needs without placing blame. Saying things like: "You hurt me," "You drive me crazy," "You embarrass me," is counterproductive and only angers the other person. The following guidelines will help you communicate your needs productively.

When you... Because people often act without realizing that their behavior is frustrating, you must specify what upsets you. Say, "When you furrow your brow at me and give me a dirty look; when you scream; when you make sarcastic remarks..." rather than generalities such as, "When you get mad; when you embarrass me..."

I feel... It is important to own your right to speak up and express your feelings. By saying, "I feel scared, isolated, vulnerable, hurt, angry, frustrated, ignored, unloved, and so forth, you begin to "own" that feeling, affirming to yourself the right to feel that way. As important as it is for the other person to hear and understand your feelings, it is even more crucial for you to gain ownership of those feelings.

I want... Here again you must specify the behavior that you want from the other person. Saying, "I want to feel loved; I want to know you need me; I want you to fulfill my emotional needs" is too general. You need to say things like, "I want you to tell me you love me; I want you to call me during your breaks; I want you to ask my advice; I want you to take my suggestions seriously; I want you to look up and smile at me when I walk in the door."

Recognize that a person can only control his/her own behavior; you cannot make someone else behave in a certain way. Therefore, if your partner continues to behave improperly, you need to take action to protect yourself. This is a three-step process:

1. If you... Making your partner aware of your feelings is the first step. Share your feelings about his/

her improper behavior, explicitly describing it. For example, you might say, "If you lose your temper and scream at me; if you lift a hand against me," etc.

2. I will... Describe the action you will take in order to protect yourself when your boundaries are violated: "I will leave the room; ask you to leave; stop listening to you; call the police," etc.

3. If you continue this behavior... You must decide on a plan of action if the behavior continues, although you need not divulge the information if you prefer not to do so. Whether or not you voice it aloud, you must at least say to yourself, "If this continues I will break off contact with you; end this relationship by filing for divorce," etc.

Setting consequences if your boundaries are violated will only work if you establish consequences that you are ready to enforce. Don't threaten to leave a relationship when you are not prepared to leave. Empty threats give the other person an excuse to continue the same old behavior. Choose consequences you can abide by, which are not more detrimental to you than to the other person. If you do not have anywhere to go, do not say, "If you keep embarrassing me I will move out of the house for a month."

The following scenario specifically describes violating behaviors, the feelings they induce, and the proper behavior expected. It also establishes the enforcing modalities.

"When I ask you to speak to me but you throw up your hands in seeming frustration and yell at me in a fit of rage, I feel anxious, scared, unloved, and afraid that you will hit me. I want you to talk calmly, explaining what is bothering you. If something is annoying you and you won't express those feelings to me, I will confront you about that, sharing my feelings. If you continue this behavior I will insist that we speak to a marriage therapist. If you keep repeating this behavior, I will consider other options, including leaving this marriage."

Setting boundaries is not a way to manipulate someone else. Rather, it communicates the message that you cannot continue to be a victim. We always have a choice. We can choose to act powerfully, we can deny a problem and do nothing about it, or we can fall into depression. Some of these choices may be terrible, but they do exist. The more conscious we are of our choices the more empowered we are. Choosing to establish boundaries says, "I need you to change and I hope you will do so, but if you don't I have choices. I can leave the room; I can leave the friendship; I can leave the marriage."

In a healthy interdependent relationship, you can be open with your spouse: "Here is what I am willing to do and here is what I need from you." It is fruitless to expect your spouse to read your mind and guess your needs. It is also unfair to punish him/her when s/he does not anticipate your needs. But with open communication you can negotiate boundaries. Of course, you cannot expect a spouse to adjust to newly set boundaries right away. Unless the behavior is really intolerable, be patient, giving your spouse time to practice these new skills. Behavioral patterns are ingrained, and it takes time for new ones to form.

The three fastest ways in the world to communicate are: Tele-fax, Tele-phone, and Tell-a-woman. You want even faster? Ask her not to tell anyone.

Confidentiality is an important ingredient in a healthy

relationship. Both spouses must realize that their private life is not for public consumption. Arguments, disagreements, and issues may only be discussed between the couple or a therapist. Neither spouse should air their dirty laundry beyond the boundaries of their home. Each partner must view the other as his special confidant, trusting the other with his/her innermost feelings while feeling secure that his/her secrets are safe.

Because a marriage is sacred, lines must be drawn to keep it strong and healthy. These boundaries allow you to be close to someone, yet keep you from feeling invaded. Strengthening these boundaries helps the partners build one another, rather than hurt one another, because each partner treats the other courteously. Lines that should not be crossed include things like throwing things, lying, walking out, forcing someone to do things against his/her will, making derogatory remarks, getting intoxicated, self-medicating, and turning to a different relationship.

Boundaries can protect the space within you, as well as around you. Boundaries help you maintain your self-esteem by determining not only at what point you say no to others, but also at what point you say no to yourself. Boundaries can help you decide to do the right thing. You determine what makes you respect yourself by only doing things you are proud of and are comfortable doing. Then define the boundaries that you do not want to cross, which can cause you to be disappointed in yourself. You remind yourself, *I will contain my anger, not allowing myself to scream. I will control my anxiety. Your actions will not cause me to lose my equilibrium or to question my judgment. You will not cause me to do things that I do not feel right doing and which cause me to feel disappointed in myself.*

Your behavior will not cause me to act inappropriately. By determining boundaries and living within them, you keep yourself under control and feel good about your behavior. Inner boundaries will protect you, since your partner's image of you will not affect your behavior.

Choosing proper boundaries determines a relationship. Psychologist Terrence Real explains that you require boundaries, because without them you are connected without being protected (boundary-wise), but if your boundaries are too stringent you are protected but not connected. Only cultivating functioning boundaries to protect themselves can cure individuals without boundaries and those who are too insulated.

Sometimes people will erect inappropriate walls to protect themselves. These can include walls of silence, the Internet, or TV; words of anger; intoxication; humor; condescension; or fatigue. However, you should use a wall only to remove yourself from being abused. In other cases, open up and deal with the issue together with your spouse. If your spouse has erected a protective wall, you can't expect him/her to open up without being assured that you understand the value of proper boundaries. This can be accomplished with patience and time.

A rabbi of a small town, together with his wife, opened his home to any poor individual who needed a place to stay and food to eat. Some people stayed a day, others who felt downtrodden were there a week, and some truly desperate individuals stayed a month.

One day, two beggars were discussing how long they had been living at the house. The first said he'd been

in the house for six months. The second said he'd been there for nine months. Then they unknowingly turned to the owner and inquired how long he had been there. He answered, "All my life."

Staring at one another in amazement, they said, "Now that's already taking advantage!"

Boundaries affect all aspects of life and all relationships:

- We establish religious boundaries, financial boundaries, moral boundaries, emotional boundaries, and physical boundaries.
- We make boundaries about when to give in, when to stay firm, when to understand, and when to be forgiving.
- We make boundaries about how much money to spend, how much to save, and how much to give to charity.
- We make boundaries about how much news to follow, and how much time to devote to work, study or entertainment.
- We make boundaries regarding how much private time we need, how much company we should invite, how often to go out, and how often to stay in.
- We make boundaries about how much time to spend apart from our spouse, how much to spend together, how much time to devote to friends and family, and how much time to devote to our kids.
- We make boundaries regarding which people we bring into our houses and what influences to allow in our homes.

Boundaries between couples include:

- We can each do our own thing, but we consult one another on major issues.
- We don't make major decisions concerning our finances or our children without mutual agreement, but we each trust one another to make certain decisions on our own.
- We try to dress to please one another, but we don't dictate to each other what s/he must wear.
- We don't let a whole day pass without speaking to each other, nor do we stay out late without calling home to say we are running late.
- We don't go somewhere without letting our spouse know where we might be reached and when we expect to return.
- We don't take separate vacations.
- We don't go out alone with someone of the opposite gender.

Although we may adopt boundaries based on the boundaries we saw in our homes, both partners must agree to them in order to find a healthy balance. The right boundaries define who you are; they govern a marriage, giving you the space within which to function appropriately, and reining you in when you stray beyond the proper limits.

Healthy people make the right choices, appropriating their time and attention to the right things with priority given to their spouse and children. They are careful about whom they allow into their sphere of influence. They are not influenced by people with the wrong values or by those who are more concerned about their own self-interest than about others. They are able to distinguish between those who are helping and those who are hurting their marital relationship.

Examine your boundaries vis-à-vis your friends and family members. Does he visit too often, invading your privacy as a couple? Does she ask personal questions about your marriage? Does he interject his opinion on matters that concern you and your spouse? When you feel down, does she remind you of all your spouse's negative traits rather than his/her positive ones? Do your advisers help you regain your balance and restore proper judgment?

Your boundaries should remind you that only people with your spouse's and your best interest in mind should influence you. Someone who works against the growth of your relationship, advising you out of his/her personal spirit of jealousy or a need for attention, should not be allowed a listening ear. Erect boundaries to protect yourself against someone who is hurting your marriage by saying things like, "Thank you, but those suggestions are not in line with the boundaries my spouse and I have in our lives." Individuals with healthy boundaries are not swayed to act or form their opinion based on guilt, or because they feel dominated or overwhelmed. You can respond to a pushy person with this sentence, "Please allow me time so I can process your ideas. Otherwise I will feel the need to push you away."

Your comfort zone is bound by not wanting to hurt others or be hurt yourself. Staying within that zone is healthy. The desire to emulate a couple who speak respectfully to one another, give each other attention, acknowledge each other's presence and listen attentively to one another's opinions contributes to marital growth. However, expanding your boundaries too freely, without thought, can cause you to lose your real self. When your beliefs and convictions are buried under other people's thoughtless words, you become insensitive to things that truly bother you. Don't accept negative advice from people just because they offer it. If the behavior is outside your boundary lines, keep it that way. It is admirable to appreciate and add good behaviors to your moral compass, but be cautious about incorporating negative behavioral boundaries.

Make sure your boundaries are not so rigid that you strangle each other. Sue and Stan decided to carve out time for themselves as a couple every Thursday evening. One Thursday night, Stan's best friend came in from out of town. Sue refused to allow him to stop by for a visit. Rigid boundaries should only be established for issues like abuse.

With a clear, realistic understanding of one another's needs, a couple can understand one another's boundaries. Over time, together, a couple can tighten or expand their boundaries, making sure that the boundaries of each of them coincide.

After a trying day at the office, the husband was finally relaxing by sitting in his easy chair and reading the newspaper. His wife, who was working on a crossword puzzle, suddenly called out, "John, what is a female sheep?"

"Ewe," replied her husband... And that's how the fight began.

27: TLC: Talk, Listen, Care

A man tells his psychologist, "No one ever listens to me." The psychologist says, "Next."

Communication is a basis for a good marriage. Communicate your needs, fears, and frustrations and make sure your spouse hears you. Marry a person you can talk to, who hears what you are saying.

If someone feels his/her spouse is not listening to him/her, nor trying to meet his/her needs, s/he can feel helpless and become angry, depressed, and lonely. S/he may feel neglected, trapped, disappointed, stressed, overworked, and discouraged.

Make sure your marriage and your relationship is always moving forward and that you are building on a solid foundation. If things get shaky, stop, talk, and listen to each other so you can rectify your problems.

I take my wife everywhere…but she keeps finding her way back.

Studies have found that partners can live peacefully even with perpetual issues, as long as they talk about them in an open, productive way.

Talk to one another. Listen to each other. Care about one another. I call this T.L.C., tender loving care.

A woman never appears more intelligent to a man than when she is listening to him.

Often we think we are listening to someone, but we have actually decided on our response before the speaker has even finished speaking. We answer, "Oh, I know just what you mean. The same thing happened to me. Let me tell you what I did." Truly listening and putting yourself in the other person's place is a much better response. Say, "I hear what you are saying. I really feel for you. I am so sorry you are going through this." In this scenario a person feels s/he is being heard. This technique is called listening from the other person's point of view and is an excellent tool to use with your spouse or children.

Show your spouse that you want to understand the situation by asking, "How did that make you feel?" or "What was going through your mind then?" Questions show your interest and help your spouse focus. Then sympathize by saying words like, "That must have been so hard," or "That must have been so disappointing." These words show your spouse that you empathize, feeling his/her pain or frustration. Rather than just advising your spouse, give him/her the time and direction to think things through for him-/herself and come to his/her own conclusions. Being able to solve your own problems, encouraged by someone supportive at your side, builds self-esteem.

A psychiatrist asks you a lot of expensive questions that your wife asks for nothing.

—Joey Adams

According to Bill Doherty, author of *Take Back Your Marriage*, a married couple with children that has fifteen minutes of uninterrupted, non-logistical, non-problem-solving conversation every day is in the top 5 percent of all married couples. Most married couples speak to each other in this way less than twelve minutes a day.

All couples go through good times and bad times. Often the good times go unnoticed while the bad times become monumental. It is much better to talk about the good times and dismiss the bad times, and in that way the good times will far outweigh the bad ones. The success or failure of most marriages has little to do with having a good time. It is about having the good times and positive feelings outweigh the negative ones. If you only communicate your anger or resentment, your communication has only negative value. Negative or poor communication and an inability to resolve conflicts is a prime cause for divorce. Good communication skills are vital to a marriage.

If a couple's interactions develop into a constant pattern of one partner becoming critical and aggressive, while the other becomes defensive and distant, psychologist John Gottman says there is a more than 80 percent chance of this couple divorcing within the first four to five years of the marriage.

A couple must identify their negative cycle of communication. Miriam attacks Yonah, which is actually her protest against losing her bond with him. Yonah responds either by being defensive or indifferent. This stems from his fear of disappointing or losing Miriam. The more Yonah acts angry or indifferent, the more alone Miriam feels. If they are both actively aware that their actions stem from a fear of disconnection, each can take a softer stance. Yonah can calmly and sensitively say, "You're right. Rather than recognizing your hurt, all I heard was your anger. I felt that I had disappointed you again, which brings out my fear of losing you." Now Miriam knows that it is not that Yonah doesn't care about or need her, but rather that Yonah cannot deal with his fear of losing her.

By talking it out, Miriam and Yonah learn what sets each of them off. Miriam says, "When you do that, it reminds me of my father who walked out on my mother when I was eight" (see chapter 30, "Major Issues: Sensitivities and Insecurities"). Yonah now understands and interprets Miriam's reaction as fear rather than anger. Now, they can connect on a deeper, more mature level.

Now that I am married I know why they call English the "mother tongue." Father never gets to use it.

Couples must always keep in mind that talking together will bring them closer together. One person should not completely dominate the conversation, although women are more likely to bring up issues, while men try to avoid them.

Talk about the things that bother you, and truly hear what the other person is saying. Tell your spouse when something makes you happy. Tell your spouse if something makes you sad, confused, indecisive, frustrated, anxious, giddy, or ecstatic. When your spouse responds with understanding, calming you and helping you analyze your feelings, being happy with you or commiserating with you, show that you appreciate his/her understanding. If the response is not what you hoped for, reexplain the point of your story, stating, "I was hoping for some sympathy," or "I just wanted you to appreciate the comedy of the situation." Reiterate the episode or problem now that your spouse is aware of the response you are hoping to elicit. Oftentimes a man will think his wife wants help solving a problem, not realizing that she only wants a sympathetic ear.

I am woman. I am invincible. I am tired.

A woman facing a problem needs a sounding board. She wants her husband to listen, understand, and empathize with her. Husbands usually go into problem-solving mode, offering suggestions: *This is what you should do.* But a woman who is hurting does not want advice, nor does she have the patience to listen to suggestions at that time. She doesn't want her husband to bolster her courage or belittle her problem. She just wants compassion and an arm around her. That connection shows her they are on the same wavelength.

Women need reassurance that they are loved. A smart husband will take a moment to call home during the day to let his wife know he is thinking of her. "I just wanted to see how your meeting at school went," makes a wife feel she is part of his life. A man who takes the time to assure his wife of his feelings for her will have a much calmer life. Spending a few moments a day truly connecting to a wife will save a man many hours later of reassuring her that he really does still love her.

We've been married three months. I'm just not used to being wrong so often.

—Dennis Regan

Men need reassurance that they are respected. They want to feel needed but they don't want to feel pressured, smothered, or questioned.

The deaf man and his wife were having a fight but he couldn't get a finger in edgewise.

One's instinctive reaction may not be what his/her spouse wants. The correct response comes naturally to some people, but usually spouses have to teach each other what reaction works for them.

One wife may be happy to receive a reply like, "I see your point," while another wife wants something more concrete. Glenda told Bob she was upset because their son Jeff had said something inappropriate. Bob agreed with Glenda that she was right to feel upset. But Glenda was not happy. "It's fine that you agree with me, but why don't you explain to Jeff how he upset his mother?" Glenda needs to teach her husband why she is confiding in him. She appreciates when he validates her feelings, but she also wants him to take the appropriate action.

One man may complain about his bad back and be satisfied if his wife says, "Oh that's so painful." Another may be hoping for a massage.

A husband who comes home from work complaining about his lousy day and tough boss may want his wife to sympathize, without offering constructive criticism or confusing him with suggestions to quit his job.

It took a lot of willpower, but I finally gave up dieting.

Use your brains when you answer one another. When a woman asks her husband whether she looks fat, a smart husband will look at his wife bursting at the seams and say, "You look lovely."

The more experiences a couple shares, the better they get to know one another. The more they communicate their needs, teaching each other the appropriate responses, the more sensitive each will be to the other. They will feel in sync and their bond as a couple will be strengthened.

For a marriage to have any chance, at least six things should go unsaid every day.

Remember to articulate your thoughts. Don't just think that it was nice of Ralph to help you with your packages. Say to him: "Ralph, thanks so much! I really appreciate that you helped me with the packages."

Discuss issues with each other. Some individuals react to a disagreement by walking out rather than talking about the issue. Because they are angry, they shut out their spouse. It is okay to need some time out to calm down and reorganize your thoughts, and your spouse should understand that, but a conversation should take place.

People who never discuss anything with each other will not have a relationship; a marriage like that will be a lonely marriage. Informative and friendly discussions enhance your involvement in each other's thoughts and lives.

A couple was married for forty-five years, raised eleven children, and was blessed with twenty-two grandchildren. When asked their secret for staying together all that time, the wife replied, "Many years ago we made a promise to each other: The first one to

pack up and leave has to take all the kids."

Teach one another what makes you happy. Delicately show by your actions and your responses what pleases you. Make your needs and wishes clear to your spouse. Be specific. Don't say, "I want you to be more helpful." Say, "When you come home I'd appreciate help giving the kids baths," or "If you stopped at the supermarket on the way home it would make my life so much easier."

Make life easy for yourself and your partner. Don't force your spouse to guess what you want. Don't expect him/her to read your mind. Subtle hints do not work, and even obvious hints may not be effective. Husbands especially want to be told in a straightforward manner what is expected of them.

My wife suffers in silence louder than anyone I know.

Therapists have perfected speaking techniques. Questioning a husband who doesn't want to be confronted usually causes him to erect a wall. Resenting his silence or feeling personally inadequate is not the proper response. A wife should say, "I realize you don't feel like talking now, but when you are ready I would love to talk to you. Perhaps I can be of some help." His answer should be, "I don't mean to shut you out. After I work things through in my mind, I will gladly discuss it with you." With this response, his wife will feel secure in his love, which is essential to a successful marriage.

When you are discussing a matter of importance, think before you speak. If you feel your spouse is opposing, drilling, or attacking you, don't lose control. You are entitled to stop, get in touch with your feelings, and consider your response. You are entitled to say, "Let me consider your point of view. Let's sleep on it and discuss it tomorrow, or

"Let me do some research into the matter."

If you are trying to make a point but your spouse is not listening, don't get upset. Repeat your statement. If your spouse still doesn't respond or s/he is speaking right through your response, stay focused. Do not raise your voice. Do not ignore what s/he is answering. Repeat your statement again with more conviction. Continue the repetition with greater conviction until your feelings are acknowledged. For example, if your response is "I'd like to think about it," and your spouse shouts, "Why can't you just make a decision?" say, "I hear your point, but I'd like to think about it." If s/he yells, "I want a decision now!" your answer should be a very calm but firm "I realize you would like a decision now, but as I said, I need to think about it. I will let you know my decision tomorrow." No matter how aggressive s/he may get, your answer still has to be a firm, "I said I'd like to think about it."

If your spouse starts to scream, curse, or berate you, draw the line. Set boundaries. Say, "I would not speak to you like that and I would appreciate if you would not speak to me like that." If s/he continues berating you, repeat yourself. If s/he persists say, "If you continue speaking to me in this manner I am leaving the room," and walk out of the room if the tirade does continue. Even if s/he follows you out of the room, say, "When you speak to me with respect, I will be happy to speak to you." Stand by this conviction (see chapter 26, "Boundaries").

After an argument, a man and his wife were giving each other the silent treatment. Suddenly, the man realized he would need his wife to wake him at 5:00 a.m. the next day for an early morning business flight.

Not wanting to be the first to break the silence, he wrote "Please wake me at 5:00 a.m.," leaving the note where he knew his wife would find it.

The next morning the man woke up, only to discover it was nine o'clock and he had missed his flight. Furious, he was about to confront his wife when he noticed a piece of paper by the bed. The paper said, "It is 5:00 a.m. Wake up."

Never become impervious to your spouse's needs and sensitivities. Even after years of marriage, even when a husband and wife are secure in one another's love, they can unintentionally hurt one another. If a wife goes out of her way to buy her husband a new shirt and his reaction is, "Why do I need another shirt?" his wife may be upset. There are loads of ways to make a spouse feel special. Saying the right thing at the right time and showing appreciation are positive reinforcement actions. In this case her husband's reaction might have sounded better had he said, "You are so thoughtful for buying me this shirt, and I really like it, but considering our budget, would you mind if I keep the thought but return the shirt?" His wife will probably feel better this way.

Here is a handy guide on how to speak to a woman, especially when her hormones are acting up.

DANGEROUS: What's for dinner?
SAFER: Can I help you with dinner?
SAFEST: Where would you like to go for dinner?

DANGEROUS: What are you so worked up about?
SAFER: Could we be overreacting?
SAFEST: Here's fifty dollars.

DANGEROUS: Should you be eating that?
SAFER: You know, there are a lot of apples left.
SAFEST: Can I get you a glass of wine with that?
DANGEROUS: What did you do all day?
SAFER: I hope you didn't overdo it today.
SAFEST: I've always loved you in that robe.

—Anonymous

If one of you is overwhelmed by the discussion, take a break, calling a time-out. Say, "Honey, I'm tired. Can we discuss this later?" or "Do you mind if we get the kids to bed before we discuss this?" or "We need a time-out." Never take the stance of, "You need a time-out," or "Can't you just relax?" Don't reach the point where you feel your spouse is attacking you for no reason and all you want to do is escape. Meditate, listen to some soothing music, savor a cup of coffee, or just say, "Give me a moment to relax." Create an atmosphere of acceptance. Calm one another. Offer each other a glass of wine, or at least a cup of tea. Then you will be in a mood to look for the part of your spouse's perspective that is reasonable and find common ground or ways you can compromise.

Never argue with a woman when she's tired…or when she's rested.

Don't harp on your issues. If you are not careful, your differences can become the focus of all your conversations. If matters of concern can't be resolved immediately, put them on hold. Have some fun, enjoy one another, and remind each other of the issues on which you do *see eye to eye*. Assure one another that your marriage is solid and that a solution or compromise can be reached.

If Gloria bursts out that she hates Yaakov, he shouldn't fall into the trap of answering, "I hate you too." Rather, he should stay calm and say, "I know you are angry now and I am sorry. I love you and hope when we both feel calmer we can revisit the issue."

Couples tend to have the same arguments over and over again. If you feel you are being trapped into the same fight once again, pull out. Say, "I know this issue bothers you, and I am working on resolving it. Let's not get into the same fight again," or "This is always a sore issue with us. Let's leave it for now and deal with it when we are emotionally in a better place."

Learning to speak to one another with care and sensitivity is an art worth mastering.

My parents have been married for fifty years. I asked my mother how they did it. She said, "You just close your eyes and pretend it's not happening."

—Rita Rudner

Stay involved in each other's lives. Tell each other about your day, your work, and the kids. A father should not be made to feel that his only involvement with his children is to give life. A wife should not feel like her only purpose is to be the housekeeper.

Discuss your work or your studies. Talk about what's happening in the community. Talk politics. Discuss family. Talk about the news. Discuss feelings. Laugh and cry together. Make life fun rather than monotonous. Pamper each other by communicating your thoughts, your convictions, your frustrations, your desires, and your emotions. After all, what is a best friend for?

My husband and I never considered divorce...murder maybe, but never divorce.
—Dr. Joyce Brothers

When your spouse speaks, hear what s/he is truly saying. And vice versa, always examine your own words; remember that what you say can differ from what your spouse hears. Furthermore, don't think that if something can be interpreted in two ways your spouse will always know you meant it positively.

Always be *dan l'chaf zechus*, judge a person favorably. Practice this especially with your own spouse, giving him/her the benefit of the doubt, interpreting everything s/he says or does with an *ayin tova*, a good eye.

Married life teaches one invaluable lesson: to think of things far enough in advance not to say them.

Husbands and wives often do not understand each other. Lawyers will be the first to tell you there is a world of difference between what one says and what the other hears. An elderly man received a letter from his son in college. Having lost his reading glasses, he asked his friend to read the letter. Impatient to leave already, his friend read gruffly: *Dear Dad. Send money immediately. I really need it right away. I have loads of debts to repay. I will write you when I get a chance. Your son, Abe.* Horrified that his son had the nerve to write such a rough, demanding letter, the father decided not to send the money. A few days later another friend visited and the man showed him his son's letter. This friend was a soft-spoken fellow and he read the exact same words in a pleading voice. "Ah," said the father, "now he is asking nicely and respectfully. Now I will send him the money."

Text messaging, rather than speaking to one another, also causes misinterpretation and misunderstanding. Additionally, it establishes an escape from real speaking and communicating.

My wife never repeats gossip. You've got to listen the first time she tells you.

The popular game of broken telephone is a great example of the difference between what is said and how it is heard and interpreted. Especially in the heat of a disagreement, the discrepancy between what is said and what is heard can be major.

The Sages (*Tamid* 32a) teach us: "Who is wise? He who foresees consequences." Rabbi Zelig Pliskin terms this "outcome thinking." Before saying or doing something, anticipate the effect that your words or deeds will have. If there is any possibility of your words or actions hurting or offending your spouse, be smart, consider the consequences, and keep yourself in check.

He ran after the garbage truck, yelling, "Am I too late?"

The driver said, "No, hop in!"

A spouse who shouts usually causes his/her spouse to shout back. Although it can be difficult, it is much more effective to speak calmly and clearly to one another. This allows the other person to hear what you are saying. People don't usually listen to those who scream, and the screamer likewise doesn't listen to a response. Each one misinterprets what s/he hears, becoming defensive and offensive. When you approach your spouse lovingly and with understanding, your spouse will feel less threatened and will be more willing to please you.

Make sure that you hear what your spouse is saying. Understanding your spouse's words and feelings is a fundamental part of marriage. Concentrate on what your spouse is saying, especially if s/he says this is important to him/her. This advice works for all issues, not only marital ones, since a spouse should be a friend and confidant for every issue.

Couples should never have a serious discussion if one partner is not focused. Even happy couples can't listen when they are upset. If your spouse is distracted by something else and not making eye contact with you, stop the discussion. Ask for a better time to discuss the issue, explaining that this topic needs serious attention. Explain that you need your spouse to help clarify your thinking, work through a dilemma with you, confirm your feelings, offer you a shoulder to cry on, or help you vent.

When a man says "Fine," he means "Everything is fine." When a woman says "Fine," she means, "I'm really angry, and you have to figure out why."

Men and women have totally different vocabularies. Here are some definitions I found that may help you understand your spouse.

What a woman says usually has very little to do with what she really means:

"Yes" = "No."

"No" = "Yes."

"Maybe" = "No."

"I'm sorry" = "You'll be sorry."

"We need" = "I want."

"It's your decision" = "The correct decision should be obvious by now."

"Do what you want" = "You'll pay for this later."

"We need to talk" = "I need to complain."

"Sure, go ahead" = "I don't want you to."

"I'll be dressed in five minutes" = "I'll be dressed in an hour."

"Nothing" = "Something." (Be on your toes: arguments that begin with "nothing" usually end in "fine.")

"Go ahead" = This is a dare, not permission. Don't do it!

Loud sigh = This means she thinks you are an idiot and is wondering why she is wasting her time standing here and arguing with you about "nothing."

"That's okay" = This is one of the worst statements a woman can make. It means, "I want to think long and hard before deciding how and when you will pay for your mistake."

"Thanks" = This is a woman thanking you. Do not question. Do not faint. Just say, "You're welcome."

"Thanks a lot" = This is pure sarcasm. She is not thanking you at all. Do not say "You're welcome," because that will only bring on a "whatever."

"Whatever" = "You know where you can go."

"Don't worry about it. I got it." = "I'm sick of waiting for you to do it, so I'll do it myself." This will lead to the man later asking, "What's wrong?" and being told "Nothing!"

"I'm not upset" = "Are you blind? Of course I'm upset!"

"How much do you love me?" = "I did something today you're really not going to like."

"Do you love me?" = "I am going to ask for something expensive."

"I want new curtains" = "and carpeting, and furniture and wallpaper."

"The kitchen is so inconvenient" = "I want a new house."

"I heard a noise" = "I noticed you were almost asleep."

"I'll be ready in a minute" = "Kick off your shoes and stop checking your watch. I'll be ready when I'm ready."

"Do I look heavy?" = "Tell me I'm beautiful."

"You have to learn to communicate" = "Just agree with me."

"Are you listening to me?" = "Too late, you're dead."

What a man says and what he means is usually completely different. Here is a list of things a man means when he says something:

"I'm hungry" = "I'm hungry."

"I'm sleepy" = "I'm sleepy."

"I'm tired" = "I'm tired."

"What's wrong?" = "I don't see why you are making such a big deal."

"What's wrong?" = "What meaningless, self-inflicted

trauma are you going through now?"

"Can I help with dinner?" = "Why isn't it already on the table?"

"Uh-huh," "Sure, honey," or "Yes, dear," really means absolutely nothing. It's a conditional response like Pavlov's dogs drooling.

"Have you lost weight?" = "I've just spent our last thirty dollars on a cordless drill."

"My wife doesn't really understand me" = "She's heard all my stories before and is tired of them."

"We're going to be late" = "Now I have a legitimate excuse to drive like a maniac."

"Take a break, honey. You are working too hard." = "I don't hear the game over the vacuum cleaner."

"That's interesting, dear." = "Are you still talking?"

"You know how bad my memory is" = "I remember the theme song to *Gone with the Wind*, the address of my first doctor, and the vehicle identification number of every car I've ever known, but I forgot your birthday."

"Honey, we don't need material things to prove our love" = "I forgot our anniversary again."

"I do help around the house" = "I once put a dirty towel in the laundry basket."

"I can't find it" = "It didn't fall into my outstretched hands, so I'm completely clueless."

"What did I do this time?" = "What did you catch me at?"

"I heard you" = "I haven't the foggiest clue what you said and am hoping desperately that I can take it well enough so that you don't spend the next three days yelling at me."

"You look terrific" = "Oh, G-d, please don't try on one more outfit. I'm starving."

"I missed you" = "I can't find my socks drawer, the kids are hungry, and we are out of toilet paper."

"We share the housework" = "I make the messes, she cleans them up."

"I broke up with her" = "She dumped me."

—*Anonymous*

My wife says I never listen to her…at least I think that's what she said.

Listening techniques have been introduced into marriage therapy. A wife says something and her husband responds, "I hear what you are saying" and then repeats what he thinks his wife said. She answers, "That is not exactly what I mean" and then clarifies her words. This exchange continues until the wife feels her husband has grasped her meaning. Then it is her husband's turn to say something, and she repeats what she thinks he said. This type of training helps communication become more accurate and thereby improves the couple's interaction with each other. A therapist can train a couple in this technique, and soon enough a couple should be able to do this on their own.

A husband answered a phone call: "No, I'm afraid she's not in at the moment. Whom shall I say was going to listen?"

Good communication may be a key to a successful marriage, but the manner in which this communication is carried out is the true secret. If both partners truly listen to each other and hear what the other is trying to say, they can create a great marriage.

The swami said, "Life is a bowl of fruit."

"And?"

"There is no 'and,' my son. Life is a bowl of fruit."

The young man said, "Swami, I sold my worldly possessions, I traveled through all kinds of terrain, I suffered, and all you can say is: Life is a bowl of fruit?"

The swami said "All right. Life is not a bowl of fruit!"

Try to understand what your spouse is telling you, getting the contents and the meaning right. Abandoning the discussion and just agreeing will eventually lead to misunderstandings. The first step is to understand what is bothering your spouse, and then try to do something about it, if you can. This will show that you care and respect his/her feelings about the matter, even if you cannot fully change the situation.

When women are depressed they either eat or go shopping. Men invade another country.

—Elaine Booster

Often a woman will complain in order to get her husband's attention, especially if her husband is prone to quick, flippant answers, as if he were doing her a major favor by responding to her in the first place.

It is common for people to misinterpret language and

gestures. Couples need to learn each other's language, understanding one another's signals. Subtle hints that are not recognized can lead to arguments. A wife should recognize that a husband who is pacing or tapping his fingers is nervous. A husband should recognize that a wife who has changed her outfit six times is feeling insecure and needs to be told she looks great. A wife should notice when her husband is getting edgy and realize he might need some time alone with her without the kids. A husband should realize that a wife who is suddenly sarcastic wants to be asked what is bothering her.

The judge said, "I understand that you and your wife had some words."

The defendant said, "I had some, but I didn't get to use them!"

Express yourself clearly. Asking your spouse if s/he is able to do something does not necessarily mean your spouse plans to do it. Specify what you want. "Will you pick me up?" "Can you come home early?" If you add words like "honey" or "dear" before your request and put the word "please" in the center, you will usually get a more cooperative response. People often nod their head to show they are listening. Don't take that gesture as agreement; make sure your spouse is not just hearing words but understands your request.

Watch what you say to one another. Speech has repercussions. The goal is to have a conversation today in a way that allows you to have another conversation tomorrow.

The efficiency expert concluded his lecture with a word of caution. "You may not want to try these techniques at home."

27: TLC: TALK, LISTEN, CARE • 217

"Why not?" asked someone in the audience.

"I watched my wife's routine at breakfast for years," the expert explained. "She made lots of trips to the table, to the refrigerator, stove and cabinets, often carrying just a single item."

"Hon," I suggested, "Why don't you try carrying a couple of things at once?"

The voice from the audience asked, "Did it save time?"

The expert replied, "Actually, yes. It used to take her twenty minutes to get breakfast ready. Now I do it in seven."

Compliments soften an accusation, so always offer compliments with any criticism. Remember: "A spoonful of sugar helps the medicine go down." For example, tell your spouse that s/he is too loud by saying, "Your ideas are really on target. I think the boss might hear them better if you spoke a little softer." Your spouse will feel good and s/he will get the message.

It is a time-tested truth that flattery will get you everywhere, so make your spouse feel good, even while criticizing him/her. Use the sandwich method: Begin with a compliment, add a rebuke and then end with a compliment. If your spouse yells, you might say, "You are such a caring person. Hearing the yelling really bothers me. It is against your nature to hurt other people."

There is a great difference between a complaint and some types of criticism. A complaint is directed at a specific problem or action, such as, "You forgot to pick me up." But some criticisms are global complaints directed against all of a person's actions or his character. "I knew you would forget to pick me up. I can't count on you for anything. You are always so unreliable." Although a person can forgive a specific complaint, s/he is totally wounded by global criticism. If you attack a person's weak spot by saying things like, "You never earn enough," you are smashing a delicate ego. Be specific when you criticize. Do not globalize by accusing someone with the words "always" or "never."

Global criticism reflects a contemptuous attitude, and builds resentment because it attacks a person's character. Global criticism doesn't say, "You are acting silly now." It describes you as a silly person. You are not acting stubborn now; you are a stubborn person. It is an affront to one's self-esteem and inevitably evokes either an angry or defensive response, or indifference. A spouse might respond with, "Look who is criticizing. You, who are a loser and can't even make a living!" or "I didn't pick you up because I can't stand being with you!" Or your spouse might just walk out the door, tuning you out completely.

If you want your spouse to accept criticism calmly, you must also accept criticism graciously. Be able to listen to criticism and apologize, or at least validate that you are sorry for upsetting him/her. Appreciate the constructive element and agree to work on it.

Marriage is the process of finding out what kind of man your wife would have preferred.

Accusing someone of doing something wrong will not endear you to that person. Even if you are right, you must be careful not to push this down your spouse's throat. Sometimes you have to be smart enough to ignore your spouse's faults, not mentioning them at all.

Mary was annoyed that Oscar always came home late. But angrily confronting him with the complaint that he always walked in every evening at eight o'clock expecting a full dinner while boring her to death with his rendition of what happened at work was not productive. Had Mary said, "I wish you would come home earlier, because I look forward to hearing what happened to you at work," she would have encouraged Oscar to alter his schedule, rather than discouraging him.

On the flip side of the coin, we cannot ignore all our spouse's faults or we will give him/her a false sense of security and s/he will never see reason to change a behavior, thus continually aggravating you. You can sympathize with your spouse's position and still calmly explain your position. By saying, "I see what you are getting at," you give credibility to your spouse's concerns while expressing your own. Talk about your feelings, using "I" rather than "you." Say, "I feel let down," rather than "You let me down," or "I found clothing on the floor, and it would help me a lot if clothing went right into the hamper," rather than, "You left your clothing on the floor."

A simple technique such as using the word "we" rather than "you" can improve your relationship. Instead of saying, "You should be more aware," say, "It would be great if we could both be more aware." Rather than an accusation, the issue has now become something both partners are working to fix.

Use the word "and" rather than "but." If you compliment your spouse by saying, "You are wonderful but you react so slowly," you have negated your compliment. The word "but" places a negative spin on the entire statement, and all your spouse hears is that s/he is slow. However, if you say, "You are wonderful, and if you could react a little more quickly it would be amazing," the message can be heard and accepted.

Another smart move is to switch all negatives to positives. Rather than saying, "Do not talk while I'm talking," say, "I would appreciate it if you would wait until I finish speaking before you say what is on your mind."

Soften the critical blow by criticizing the action and not the person. "Screaming is bothersome to me" sounds better than "Your screaming sounded horrible."

All a bachelor has to do to discover his hidden faults is get married.

Timing is essential. It is not a good idea to criticize someone who is angry or hurting. Wait until things are calm and tempers are under control in order to discuss problems. The time to discuss differences is not when a man wants to watch a game or a woman is preparing for company.

It is also counterproductive to criticize someone when s/he cannot do anything about it. If you think your wife's shirt clashes with her skirt, you can ask, "Are you sure that shirt and skirt go together?" if you are still home. Once you have left the house and there is no turning back, do not mention the outfit or you will only cause her to be self-conscious and frustrated, in addition to being angry that you didn't mention it when she could have done something about it.

A monk joins a monastery where his superior tells him that he is permitted to speak only three words per year.

At the end of the first year he tells his superior, "Bed too hard."

At the end of the second year he tells his superior, "Food no good."

At the end of the third year he tells his superior, "Want to leave."

His superior says, "I'm not surprised. All you've done since you got here is complain, complain, complain!"

Sometimes people shut down because their spouse unwisely raises a topic at an inappropriate time. Aaron had just argued with Brenda's father, who accused him of being a disappointment. Needless to say, when Brenda asked Aaron to spend the weekend with her parents it was out of the question.

Be careful about broaching sensitive topics. Rather than telling Ben she heard about a great job opportunity, Pam opened the discussion with a rant about his mediocre earning abilities. By the time she got around to the new job opportunity, Ben was no longer listening to anything she had to say.

A smart husband is one who thinks twice before saying nothing.

Speak with forethought. Rather than saying, "Do it like this. It's the only way," say, "It appears to me that this way may be better." Say, "I don't remember it being said that way," rather than, "You are a liar."

Speak courteously. Using words like "please," "thank you," and "excuse me" makes your spouse feel respected and makes you deserving of respect.

Speaking to one another with sensitivity and respect helps you retain your favorable feelings toward each other, strengthening them so they will overpower any negative feelings. Control how you think and what you say. If your spouse disappoints you, assume s/he had good reason. If you must tell your spouse something disappointing, don't procrastinate if it is inevitable. If you were planning a vacation and your boss tells you that you can't take off, tell your spouse in a delicate and caring manner. "Honey, I am so sorry to disappoint you. I was also looking forward to spending the time alone with you. Hopefully, we will be able to go in a few months."

If a spouse keeps disappointing you, broach the problem in a non-accusatory manner. Rather than saying, "You don't care," say, "I feel sad when you don't seem bothered by the situation."

Some women pick men to marry...others pick them to pieces.

—Mae West

In *Seven Principles of Marriage,* John Gottman describes how bad discussions can degenerate. An individual who feels attacked will first be defensive about his actions, then feel contempt for the speaker, which will lead him to criticize the attacker and finally tune out of the discussion. John Gottman terms the actions criticism, contempt, defensiveness, and stonewalling, or the four horsemen, because they march into your marriage and destroy it. He advises that when your partner makes a bid for attention, you should respond reassuringly with a kind comment or gesture at least 60 to 70 percent of the time.

By analyzing fifteen minutes of a couple talking to each other, John Gottman can predict with 90 percent accuracy whether the couple will still be married fifteen years later.

After watching for an hour, his success rate goes up to 95 percent. Gottman found that all marriages have a distinctive pattern that surfaces during a couple's interaction. He identifies, tracks, and codes twenty different emotions such as disgust, anger, sadness, defensiveness, and so on. Then he compares these codes to measurements taken by electrodes and sensors attached to each partner that identify at what point in their dialogue each of them is either sweating, fidgeting, or whose heart is racing. In this way, Gottman forms an equation that determines his prediction.

People, he believes, are in a state of either positive- or negative-sentiment override, where they choose to judge their spouse in a positive or negative light. For a marriage to survive, the ratio of positive to negative emotion in a given encounter has to be at least five to one. The single most telling sign that a marriage is in trouble is if one or both partners show contempt, if one speaks from a superior plane and puts his/her spouse on a lower plane. Women are more critical; men are more likely to stonewall, but there is no gender difference when it comes to contempt. Anytime one spouse makes the other feel inferior, looks down on the other, belittles, or rolls his/her eyes when the other speaks, it predicts the deterioration of the marriage.

Q: Your dog's barking at the back door. Your wife's barking at the front door. Who do you let in?

A: Well, it's your call...but the dog'll stop barking when you let him in.

Any discussion in which you plan to correct or criticize your spouse should be opened with a soft start, as opposed to what John Gottman terms a "harsh start up." Rather than beginning with an attack, it is advisable to begin gently and with care. "Darling, can we discuss why your boss canceled your vacation?" If you start kindly, your spouse won't feel attacked and react harshly. S/he will be able to listen rather than feel overpowered and overwhelmed, forced to fight back or tune you out. People who feel attacked become physically flooded: their heart rate speeds up, they begin to perspire, and their blood pressure rises. Marriages do not survive when people feel attacked by their spouses because the physical reaction is so disturbing that a person can no longer deal rationally and work out differences.

In all arguments, the presence and acceptance of what John Gottman terms "repair attempts" determines the damage or recovery to the relationship. If there is a solid friendship between the couple, repair attempts will work and will diffuse the harshness of the quarrel. Repair attempts are any words or actions that break up the tension. It is a way to de-escalate the argument, by saying things like, "Let's take a break," or "I think it's time for chocolate," or by interjecting a joke. If your spouse responds to these repair attempts, the force of the dispute is diminished. When you clash, be sure that you interject repair attempts and listen for your partner's repair attempts, responding positively to them.

A wife is standing in front of a full-length mirror taking a hard look at herself.

"You know, dear," she says, "I look in the mirror, and I see an old woman. My face is all wrinkled, my hair is gray, my shoulders are hunched over, I've got fat legs, and my arms are all flabby."

She turns to her husband and says, "Tell me

something positive to make me feel better about myself."

He studies her carefully for a minute, thinking about it, and then he says in a soft, thoughtful voice, "Well, there's nothing wrong with your eyesight."

Never say anything that goes to the core of a person. If you have done something that will hurt your spouse by confessing it, keep it to yourself. Perhaps you will feel less guilty by coming clean, but it will only damage your marriage.

A policeman stops a man driving along the highway. He says, "Mister, did you know that your wife fell out of the car ten miles back?"

The man takes a deep sigh and replies, "Thank G-d. I thought I was going deaf."

Yaron told Bracha that he was no longer attracted to her because she had become sloppy and slovenly. Bracha was hurt and angry, and returned fire by saying that he no longer excited her and therefore she didn't care about her appearance. Perhaps they communicated their feelings to each other, but they also destroyed their relationship.

The goal is to communicate in a manner that will improve a marriage. Yaron and Bracha's conversation should have gone like this, "Darling, you can be so attractive. I realize you are overwhelmed by your work and the kids and no longer have the time to pamper yourself. How can I help you find the time and energy to take better care of yourself?" A soft approach like this will get the message across. It may still hurt a little, but it does not elicit the resentment and anger that a harsh opening does.

The newlyweds were strolling along the beach. The young man looked out to the sea and eloquently said, "Roll on, thou deep, dark, blue ocean – roll on."

His wife looked at him with admiring eyes and spoke, "Oh, Herman. You're wonderful. It's doing it!"

Get in the habit of complimenting one another.

A woman who continually advises her husband may make him feel babied or inadequate. Your spouse does not need another parent. Be wary of advising too much or by-passing him to do things yourself.

A good wife laughs at her husband's jokes, not because they are clever, but because she is.

Some smart women act weaker and a bit more helpless in certain areas in order to make their husbands feel stronger and more needed.

There are various methods to have a spouse respond in the way you would like without resorting to commands. Rather than saying, "You have to do the car pool," provide information, such as, "Paula is unable to do the car pool today." Hopefully your spouse will process this information and volunteer to do the car pool. There is also the question form. "Do you have any idea who might be able to do the car pool?" S/he may volunteer to drive or suggest someone else. You can also state how you feel without accusation or guilt. "I really would appreciate it if you could help me with the car pool." Speaking respectfully is the best way to elicit a positive response.

A short story for men only… One day, long, long ago, there lived a woman who did not nag, whine, or complain. But it was a long time ago, and just that one day. The End

A smart wife knows how to accomplish what she wants in a subtle way. She may say, "I know you are tired from working all day, but you are so strong and the garbage is heavy for me. You are so good I'm sure you won't mind taking it out." Or if a wife needs a break she might say, "I know money is tight, but you deserve a dinner out for a change."

A smart husband also knows the art of diplomacy. Rather than telling his wife she gained weight, he might say, "I know you are frustrated that you haven't lost the weight you gained from giving birth. Maybe I can come home early some nights and we'll go walking together. I can also use the exercise." When your words are complimentary or helpful, they accomplish your objective.

A farmer and his wife were discussing how to celebrate their silver wedding anniversary. The husband said, "Should I kill a chicken?"

The wife replied, "Why blame some innocent old bird for what happened twenty-five years ago?"

Couples must make one another feel special. Talk pleasantly, laugh with each other, share secrets, make eye contact, and wink at one another. Discussions should be used for connection, not just as a way to complete household chores. Discussions about your personal life, your spouse's flaws, your private experiences, your little secrets, must be kept personal. Only the two of you, or a professional if need be, should be privy to those talks.

What's the difference between a new husband and a new dog? A dog takes only a couple of months to train, and after a year is still excited to see you.

Some writers have suggested you treat a spouse like

a pet. Take care of him/her, feed him/her, play with him/her, cuddle him/her, and reward him/her every time s/he treats you as you would like to be treated, just as you would reward your dog for learning tricks. If your wife cooks a delicious dinner, sing her praises. If your husband comes home early to help with the kids, give him an enthusiastic welcome and tell the kids what a terrific father they have. Every so often, a reward of a red rose, a dinner out, or a romantic evening is a great response.

Conditioning your spouse, and training him/her that nice behavior is rewarded keeps the behavior going.

Before marriage, a man will lie awake all night thinking about something you said. After marriage, he'll fall asleep before you finish saying it.

—Helen Rowland

Although couples should share their secrets, each individual is entitled to his/her own thoughts. A wife who thinks her husband is not worldly enough can encourage him to read more, but if she doesn't think he's bright enough to learn well, telling him so will only damage their marriage. A smart wife will keep her feelings to herself and focus on her husband's other positive characteristics. If a husband feels his wife is no longer attractive he can suggest a relaxing day at a spa, a fun makeover or the advantages of joining a health club, but explicitly stating that she is unattractive will injure their relationship. Be smart and diplomatic. Know what to say and what not to say to achieve your goal without damaging your relationship.

I love you. You're perfect. Now change!

It is important for a husband to know he is doing a good

job as a provider, a husband, a father, and even as a son-in-law. Tell him he's doing a great job.

It is important for a wife to feel she looks good, and she's doing a good job with the kids, the house, and her job. Tell her so.

Most wives lead double lives – their husband's and their own.

Show your spouse that you like, love, and appreciate him/her. Most people need to have this verbalized, so train yourself to say nice things to your spouse. When a wife is dressed up she appreciates her husband's smile of approval, but most woman want to hear it verbalized. "Wow, you look great!" If your husband helps clean up, make sure to thank him with words, "You are such a great help. I really appreciate it."

You agreed to marry your spouse, so obviously you like him/her. But s/he still likes to hear you say, "I like being married to you because you are such a fine person and at the same time you are so much fun to be with." A wife assumes you enjoyed her cooking because you took a second helping, but she would still like to hear you say, "Thanks for the delicious meal. You are one great cook." A straightforward compliment like "Dinner was delicious" can't be misinterpreted. Without it, your wife may think, "I know he ate two portions, but maybe he was just starving."

Just as you enjoy compliments, praise, and loving gestures from your spouse, so does s/he. Put yourself in your spouse's shoes. If it makes you feel good to hear a compliment, it also makes your spouse feel good.

Then there was the guy who loved his wife so much, he almost told her.

Non-expressive individuals must also learn to be complimentary, even if they are not naturally talkative.

Shmuli was a nice, easygoing, but quiet guy. Frieda felt he was too quiet. Because he was non-expressive she felt unfulfilled and lonely. A therapist worked with Shmuli to make him more expressive. For one exercise, Shmuli had to compliment Frieda three times a day. At first, expressing his feelings this way felt forced and fake, but once Shmuli got used to it and saw how talking made his wife feel connected, he became more comfortable with it. Their relationship quickly improved.

Compliments should include praising your wife's great pancakes or your husband's neat job of fixing the storm door, but that's only the beginning. Tell your husband you admire his business acumen. Tell your wife she is intuitive. Tell your husband you value his opinion. Tell your wife she stands out in a crowd. A global complaint is detrimental to a marriage, but a global compliment does wonders. Instead of "You are a good husband," better yet, say, "You are a good husband because you tune in to when I'm feeling down and always give me just the right compliment." Try: "You are a great wife because after a hard day, you always try to have a hot bath ready for me." Noticing and appreciating reinforces the behavior, strengthens one's self-esteem, and directs a person's actions.

Compliments should also be private and personal. "I love the way your face lights up when you are excited. I love being with you. I love when you laugh," and so forth. Making your spouse feel good costs you nothing, and you are the beneficiary. Your spouse will appreciate it and reciprocate. One's tone, expression, and wording all convey an attitude. Saying something lovely without any warmth in your voice makes the compliment seem forced and chore-like and it will be received that way. If you don't know how to express yourself well but you speak softly, with concern and a twinkle in your eye, you will convey affection and sincerity.

Dave said to Mike, "I had such a crazy day. I was at the airport buying an airline ticket and I just wanted to say to this extremely overweight ticket agent, 'I need two tickets to Orlando, but what came out was, 'I need two tickets to obesity.' I couldn't believe I'd said that right in front of this woman. Has anything like that ever happened to you?"

Mike said, "Did it ever! Something like that happened just this morning. I was sitting across from my wife at the breakfast table and all I wanted to say to her was, 'Could you please pass the French toast,' and instead what came out was, 'You impossible woman, you've ruined my life!'"

Speak respectfully to your spouse. Do not curse or call one another derogatory names. Do not whine and constantly complain.

Don't be too hard on your spouse. You will not bring about peace by being impatient, stern, or strict. Don't try to teach lessons by arguing. Any victory attained through an argument is short-lived. Arguing only makes a bad situation worse and usually causes a spouse to fight back.

A short temper can cause your spouse to shut down, but encouragement makes him/her want to live up to your expectations. Shouting, "Get out of bed and get to work! How are we supposed to pay the bills?" won't help. Rather say, "Honey, I realize you are tired and your job is draining, but I'm sure your boss notices how reliable you are and you wouldn't want to disappoint him." A positive approach is a proven motivating technique.

Just as you should not put your spouse down, you should not put yourself down. You can apologize by saying, "I'm sorry for jumping at you. I was very tired." But don't say, "I don't know why you put up with me. I am always jumping down your throat." This can plant a seed of doubt in your spouse's mind: *Why do I put up with him/her?* Don't say, "I know I'm such a slob." This might reaffirm your spouse's negative thoughts about you. Additionally, there's no need to repeat derogatory things that people have said about you, which can make you look bad in your spouse's eyes. Don't ever make your spouse question your mental health, your competence, or your loyalty.

In a non-conceited manner, you can even compliment yourself once in a while, saying, "I must say, I really pulled this house together," or "That deal I managed was really tough but I did it." A smart partner, or one who is reading this book and cleverly incorporating the advice, will chime in and say, "It sure was. I too am so proud of you."

You can tell when he's lying. His lips are moving.

Marriage must be based on honesty. You must be truthful because your partner needs to trust you. A liar eventually loses credibility, since one lie usually leads to another. Honesty is the best policy and leads to the best relationship. Once in a while, you may need to tell a little white lie so your spouse is not hurt. This is permitted, since the *baraisa* says, *Mutar leshaker bishvil shalom,* All lies are forbidden, but for the sake of peace.

Sometimes someone may be afraid of his/her spouse's

reaction; s/he finds it easier to lie than to say where s/he is, what s/he is doing, or what s/he is thinking. Lying is a form of withdrawal, in that you are erecting a barrier and hiding your needs. If you think you are doing the right thing, tell the truth and explain why your actions are justified. If you recognize that you are doing the wrong thing, own up to it, apologize, accept the berating, and promise him/her that you will try to act better.

If you realize your spouse is lying to you, find out why your spouse can't tell you the truth. Is it because s/he is truly doing something horrifically wrong, or is it because s/he can't trust you not to misinterpret the truth? Is s/he afraid that there is no option of calmly discussing the infraction? Do you need to handle situations with more calm and understanding, so you can engender trust? Once a spouse can confide in you, then the two of you can speak things out and work on a method of dealing with the issue as a caring couple.

If you know the answer, don't question your spouse merely to embarrass or discredit him/her. Don't make it your goal to catch your spouse in a lie. Aim to gain your spouse's confidence. Then, whatever the issue, together you can handle it.

If your spouse turns to drugs, drinking, or to another individual, s/he has not turned to you for the comfort s/he requires. Clear, open, honest, and understanding dialogue helps to prevent these vices from invading a marriage.

The party that answered the phone after I dialed told me that I had the wrong number.

I asked, "Are you sure?"

The party said, "Did I ever lie to you before?"

If you find yourself acting in a malicious, vengeful, disrespectful, or disloyal manner, you must ask yourself why you are acting this way. "Is this my problem, or is my spouse inciting this behavior?" Likewise, the spouse being hurt should question, "Is this his/her issue, or am I causing my spouse to act in this unseemly manner?"

Your words cause your spouse's reactions, and your reactions cause your spouse's words. Despite the fact that your spouse may react inappropriately, you are responsible for seeing to it that your actions are appropriate. Clearly, calmly, and truthfully say what you want your spouse to hear and understand. Clearly and carefully try to understand your spouse's words and intentions.

I can't believe I'm married eighteen years. It feels like one hour. One hour under water!

28: Love Each Other

One woman said to her husband, "You never tell me you love me."

Her husband said, "I told you I loved you when I married you. If things change I'll let you know."

Love grows when you give to one another; raise a family together, creating memories; and share your lives, feelings, insights, experiences, and dreams.

According to Rabbi Dr. Abraham Twerski, in today's culture, the word "love" has lost its meaning. He tells a story of the Rebbe of Kotzk, who sees a young man enjoying a piece of fish. He asks the man why he is eating the fish and the young man replies, "Because I love fish." The Rebbe replies, "You pulled the fish from the water, killed it, and broiled it because you love it? You don't love the fish. You love yourself. You are eating it because it tastes good to you, and you are satisfying your own desires."

Rabbi Twerski goes on to explain that this is true of today's young couples. A man loves a woman because he sees in her someone who can provide for all his emotional and physical needs. The same holds for a woman. Each, in essence, is looking out for his/her own self-gratification. "However, true love", says Dr. Twerski, "is not about what I am going to get, but rather what I am going to give."

In the same vein, Rav Eliyahu Dessler says, "It is a mistake to think that you give to those whom you love. Rather, the truth is, we love those to whom we give." This is because when one gives, he invests a part of himself in the other person. Since everyone loves himself, and now a part of himself is in his spouse, he now loves his spouse.

I fall in love really quickly, and this scares guys away. I'm like, "I'm in love with you. I'm crazy about you. I want to marry you."

And they're like, "Ma'am, could you give me the ten bucks for the pizza, and I'll be outta here."

—*Penny Wiggins*

There are periods of time during a marriage when passionate love is at a low ebb, sometimes temporarily and sometimes for extended periods. All that you have built together and share together sustains a marriage. No one else has your shared memories, no one else feels as you do about your children, no one else has experienced your growth as a couple, no one else can understand your conflicts. During these times both spouses can express their love by demonstrating a caring and supportive manner, and by helping one another.

28: Love Each Other • 237

Love is an unusual game. There are either two winners or there are none.

Susan said, "I went into this marriage wanting to be married. I was committed to forging a relationship, building a home, deepening our friendship, learning to rely on one another, and raising children. Stuie entered this marriage feeling that it would be fun, but he was totally unprepared to take on any of the responsibilities. He doesn't want to feel tied down; he still wants to hang out with his friends, bowling, drinking, or partying every night. He is married without taking on the mind-set of a married man. Even if he does love me and is loyal to me, a marriage can't survive that way."

It was another typical visiting day at the Happy Home. A patient said to his wife, "I'd like a watch that tells time."

The wife asked, "Don't you have a watch that tells time?"

"No. You have to look at it!"

Listen closely to your spouse, look closely at your marriage, and make certain that it is based on a solid friendship, with the positive feelings outweighing the negative ones and both partners agreeing that, despite their differences, each likes the other person.

Think about the type of person you would like your spouse to be, and then you act that way. If you love your partner enough to put yourself in his/her shoes, and try to make him/her happy and satisfied, you will make yourself happy and fulfilled as well. Consider things from your spouse's point of view and you will have an easier time meeting his/her needs. You will also find it easier to love him/her.

Man to friend: "When did you first realize your wife had stopped caring about you?"

Friend: "When she pushed me through the window and wrote for an ambulance."

Couples should be best friends. A woman should not spend all her time talking with girlfriends, nor should a man confide all his secrets to his pals. Save your secrets for your spouse. It is wonderful to have friends, but it is even more wonderful when your spouse is your best friend and confidant.

Couples should know the ins and outs of their spouse's life. Know your partner's likes and dislikes, hopes, dreams, goals, challenges, fears, and quirks. What is her soft spot, what sets him off and angers him, what excites her, what makes him laugh or cry, what makes her hurt, and what encourages him? Be aware of his beliefs, values, and passions; what she enjoys doing; which people he likes to be with; what bothers her; and what makes him happy. Your spouse's past, his upbringing, her favorite memories, his greatest disappointments, and her deepest thoughts should also be a part of your life.

Discuss your feelings, your opinions, and your impressions. When you are deeply involved in each other's lives and thoughts, it will be much more difficult to damage your relationship. Therefore, always work at being a part of each other's lives, sharing yourself with your spouse and drawing your spouse into your life. It is the responsibility of both partners to build and nourish this wonderfully rewarding relationship.

Because Adam had come home late, Eve started to berate him, "You've been unfaithful to me!"

Adam looked at her, puzzled. "With whom?"

Couples must take time to cultivate an enjoyable physical relationship. This helps a marriage thrive and endure. It adds an element of pleasure and excitement while forging a powerful and intimate bond. Keeping the spark alive in a marriage must be a priority. As life becomes more complicated, couples often have less time, energy, and privacy. Life's daily routines and responsibilities intrude, and with careers, children, and financial matters to challenge them, couples find it more difficult to keep the flame alive.

The physical relationship is an essential part of a marriage that both partners need, because nothing else can create that deep closeness and love that is critical to a solid marriage. This need is biological and emotional, and when it is fulfilled it strengthens a marriage. It is the responsibility of both partners to build and nourish this wonderfully rewarding relationship.

Abstaining from intimacy during the time a woman is a *niddah* (during the menstrual cycle and seven days beyond) has been proven to benefit the marriage relationship. There are experienced teachers and many books to consult on this essential topic.

Rebbetzin Feige Twerski writes: "Intimacy in marriage is very important, and sorting it out is crucial to the relationship." She writes that from a Torah perspective: "Intimacy between a husband and wife can be the most powerful expression of love between two people. The biblical mandate for the couple to be 'one flesh' speaks to holistic union of heart, mind, and soul. The Torah view stands in stark contrast to other religions that consider physical intimacy a contamination of the soul, albeit a necessary evil for the sake of procreation. It is for these reasons that in certain sects, spiritual leaders remain celibate and are enjoined from the marriage relationship. By contrast, the elite spiritual leader in the Jewish religious hierarchy, the *Kohen Gadol*, High Priest, qualified for that position only if he was married."

Rebbetzin Twerski goes on to say, "The objective of intimacy in Judaism is not exclusively for procreation, but is seen as integral and necessary for the well-being and felicity of the relationship. The Torah considers marriage and all that it entails a sacred bond. This is signified by the names attributed to betrothal and marriage, *kiddushin* and *nesu'in*, which mean, respectively, 'sanctification' and 'uplifting.' Moreover, our Sages teach that when a husband and wife live together in peace and tranquillity, the Shechinah, the Divine Presence, joins them."

Rebbetzin Twerski further says, "Emotional intimacy will create and shape the nature of the physical encounter. The quality of intimacy in marriage is, generally speaking, a product of the overall interaction between spouses. It doesn't exist in a vacuum. Respect, love, and caring are the essential components that must be cultivated and become integral to the union. It is the emotional intimacy that will create and shape the nature of their physical encounter. One cannot expect to be unavailable, inattentive, and insensitive by day and still unite successfully and meaningfully at night. Since emotions are influenced by physical and psychological events, rather than trying to reach someone exclusively through verbal and intellectual means, the body can often be the primary pathway to connecting, i.e., holding hands, hugging, a caring touch, and even non-verbal communication (posture, gesture, facial expressions, and so forth). A caring touch is important to all of us."

She concludes by saying, "Physical intimacy is most often a barometer of the relationship as a whole. It provides the couple with the energy necessary to engage life productively and effectively. Therefore, it behooves all of us to pay close attention, watch for danger signals in the relationship, and respond accordingly."

Rebbetzin Emuna Braverman writes, "While every marriage and every relationship is different, a marriage without physical intimacy is unlikely to survive, let alone thrive. We call it intimacy not just to use more appropriate language but because it is an accurate description. It is a deep and profound way for a couple to connect, and if it is missing from the marriage, then the union itself is dramatically limited."

Mr. Cohen was very ill. The doctor walked into his hospital room and asked Mrs. Cohen if he might have a word with her. Outside, he said to her, "Mrs. Cohen, your husband is going to die unless you do certain things."

"Just tell me," said Mrs. Cohen.

"You must do whatever it takes to keep him happy. Wait on him hand and foot, cook anything he likes, stay with him, coddle him, and fulfill his every whim."

"I understand," said Mrs. Cohen. She then returned to her husband's hospital room.

"Please, dear," said Mr. Cohen, "tell me, what did the doctor say?"

Said Mrs. Cohen, "The doctor said you are going to die!"

29: SHARE RESPONSIBILITIES

―――‹‹◉››―――

A wife calls her husband to come home immediately.

Husband: "Why?"

Wife: "Because there's something wrong with the car. The carburetor is flooded."

Husband: "You don't know anything about cars. How do you know the carburetor is flooded?"

Wife: "Just come home, dear. I'm telling you the carburetor is flooded."

Husband: "Darling, you don't know the engine from the trunk. How do you know the carburetor is flooded?"

Wife: "Dear, just come home. I'm telling you the carburetor is flooded."

Husband: "Darling, you don't know the windshield

wiper from the horn. How do you know the carburetor is flooded?"

Wife: "I'm telling you the carburetor is flooded."

Husband: "Darling, you don't know the steering wheel from the tires. How on earth can you be so sure the carburetor is flooded?"

Wife: "Because, dear, the car is in the swimming pool!"

Assume your wife knows what she is talking about and treat her with respect. Do not act as if she were inferior.

A housewife is someone who spends seven days a week scrubbing the floors, shopping for food, cooking the meals, washing the dishes, doing homework, doing car pools, disciplining kids, and being a valet, maid, and chauffeur for the kids. But that isn't what hurts. It's when someone asks her husband, "Does your wife work?" and he says, "No."

Running a house is a big job, no matter how large or small it is or how many children there are. It is a huge responsibility even with a housekeeper or a babysitter to help. This responsibility should be respected.

Sara, a newlywed, calls her mother crying and says, "Please take me home."

"Why?" asks her Mom.

"Because," says Sara, "the honeymoon was wonderful, but now that we are home Ira keeps saying things that I never hoped to hear. He's using terrible language…all those four-letter words that are too awful to repeat."

"Sweetie," says her mother, "what did he say that is worth leaving him for? What four letter words?"

Still crying, Sara replies, "Oh, Ma, he used words like wash, cook, iron, dust…"

Work together, sharing the chores and responsibilities. A wife is not a slave. A husband is not a hired hand.

A woman once complained to Rabbi Mordechai Gifter, of blessed memory, that her husband refused to help her take out the trash, believing it to be beneath his dignity. The following morning the rabbi showed up at the woman's home and insisted on taking out the garbage. Rabbi Gifter wanted to show the husband that if it was not beneath a great rabbi's dignity to help with the garbage, it certainly should not be beneath a husband's dignity to do so.

Remember, you married her. You didn't hire her.

Men and women should share the housework, especially things like taking out the trash, which neither spouse loves to do. A husband who is willing to do this task shows he is willing to invest in the marriage, because he is doing this job only to make his wife happy. His wife should continually thank her husband, recognizing his investment in the marriage. Thanking him will encourage him to continue and will keep him feeling that his actions are appreciated.

My wife and I have a perfect understanding. I don't try to run her life and I don't try to run mine.

The man in the house also needs respect. There are many men who give the orders at work and take the orders at home. A man can be the CEO of his company, president of his bank, or the owner of a large firm, and be obeyed and even feared at work, yet he can come home to a wife who tells him what to do, how to dress, and even where to sit. He may ask, "Can I sit here?" and his wife will answer, "No, that chair is getting too worn out." "Can I eat this?" "Don't touch that. It's for company." There are plenty of men who can handle this, but each wife should make sure her husband does not mind.

An office clerk crept meekly into the boss's office.

"Excuse me, sir," he said. "I'm sorry to bother you, but my wife told me that I had to ask you for a raise."

"All right," said the boss, "I'll ask my wife if I can give you one."

When a husband returns from work, a wife shouldn't hand him the baby with the words, "You change him. You put the kids to bed. I've taken care of these children all day." A husband has also worked all day. Husband and wife must work together to care for their children. Don't use the children as a tool to train or punish one another. Respect each other. Be considerate of each other's pressures and responsibilities and make your children feel loved.

Sharing household responsibilities is even more important if both spouses work outside the home.

The division of responsibilities usually evolves naturally in a solid marriage. Certain chores become the job of one spouse, the other spouse takes on other jobs, and you continually consult each other about a third group.

Sometimes one spouse will be the one to makes specific types of decisions. Who deals with the mail? Who takes care of the car? Who pays the bills? Who takes care of the gardening? Who changes the bulbs? Who arranges trips? There are thousands of responsibilities that come with a marriage. Discuss them and work them through to help avoid the blame game: "I thought you were going to take care of it!"

"Is your husband hard to please?"

"I don't know. I never tried!"

Help one another. Don't measure how much you give or how much you get from each other. The way for a marriage to succeed is for each one to try to do the most s/he can for the other person.

Of course, even if one spouse has certain responsibilities, major issues should still be discussed. Perhaps the wife makes the meal decisions, yet she should consult her spouse before deciding that the family is going vegetarian.

My husband says I treat him like he's a god. Every meal is a burnt offering.

—Rhonda Hansome

A wife, who is responsible for meals and basically knows her husband's likes and dislikes, should still remember to ask him occasionally if there is something special he would like her to prepare.

A little boy went up to his father and asked, "Dad, where did my intelligence come from?"

The father replied, "Well, son, you must have gotten it from your mother, because I still have mine."

In many homes the wife is responsible for the interior decorating, with the husband wanting only minimal involvement. In some instances though, husbands will want much more control in this area. Each couple must find the right balance that works for them. If their tastes are totally at odds, perhaps the wife will decorate the kitchen and the husband will decorate his study. Since interior design is usually considered the wife's domain, she might end up making the decorating decisions about the other rooms. Of course, she should not choose a style that makes her husband feel uncomfortable; rather, she should incorporate things that would please her husband. A magnificent home with a hostile ambience is counterproductive. It is much better to have a less beautiful home and a more beautiful marriage.

It doesn't matter if you are born poor and die poor, as long as you're rich in between.

Some husbands make all the financial decisions for the couple, while other couples believe these decisions should be made jointly. In some instances, the woman takes charge of the finances. Still other couples share the decision making, with the man deciding the business investments while the wife decides on the expenditures. No matter how these decisions are made, there must be a system and budget that both partners agree to and abide by, so that the money coming in is sufficient to cover the money going out.

Talk about economy… One gent got married and, starting out for the honeymoon, bought a bag of peanuts to nibble on. After biting into the third one he told his bride, "It's a big bag. Let's save some for the children."

A wife who wants to share the responsibility of dealing with the family income and the budgeting is entitled to do so, since this affects her and her children's well-being. She can expect her husband to accept that she may make some worthwhile suggestions and discuss it with her. Both spouses must display maturity in these discussions.

A man takes an assertiveness training course. He calls his wife and says, "Honey, I am coming home, and you better have the house cleaned, the kids bathed, and dinner on the table. You had better have my chair fluffed and a martini ready. And do you know who is going to brush my hair and shave my beard?" "Yes," says his wife, "the undertaker!"

Over time, couples learn which issues each partner feels are important, which each partner wants to handle by him-/herself, and which should be a joint decision. If your spouse is excluding you from decisions that you would like to be a part of, open your mouth and communicate that. Do not take it for granted that your spouse knows you want to be involved. Perhaps things were run that way in his/her family and s/he doesn't realize you have different expectations.

Husbands and wives need to discuss endless issues. If one spouse is happy with the way the other is handling something, s/he may choose not to question the decisions. Of course this does not mean s/he should not be consulted; s/he should feel part of the decision making, with his/her preferences being considered. Giving your spouse the impression that his/her feelings are inconsequential creates a spouse who feels frustrated, intimidated, or resentful.

The other spouse should not be offended with any questions; rather s/he should be open-minded enough to hear his/her thoughts on the matter. This strengthens a couple's connection.

The doctor gave Beryl three months to live. He sent Margie away for twelve weeks.

Make all your vacation plans together, unless one spouse

truly wants the other to make all the arrangements. Never accept an invitation without checking with your spouse to see if it is convenient, unless you are positive your spouse is happy to be relieved of the responsibility of handling his/her calendar. You must know how your spouse feels about these matters, since different people wish to be consulted about different aspects of their lives.

One wife may be relieved if her husband makes all the medical decisions for the family but may be horrified if he chooses the household appliances. One husband may agree to any decision his wife makes concerning visiting relatives, but she dare not get involved in what model car the family will use.

It is unrealistic to discuss everything. A woman who wants to buy a new brand of mascara should not need to discuss it with her husband. Only a control freak conducts a marriage like this. On the other hand, a blond woman who wants to become a brunette and surprise her spouse should be prepared to dye her hair back to its original color if he is upset about it. You want to retain your own individuality after marriage, yet consult one another and always consider each other's taste and opinions.

When you are negotiating what decisions to be involved in, there must be understanding, compromise, fairness, and respect.

There are no fixed rules for dividing or sharing household responsibilities between spouses. There are homes where the husband does all the shopping and cooking, homes where the wife is the only breadwinner, homes where the wife does all the driving and home improvements, and homes where the husband spends all his time raising the children. As long as the couple is comfortable with the arrangement it is perfectly fine.

She got a mudpack and looked great for two days... Then the mud fell off.

My grandfather always said it's simpler after you get married. Before marriage you have to please everyone. After marriage you only have to please one person: your spouse. Together, decide what works for the two of you and share the responsibility of making your marriage a strong and loving one.

If you want a guy to do something for you, all you have to do is introduce an element of senseless danger, and it becomes a sport.

"Honey, why don't you try to take out the trash while I chase you on rollerblades with a chainsaw!"

—*C. Lynn Mitchell*

30: Major Issues: Sensitivities and Insecurities

"How'd you come out in the fight with your wife?"
"She came crawling to me on hands and knees."
"Yeah? What did she say?"
"Come out from under the bed, you coward!"

    Everyone comes with baggage, emotional and psychological. All your past experiences, whether positive or negative, qualify as baggage, because each one of us is affected by our upbringing and our past relationships with family, friends, teachers, employers, and other people we've dated. We are affected by our wonderful experiences and our significant traumas, our fears, insecurities, sensitivities, and self-image. Accepting that all these feelings play into your reactions toward your spouse can help you understand yourself and your emotions. Using that knowledge, either to change or clarify your attitude toward your spouse, is a critical ingredient to forming a good marriage.

Everyone's upbringing has a profound influence on his/her relationships and married life. Your positive experiences make you dream of reenacting them. Your negative experiences can scar you and can even bring conflict into the marriage. If you loved eating dinner together with your family, you will want to create a family where your spouse and children enjoy that same experience. If eating together with your family always felt like a rigid and demanding ritual, you may want a home where mealtime is looser and attendance is not mandatory. By being cognizant of any issue, you can work to rectify it.

A guy walks into work, and both of his ears are all bandaged up. The boss asks, "What happened to your ears?"

He says, "Yesterday I was ironing a shirt when the phone rang and I accidentally answered the iron."

The boss says, "Well, that explains one ear, but what happened to your other ear?"

The guy says, "Well, gosh, I had to call a doctor!"

It is crucial to understand your issues so you can deal with them. Both Debbie and Dave had birthday parties that only their relatives attended. Debbie resented the fact that her friends were never invited, but Dave loved the intimacy of a small family party. Although Debbie and Dave had the same experience, their reactions were totally different. Now, as they are planning their son's birthday party, they need to work together to decide whether they should include friends or invite only relatives.

Part and parcel of the baggage people carry with them into marriage is the dreams and expectations they have. Tania grew up in a cramped, three-bedroom apartment with six siblings and no privacy. When she married Steve she hoped he would make enough money to buy a house where each child could have his own room. However, Steve's father was a workaholic, never spending any time with his children. Steve preferred to make less money and have a smaller home with ample time to devote to his kids. Both dreams make sense, but they conflict with each other.

Although differences like these can be worked out, they can also be a source of friction if they are not dealt with properly. Steve can work a bit more than he would have originally planned, and Tania can adjust to having two children in a room. If the couple discuss their expectations and explain their reasoning, they are more easily able to understand one another's feelings, making negotiating a compromise easier.

It is important for each spouse to define his/her dream. If there is friction in the marriage, they can see how and why the dream might be interfering with the relationship. Recognize your own dream and its source and your spouse's dream and its source, and hopefully this understanding can lead to compromise.

When I woke up this morning my wife asked me, "Did you sleep well?"
I said, "No, I made a few mistakes."
—Steve Wright

Each person should be aware of his/her own sensitivities so that s/he is not hurt, insulted, or outraged when those sensitive areas are touched. S/he must also be aware of and careful of his/her spouse's needs and sensitivities.

My wife is always buying clothes. You'd think that as a child she was once frightened by an empty hanger.

Many people are immature and insecure when they marry. They must grow together, realizing their own as well as their spouse's sensitivities.

Janet lost her mother at an early age, and the loss scarred her. Every time Rob mentioned his mother, Janet felt anger, jealousy, and resentment. Of course Rob could not be expected to ignore his mother's existence because of Janet's sensitivity in this area; Janet had to seek help to accept her mother's death. However, Rob did have to tread lightly when discussing the advantages he experienced by having a mother. Janet had to be mature enough to deal with this terrible tragedy, and Rob had to be aware of Janet's sensitivity and not evoke unnecessary pain or anger in her.

When we started out, my ex and I decided we wanted to keep growing as people. I just never imagined he would grow to three hundred pounds.

If a person is self-conscious in some area, such as intelligence, looks, or weight, marriage may not give her/him enough security to feel totally confident of his/her spouse's love.

Even a person's advantages can cause insecurities. A rich man may believe his wife loves him only for his money. A beautiful woman may feel her husband appreciates her looks but not her intelligence. This can cause a person to torture him-/herself and in turn his/her spouse.

Mature adults tune into one another's sensitivities, learning to cope with them. Because an emotional hurt is devastating, as we mature into more secure, well-adjusted adults, we develop the ability to work through our own issues more effectively and understand those of our spouse, thus creating a good marriage.

My daughter, Tova R. Katz, a marriage and family therapist, taught me, among other things, that recognizing what will hurt your spouse is like identifying his/her emotional sunburn. When a friend, with the best of intentions, slaps you warmly on the back, if you happen to have a sunburn under your shirt, you will experience pain. If a spouse unintentionally hits a sensitive chord within you, although done with the best of intentions, s/he may hit a sore spot, causing you great pain. Each partner, being cognizant of and compassionate of which sensitive areas, which emotional baggage, lie underneath his/her spouse's protective layer, makes for a mutually rewarding marriage.

If one spouse is always upset and frustrated, his/her partner may be doing something wrong, or perhaps the angry spouse has unrealistic expectations or is overly sensitive or insecure. The couple must analyze these disagreements to determine their true cause. Some argumentation in a marriage is acceptable, but constant arguing, relentless criticizing, and continuous correcting wear away at a relationship.

We were incompatible in a lot of ways. Like, for example, I was a night person, and he didn't like me.
—*Wendy Liebman*

If someone was raised in an abusive or dysfunctional home, s/he may bring that emotional baggage to the marriage and cause major turmoil. Professional intervention with these issues is a must before one contemplates getting married. Although everyone enters marriage with some baggage, a person coming with overweight luggage must be prepared to shed some of it beforehand to have a successful marriage.

"How can you talk to me like that," he wailed, "after I've given you the best years of my life?"

"Yeah," returned the wife, "and who made them the best years of your life?"

31: Different Backgrounds and Outlooks

Losing a wife can be hard. In my case, it was impossible.

Ira said, "Lisa and I are alike in many ways, but we are waiting to get engaged because we want to work out our differences." A couple may share a lot of similarities, but they are still different people and will always have some differences. People are brought up in different homes with different policies, different disciplinary approaches, and different values. Each home emphasizes different goals, respects different characteristics, and stresses different qualities. One family may believe in saving money to prepare for their children's futures, while the other believes in spending it so the kids enjoy life now; both parents feel they are doing what is best for their family. Although a person may view the way he was taught as the only right way, one approach is neither better nor worse than another; they are merely different orientations. However, this can cause problems if it is not explored and managed.

If it weren't for marriage, most men would go through life thinking they had no faults at all.

Every marriage has conflicts based on personality or lifestyle differences. These issues can include disagreements over money and household chores, employment, lifestyle, relationships, religion, raising children, and matters of intimacy.

A husband may feel he should run the family and may demand to be in charge, or he may be quite happy to allow his wife to take charge. A wife may feel her husband should take charge and resent if he doesn't, or she may appreciate a husband who allows her to run the show.

I'd love to get my wife everything she wants for her birthday, but I just don't know how to gift wrap Bloomingdales.

Some women feel they should buy everything for the home; they become furious if their husbands buy a piece of furniture. Other women are thrilled when their husbands come home with a new item for the house. Some individuals think only the wife is responsible for the children's upbringing, although most people feel both parents should be involved. Some people feel only the man is responsible for earning a living while others believe both husband and wife should contribute. Couples have to work out these matters. Although a person may have been raised in a home where the husband worked and the wife was in charge of raising the children, that does not necessarily mean this is the right way. Do not be insulted or angered should your spouse's beliefs differ from yours. In all instances, the couple must examine the different ways they were each raised and decide together what works for them as a couple.

Your value system forms your behavior, so if you change your values you can change your rules of behavior. Each spouse must understand his/her own value system and his/her spouse's values, and each must be willing to analyze these beliefs. The couple can then work on a direction that is right for both of them.

A woman asked her husband, "What are you going to do today?"

He said, "Nothing."

She said, "But you did that yesterday."

"So," he said, "I didn't finish!"

A wife who was raised in a home where her father worked and never had time for the kids – to help change diapers, put the children to bed, or assist with homework – may decide it is very important to have a father involved with the children. Her behavior and rules will be based on that decision. Of course these discussions must include consideration of the couple's lifestyle, their financial needs, and their job requirements as well as their goals.

If you come from a home where the modus operandi in the family included shouting, cursing at one another, and continually showing anger or throwing tantrums, but your spouse comes from a home where shouting and curse words were discouraged and conversation and compromise were encouraged, both partners should be able to recognize what is preferable for their home and children. Just because something was accepted in one's home does not mean it is necessarily correct. Do not feel attacked if your way of life is not the one chosen for your joint family.

Get in touch with your own feelings and determine if this behavior is in line with what you truly believe, or if is merely what you are used to seeing. You are not a puppet. Think for yourself. Discuss the issues with your spouse and with experts. Dance to a tune you like, but be willing to change some steps. Be prepared. Questioning your own beliefs, or having your beliefs questioned, may cause some stress and anxiety but may also yield better results.

Do not expect your spouse to accept a statement such as: "You only feel that way because your parents forced those beliefs on you." Naturally s/he will become defensive. People tend to defend even the worst parents because it hurts too much to see reality. Neither can you say things like: "Just because your parents controlled you doesn't mean I'm controlling you." "Don't think I am lying to you because your parents always lied to you." "Your family may have never respected your opinion but that doesn't mean I am not listening to you." "Just because your parents always fought and caused sibling rivalry doesn't mean that's the right way to raise kids."

Although you want to help your spouse understand where you are coming from and what his/her issues are, you must be delicate with your spouse if you are challenging lifelong beliefs. The truth comes to a person slowly as s/he learns about him-/herself and his/her upbringing. S/he must be able to process the new information in a way that allows him/her to still love his/her parents and siblings. This is especially true when a spouse was brought up in a home where the children never questioned the parents' rules and beliefs.

How many sons does it take to change a Jewish mother's lightbulb? None.

"It's okay, son. Don't bother. I'll just sit here in the dark."

Some parents raise their children on guilt. These children go on to become spouses who use guilt for control. Since guilt works only if the other person responds to the guilt, the other spouse must learn to be sensitive but not be manipulated by guilt.

If parents raise children with bad values, for example, if they raise them to believe that wealth is more important than love or goodness, or that making a good impression is more important than truly being a good person, the children can come to a marriage prepared to fool, hurt, and cause conflict. These people must learn to accept new values, perhaps deciding that their spouse's values are better, or that a set of values that neither was raised with is preferred.

Some parents raise their children on forced obedience and conditional love. They force conformity of thought and action, instill fear of recrimination and revenge, and exhibit uncontrolled anger. These parents often buy love, withhold love, or vie for love. When these children grow up and marry, they often treat their spouses and children in like manner. Individuals who were raised in a family where approval was unattainable feel like nobodies without their spouse's approval.

It is counterproductive to expose the truth to someone who has been raised in any of these harmful ways. Your spouse will make you feel that you don't know what you are saying. The result will be anger, blame, distance, and a perpetuation of the abusive cycle. To help a person from a dysfunctional home understand where s/he is coming from, professional help is usually required.

An individual must recognize the negative parts inherent in his value system to realize that his/her marriage and parenting methods need to be revamped. If one's upbringing is the cause of the problem, s/he must first accept that reality, and then go through a step-by-step process to ultimately change and create a good marriage and parenting method.

Professional help is required so s/he can stop discounting the damage, release him-/herself from the family's control, place the responsibility where it belongs, and forgive him-/herself. Hashem blessed each of us with *bechirah chofshit*, free will. One can determine to be different and do better than his/her parents did. Eventually s/he may also be able to forgive his/her parents.

In order to change an abusive cycle, a person must take responsibility for his/her actions even if it was his/her upbringing that caused those actions. Each individual can choose to change what exists. People who are taught things that are wrong still can choose to do right. People who are abused can still choose to fight back and not accept the abuse. These are not simple matters, but by acknowledging the existence of the problem one can bring about change. A spouse who is being abused must open his/her eyes and fight for his/her dignity.

Marriage is a very expensive way to get your laundry done free.

There are many instances where both spouses have had a good upbringing but some of their ideals are different.

Discussion, cooperation, and compromise help couples plan a strategy for these aspects of their life.

With these couples, it is neither stubbornness nor insecurity, but rather strong, solid values that cause each partner to remain firm in his viewpoint. Understanding the importance of religion, family ties, raising a family, and respectful treatment, each spouse firmly defends his/her position.

Gary felt strongly about the benefits of religion, and Sandra agreed with him at first. But when their child reached school age, Sandra decided it was too expensive to pay for the yeshiva that Gary wanted his son to attend. Because religion was so important to him, Gary stayed firm and would not give in on this point. He was willing to compromise by putting in extra hours at work and doing some careful investing so Sandra would be able to continue her lifestyle without feeling pinched.

For a while we pondered whether to take a vacation or get a divorce. We decided that a trip to Bermuda is over in two weeks, but a divorce is something you always have.

—*Woody Allen*

Barry didn't get along with Shayna's parents. Although he would not discuss the reasons for his dislike, he told Shayna she would have to choose between them. If she wanted a relationship with her parents, he would consider divorce. He was not willing to compromise when Shayna suggested that she keep her relationship with her parents, without including Barry. Shayna drew the line and would not even consider totally breaking ties with her parents.

Kids? It's like living with homeless people. They're

cute but they just chase you around all day long going, "Can I have a dollar? I'm missing a shoe! I need a ride!"
—Kathleen Madigan

Linda and Michael were married two years and Linda wanted to start a family. Although he liked kids, Michael felt that a child would disrupt their lives. Linda remained steadfast in her demand that they have a child and Michael had to agree in order to hold on to Linda. He never regretted it for a moment. They now have four lovely children.

Reality is that each couple has a different dynamic and each couple has to carve out a life together.

When a couple is having difficulties, it is the responsibility of both parties to deal with the problem. Sometimes one spouse will say to the other, "It is your problem. You deal with it." An attitude of: "I know I am doing the right things. If you believe there is a problem it is your fault or it is in your head, so you deal with it" will cause the marriage to break down. This is true even if most of the problems do stem from the other spouse. Both partners still need to deal with it.

Morris is in the hospital with a heart attack. Morris turns to Sadie and says, "Sadie, you were with me when I tripped on the step and broke my arm. You were with me when I lost my job. You were with me when I fell in the snow and broke my hip. And now here you are with me when I'm lying on my deathbed. Sadie, I just want to say one thing to you. Sadie, you're a jinx!"

32: Discover Your Personality

Had Columbus been married, he might never have discovered America because of the following:
"Where are you going?
With whom?
Why?
How are you going?
To discover what?
Why you?
What do I do when you are not here?
Can I come with you?
Coming back when?
Why?
Don't lie...
Why are you making such programs?
You seem to be making a lot of such programs.
Why?
I want to go to my parents' place.

I want you to come back.

I don't want to come back...
I will never come back...
Why are you not stopping me?

I don't understand; what is this discovery chatter?
You always do this.
Last time you also did something like this.
Nowadays you always seem to do like this.
I still don't understand; what else is there to be discovered...etc.?"

—*Young Fropkian*

Understanding your own and your spouse's personality can help you accept one another and work better with each other. The Enneagram system is a good method to discover your personality type. This system divides people into nine different categories:

1. The Reformer is principled, purposeful, self-confident, and perfectionistic.
2. The Helper is demonstrative, generous, people pleasing, and possessive.
3. The Achiever is adaptive, excelling, driven, and image conscious.
4. The Individualist is expressive, dramatic, self absorbed, and temperamental.
5. The Investigator is perceptive, innovative, secretive, and isolated.
6. The Loyalist is engaging, responsible, anxious, and suspicious.

7. The Enthusiast is spontaneous, versatile, distractible, and scattered.
8. The Challenger is self-confident, decisive, willful, and confrontational.
9. The Peacemaker is receptive, reassuring, agreeable, and complacent.

If you are aware of which category a person functions in, you can understand him/her better and be more careful about provoking, frightening, worrying, or exciting him/her, since you are better able to predict his/her response. Understanding your own personality type is also helpful for developing insight into your own reactions and to help your spouse comprehend your makeup, strengths, and vulnerabilities.

No matter how much research you do, and how well you try to get to know your potential spouse, you will discover many sides of your spouse's personality after marriage that you were unaware of beforehand. In fact, throughout life we discover many aspects of our own personality that we were not consciously aware of earlier. As new situations arise, different aspects of our personality emerge.

How do you turn a dishwasher into a lawn mower? Give her a shovel!

Sara was a quiet, cooperative young lady who never spoke up to anyone. When her husband fell ill, she raced him to the emergency room where he lay unattended and in pain for hours. Her frustration mounted and she suddenly went to the medical desk and demanded help. To her amazement, the medical staff responded. Realizing that she had the power to be effective, she forced herself to keep speaking up, in order to get her husband the care he needed. She discovered a side of her personality she did not know existed. The efficacy of well-placed aggressive behavior was positively reinforced during her husband's hospital stay, causing her to incorporate it and use it more frequently.

Sometimes, discovering your personality can have negative consequences. Charles always seemed in control, shrugging off whatever bothered him, albeit somewhat angrily. One day he came home to find that his wife, Sharon, had thrown out an important document. Rather than containing his frustration, he lashed out at her. Feeling guilty for her mistake, Sharon didn't defend herself, meekly accepting the verbal abuse. This emboldened Charles and he began lashing out at Sharon over every little thing. Suddenly the dynamics of the marriage changed and Sharon became scared and much more subservient. Charles felt empowered but Sharon was miserable. She was too scared to speak up until their marriage had totally deteriorated.

What do you call a woman with an angel for a husband? A widow.

We grow, change, mature, and develop our character as circumstances arise. We can only guess how we might react in untested situations, hoping we will act in a way that we are proud of recalling. We strengthen ourselves, building our temperament and personalities so we can handle new conditions when they arise. We must hope that our spouse has developed him-/herself with the same care. Each partner must monitor his/her own change and growth, being aware of its effect on his/her spouse.

Inform your spouse if you have changed your view or attitude about something, explaining why you have changed, what you have learned, or whom you have spoken to that has made you see things differently. Don't leave your partner behind. You may be ahead, but you will be alone.

The guy in the bar is just looking at his drink when a big trouble-making truck driver sits next to him, takes the drink from the guy, and drinks it all down. The poor man starts crying.

The truck driver says, "Come on, man. I was just joking. Here, I'll buy you another drink. I just can't see a man crying."

"No, it's not that. This is the worst day of my life. First, I get fired for being late to work, then my car is stolen, and then I go home to find my wife has left me to go home to her mother. I leave home and come to this bar. And just when I was thinking about putting an end to my life, you show up and drink my poison…"

33: Can a Person Change?

Unfortunately, marriage is often a case of two people agreeing to change each other.

When my daughter was dating, I told a married man that she did not want to mold a husband. He said, "She will."

Marriage should really be a union of two people learning to accept each other and adjust to one another's different backgrounds. It should be about realizing the reasons for their differences and the benefits to be found in being different. It should be about accepting that one way is not necessarily wrong, it is just different.

If it weren't for my faults, I'd be perfect.

Many people want to be accepted for who they are but have trouble accepting others for who they are. They will make excuses for their own deficiencies in weight, sloppiness, patience, or lack of productivity, but they are unwilling to tolerate or forgive the flaws of others. Don't expect your wife to look good and keep in shape if you refuse to exercise. Don't ask your husband to stay calm and relaxed if you are always yelling. A spouse may be willing to give in sometimes, but don't expect one spouse to always give in to the other spouse. If you want a caring spouse, you need to be a caring person. Don't tell your spouse or your children, "Do as I say, not as I do."

The warden gave the burglar his best good-bye speech, since his sentence was up, reminding him how important it was to change his ways completely. When he was finished speaking, the burglar continued to stand before the desk. The warden asked, "What are you waiting for?"

The prisoner said, "My tools!"

You can't change the other person; you can only change yourself and your reaction to the other person. If a husband can't keep his stuff clean, his wife can constantly berate him or she can learn to take deep breaths and accept this fault. If it is not in his wife's nature to be on time, her husband can continuously be angry and frustrated, or he can accept this flaw in the context of the whole person.

A woman marries a man expecting he will change, but he doesn't. A man marries a woman expecting that she won't change, and she does.

You can only change your own actions, responses, and attitude, which will hopefully affect the actions, attitude, and responses of your spouse. Love is not just a feeling; it's an action. Grammatically, it is a verb. We have the ability to control what we do. We even have the capability to control our feelings, although this is more difficult. What we don't have the ability to control is what our partner does. The most we can do is try to influence, teach, and affect our partner. If you are unhappy with your partner's actions, recognize that his/her action is often a response to your behavior.

You don't marry one person; you marry three: the person you think they are, the person they are, and the person they become as a result of being married.
—Richard Needham

Lisa was always in a rage when Danny came home from work. She felt he had been out in the world all day while she was locked up in the house with nothing productive to do. Danny often suggested that she get out – either to school or a job. But Lisa worried that she would not be able to keep the apartment clean or prepare the meals if she took on another project. Dreading his welcome, Danny began to stay later and later at work, which caused Lisa's temper tantrums to escalate. After brainstorming for a while, Danny and Lisa decided that they would meet two or three times a week for lunch. This would not be simple for either of them; Danny's workday would be broken up and Lisa would have to travel a bit to meet him, but Danny thought they should make their lunch meetings a priority. This suggestion showed Lisa that Danny cared about her and also gave her a chance to get out of the house, making Lisa much calmer and happier. Their lunches gave Lisa something to anticipate and made the time at home much more tolerable. By adjusting his schedule to accommodate his wife, Danny found that his wife was happier, and therefore he was much happier.

When you adjust your behavior, you elicit a different response from your spouse. Try different approaches, because when you make your spouse happy, you make yourself happy. If each partner tries to change himself in order to make his/her spouse happy, both will be happy.

A man who is about to be released from an insane asylum is called before the approval committee. "You have been in here for five years and are about to go back into the real world. What do you think you will do?"

"Well," says the man, "I have thought a lot about it. I used to be a big doctor, so I plan to go back and reestablish my practice. If that doesn't work, I was also a macrobiologist, so I can always go back to working in a lab. If that doesn't work, after college I took my CPA exam and am a qualified accountant, so I can always go back to working in a big accounting firm. And if all else fails, I can always go back to being a teapot."

There are those who refuse to change. Stan moved from New York to California because Iris insisted on living near her parents. They had been married seven months and had not yet visited his parents in New York, so Stan wanted to spend the holidays with them. Iris insisted that during the first year of marriage the holidays are spent with the girl's parents. Stan knew that was generally done, but thought Iris might be flexible, considering they lived near her parents all year. She wouldn't hear of it.

In *The New Rules of Marriage,* psychologist Terrence Real criticizes couples that are miserable yet have no desire to change. He terms them "comfortable/miserable." If you want a good relationship you have to get out of your stale comfort zone, working to change yourself and the dynamics of the marriage.

Both men and women can be stubborn. Some people refuse to give a finger, afraid their spouse will then want a hand. Janie wanted Larry to come home for dinner every night, but Larry made it a point to always work late and miss the dinner hour. Even though eating dinner together two nights a week would have made Janie much happier, he would not even consider that idea. He was afraid that once he began coming home for supper Janie would say, "See! What's the big deal? Why can't you do this every night?" If that happened he would feel pressured, besides losing too many working hours. Discussing it together and agreeing to try eating dinner together only a few nights a week would have strengthened their relationship. But Larry would not discuss the issue because he felt no desire to change.

How many psychiatrists does it take to change a lightbulb? One, but the lightbulb really has to want to change.

Jeff was a great businessman and a great provider. He therefore believed Iris should ignore his abusive temper and his insistence that everything be done his way. But it did not take long for Iris to realize that all the luxuries in the world weren't enough to compensate for the horrible way Jeff made her feel. Because he refused to change, Iris left him.

Lois was an only child, used to being pampered and having things her own way. Whenever Mike tried discussing other options, she threw a tantrum. She wanted to do what she wanted, have what she wanted, and buy what she wanted. Mike, understanding that she had been brought up in this manner, was patient with her, and just continually explained that a couple cannot function in this manner. He did not expect her to change overnight but guided her along, constantly reminding her of all her great qualities while saying things like, "If you could just be more open-minded, you'd be unbelievable. If you would just spend a bit less, you would take some of the strain off me, which would make me love you even more – if that is possible." It took time. Change usually is gradual and takes work. But Lois was smart enough to understand and accept her own faults. Because she wanted her marriage to succeed, she worked on herself.

A man decides to make an effort to change for his wife. He knows it drives her crazy that he never puts the toothpaste cap back on the tube, so he decides that from now on he will always replace the cap. He does this for over a week and can't understand why his wife hasn't noticed or commented on his great change. Finally, his wife says to him, "What's wrong? Why did you stop brushing your teeth?"

Some people won't give in because of stubbornness, others because of pride. Some people don't want to be inconvenienced; others want everything their own way. They refuse to acknowledge the benefit of changing: it would make their spouse happier and in turn their own lives would be happier.

Giving in is not a weakness. Quite the reverse; it takes great strength of character to be the one who gives in to one's spouse. It takes the ability to understand that peace is more important than winning, that your spouse's need to be heard and respected is more important than your own need to be right, and that your marriage is more important than this particular issue.

Diplomacy is the art of letting someone have your way.

Studies show that men who allow their wives to influence them and are not too chauvinistic, hotheaded, or indifferent to their wife's opinion are four times happier than those who ignore their wives' influence (John Gottman, *Seven Principles of Marriage* p. 105).

Studies also show that most women, whether or not they are happily married, are affected by their spouse's opinion.

If a wife feels she can influence her husband, she is less frustrated and less likely to attack him. With fewer attacks, he in turn is less prone to react with a barrage of accusations, counterattacks, or indifference when his wife does complain.

A man goes into a Zen bookstore and hands the cashier $10 for a book that costs $9.95. He waits and finally says, "Where's my change?"

The cashier says, "Change must come from within."

If only one partner is willing to change, he must tell himself, "I am doing this as a gift for my spouse, without expectations. I am doing this in order to make my spouse happy." Of course, if your spouse is happy, you will also be happy. By changing course for your spouse, you get to share in the gift of happiness. Hopefully giving this gift will cause your partner to reciprocate.

Arlene said, "Danny is really trying to help me feel less cooped up, so he leaves work early once a week to take me out. Now when he comes home at the end of a long workday, I act more upbeat to let him know how much I appreciate his efforts."

Often one spouse says, "I will change if s/he will change," or "I will admit to faults if s/he will admit to faults." You can only change yourself. Recognize your own faults and work on correcting them. By so doing, you will alter the dynamics and cause your spouse to be less defensive and more open to owning up to responsibility and more willing to change.

Attitude is the key. Decide you want to be happy and make yourself happy.

G-d wanted to hide the secret of happiness, so He called the angels together and asked them for suggestions where to hide it.

The first angel said, "Hide it deep under the sea. Man will never find it there."

The second angel said, "Hide it on the highest mountain in the world. Man will never find it there."

The third angel said, "Hide it deep within the human soul. Human beings will never think to look there."

And that's exactly what G-d did.

Everyone must look deep within him-/herself and decide they want to be happy. If you have to change something about yourself to be happy or to make your spouse happy, do it. Change your actions, change your expectations, change your thinking, and change your attitude!

34: Character Counts

A man had a head that came to a sharp point, two sets of lips, three eyes, one of them under his right ear, and bright blue skin. He walked into the office of the "Believe It or Not" people and said he'd like to talk to the man in charge. The receptionist asked, "About what?"

Every individual is unique. Truthfully, some people are better than others. Some people are kinder, finer, warmer, more caring, more loving, more generous, more patient, more forgiving, more understanding, more other-directed, more appreciative, more helpful, more considerate, more compassionate, more sensitive, more intuitive, more generous, more gracious, more cooperative, more focused, more adaptive, less temperamental, less jealous, less angry, less volatile, less critical, less cynical, less spoiled, less demanding, less selfish, less vengeful, less frustrated, less stubborn, less rigid, calmer, happier individuals. However, no one is perfect. We all must work on our own faults.

Negative personality traits can be truly harmful to a relationship. An individual can hide these faults while dating, but they eventually surface in marriage and can be destructive. While a parent may adjust to or blindly accept a spoiled or jealous child, a spouse may not be as willing to do so. Inflexible, demanding, self-centered, manipulative individuals are the enemy of a happy marriage. An individual who is extreme in any direction – a neat freak or a slob, a cheapskate or a spendthrift, someone who is rigidly punctual or someone who is never on time, an inflexible person who needs everything his/her way or someone wholly carefree – can wreak havoc in a marriage.

Sadie said to Maddy, "I've had it with Albert. I can't stand how he acts. He gets me so aggravated I've lost twenty pounds."

"So," said Maddy, "why don't you just leave him then?"

"Oh, not yet," Sadie said. "I still want to lose another ten pounds."

Derech eretz kadmah laTorah, good behavior comes before Torah. Hashem created man *b'tzelem Elokim*, in His image, giving each of us the potential to replicate G-d's *middos*, His character traits. As G-d is merciful, we too must be merciful. As G-d is forgiving, we too must be forgiving. As He visits the sick, so we must visit the sick. He is compassionate, so we must learn compassion. By imitating Hashem's ways, we can properly learn to fashion ourselves and our behavior. As Hashem acts toward His beloved nation, so should we each act toward our beloved spouse, to our children, and to the entire Jewish nation. Hashem has an image of what each of us has the potential to become. At the *akeidah*, the binding of Isaac on the altar, Hashem called out, "Avraham, Avraham." The rabbis explain that Avraham's name is repeated because he lived up to his potential, becoming an identical match to the image Hashem had of him in heaven. Each of us must strive to do the same, to become the good, caring, giving person Hashem wants each one of us to become.

I can make my wife do anything she wants to do.

A self-centered person who views everything in terms of how it affects him/her rather than how it affects him/her, his/her spouse, and their marriage, is asking for that marriage to fail.

Molly had three kids, a full-time job, and a home to run. Barry expected dinner heated to the correct temperature and on the table when he walked in the door. He could not accept that, as hard as Molly tried, she could not guarantee that the food be warm when Barry came home. Barry's selfish rigidity did not let him realize that circumstances such as a child crying or the need to finish a project for work could easily throw off her timing. He took it as a personal offense, refusing to believe it had nothing to do with Molly's respect for him. Barry believed that if she really wanted to please him, she could do it. Unrealistic demands do not foster a good marriage.

I love you just the way you are. But don't get any worse.

If you think your spouse is irrational about something, arguing with him/her when s/he is still upset and cannot hear you is counterproductive and will just lead to more arguing. If you are certain you are being rational, you can mention that you are still uncomfortable, but only when your spouse is calm. Validate your spouse's feelings; this does not mean you are validating his/her behavior. Say things like, "I see you are upset. I realize you are unhappy with the situation. I'm sorry things didn't work out the way you had hoped. I'm sorry if you feel I misunderstood you."

When at least one person in the marriage has a healthy attitude, the marriage can be a good one. With time and effort, this person can help his/her partner understand many issues more clearly and with less confrontation. Of course the other partner must cooperate, taking responsibility and recognizing his/her faults.

To make a marriage work, each partner must know him-/herself, taking responsibility to improve his/her character. You must choose to overcome any negative influences or experiences that have affected your character and self-esteem. Everyone eventually faces the choice to resist change or choose to grow. You can choose to understand and learn from your past, letting it help you shape your future in a positive way.

Learning to accentuate your best qualities and control your negative ones will make you a better person and a better spouse. Channel your talents and passions to do things that make you feel happy and fulfilled. Do things you've always wanted to do, such as taking up a sport, joining a band, or going to classes. When you are happy it is easier to accept other people, appreciating and enjoying them.

You can also channel your negative character traits in positive ways. Rather than being jealous of another person's possessions, learn to be jealous of his good deeds and try to imitate them. An angry person can take up an unjust cause, fighting for justice.

If you recognize qualities in yourself that you find too difficult to use in a positive way, determine that you will change those traits. You can change when you notice how these characteristics are affecting your relationships, and when you remind yourself how you dislike this behavior when others display it. Change is possible, but only you can do it.

He stopped calling her "the little woman" when she started to call him "the big mistake."

Work on yourself to be a giving, caring person; you will like yourself and make it easier for others to like and respect you. A person who is accepting and even tempered, willing to give and able to adjust, is happy with him-/herself. His/her self-esteem enables him/her to compliment his/her partner more, be less competitive, and be less prone to misinterpret his/her partner's statements. Of course this makes marriage easier for both spouses.

People who are always dissatisfied, wanting more success, love, power, children, attention, recognition, or possessions will never be happy. Achieve real happiness and you will also make your partner happy.

In order to be happy, every person must be passionate about something, whether it is marital success, monetary success, moral success, prestige, religion, and so on. Your successes and even the struggles you engage in as you try to achieve your desires give you a sense of satisfaction. Be passionate about the right things, and this will bring you true joy.

34: Character Counts • 283

Ralph and Edna were both patients in a mental hospital. One day, while walking past the hospital swimming pool, Ralph suddenly jumped into the deep end. He sank to the bottom of the pool and stayed there. Edna promptly jumped in to save him. She swam to the bottom and pulled him out. When the head nurse became aware of Edna's heroic act, she immediately ordered her to be discharged from the hospital, since she now considered her to be mentally stable.

When this nurse went to tell Edna the news she said, "Edna, I have good news and bad news. The good news is, you're being discharged, since you were able to respond rationally to a crisis by jumping in and saving the life of the person you love. I have concluded that your act displays a sound mind. The bad news is, Ralph hanged himself in the bathroom with his bathrobe belt right after you saved him. I am so sorry, but he's dead."

Edna replied, "He didn't hang himself. I put him there to dry. Now how soon can I go home?"

Even a person with a problematic personality can have a good marriage, as long as s/he is a caring person who is sensitive to his/her spouse's needs. The key is finding a partner who understands and accepts the particular behavior and is able to deal with it. If the person with the issue accepts responsibility and is willing to work on it, the marital challenge for each spouse will not be as burdensome. Of course, major psychological problems such as borderline personality disorder may be too great a challenge for a couple to overcome.

Sharon needed to keep her home spotless; anything out of place sent her into a rage. Because she genuinely was a giving and caring person Jack married her and tried to be neat and orderly for her sake, although it was hard for him. At the same time he did encourage her to get therapeutic help.

A woman was letting her husband have it. "You're an idiot. You always were an idiot. You'll always be an idiot. If they had an idiot contest, you'd come in second."

"Why would I come in second?" the husband asked.

"Why?" she answered. "Because you're an idiot!"

If people with major hang-ups can create a strong marriage, surely the average couple should be able to establish a fine marriage!

Even if only one partner has a problem, both partners are responsible for the solution. Although one partner may be more demanding than the other, the key word is "partner." In the game of tug-of-war, the opposing teams pull and tug, and eventually one pulls the other down. Similarly, a marriage will not survive if you are not on the same team. But a husband and wife who are on the same team and who do pull together will be victorious against the forces pulling against them. Even though one may have to work harder and give more than the other, together they can be victorious. Of course, if one partner is doing all the work and the other is indifferent, problems will ensue.

Marriages can survive if each accepts the other's different or odd side with understanding and is accommodating and respectful, rather than critical and derogatory.

Life is a stress test.

People have many stresses in life, as well as psychological disorders that can be clinically treated. A person who can't control his anger, frustrations, depression, or anxiety, or who exhibits phobias, obsessive-compulsive disorder, bipolar behavior, or borderline personality disorder should be taking medication. If you or your spouse is suffering from any of these disorders, you must get help or insist that your spouse get help. This is crucial for the well-being of your family. As was mentioned, Rabbi Dr. Abraham Twerski discusses the need to recognize the many mental disorders people suffer with while the couple is still dating (see chapter 9, "Recognizing the Right and Wrong Person"). These disorders can be toxic for a marriage, and he therefore advises people with mental disorders to seek professional help.

My wife stopped taking tranquilizers. She was starting to be nice to people she didn't even want to talk to!

An insecure person may become so anxious and stressed s/he can't function properly. In these cases it is advisable to see a therapist and consider anxiety/depression medications. Proper medication, administered by a reputable doctor or psychiatrist, helps a person feel calmer and more capable of dealing with life's pressures. Marital issues become less tense. Although people rarely confide in others that they are on medication, these medications are widely used and should not carry a stigma. Information to help you recognize the many possible psychological conditions is readily available on the Web, or an expert can be consulted.

A woman took her son to a psychiatrist. "Tommy refuses to listen; he is wild and uncontrollable. He is driving me insane," cried the mother.

"Take it easy," said the psychiatrist. "You must calm down. We will deal with Tommy, but first take these Valiums I am prescribing for you, to quiet your nerves."

A week later the mother and Tommy returned to the psychologist's office. "How is Tommy doing?" asked the therapist.

The mother answered calmly, "Who cares?"

35: Common Interests or Disinterest?

"Love is one heart in two bodies." Each partner has a right to retain his/her own opinion, individuality, friends, hobbies, and tastes. But it is also important to share interests and to do things together. Learn, read, play games, travel, and take an interest in your kids together. Sharing tastes and hobbies strengthens your marriage. Discussing your different opinions and staying aware of each other's thoughts and activities will also keep you closely connected.

One woman said, "The only thing my husband and I have in common is that we were married on the same day."

In an ideal marriage both partners share all the same interests and fulfill all of each other's needs. This is rare; it is more likely that you will share many interests and have common goals, but each of you will also have your own needs and interests.

Isaac enjoys sports. Charna enjoys dancing. Isaac likes following the stock market. Charna likes reading books. Although each one can try to get the other interested in his/her hobby and likewise make an effort to take an interest in the other's hobby, they may not be successful.

I was never an athletic kid. One year I played Little League baseball, and my dad was the coach. Halfway through the season he traded me to another family.
—*David Corrado*

Some women who really have no interest in sports will still take up golf or follow baseball in order to strengthen their connection with their husbands.

I once met a man who said he and his wife knit together. He took it up to form a connection with his wife. Now he finds it both relaxing and productive.

You can usually find another person to share some interests and hobbies if your spouse is indifferent to them. If these hobbies are only a small part of your life, this is not a problem. Of course you must be aware that if you fill your life with other people, you will close out your spouse, and eventually there may be no relationship that connects the two of you.

You must be on the same page regarding your physical relationship. If you and your spouse lack a common interest in that regard, it is imperative to seek help.

A wife said to her husband, "Let's not stay home all the time. Let's go out three times a week."

The husband said, "Good idea. You go out Monday,

Wednesday, and Friday. I'll take Tuesday, Thursday, Sunday."

If a woman enjoys the spa but her husband doesn't, they can discuss the idea of her going with a girlfriend for a day or two. But if she disappears for a week her husband is likely to feel angry and abandoned, especially if he is left to watch the kids. He may also feel entitled to go off for a few days with the fellows. This might work out, or it may lead to two people growing apart.

A woman may feel her husband is not intellectually stimulating enough, while he may feel she doesn't ever want to have fun. He can try joining a book club with her and she can try jet skiing with him, or each may have to turn to relatives or friends to fill this need. It is smart to hone in on which activities the two of you can do together, making those activities a priority in your lives.

If one spouse wants to read the paper a few hours a night, learn nightly, or watch sports a few times a week, the other should accept that, figuring these times into his/her schedule. As long as the activities are within normal limits, neither spouse should feel the other is doing this to avoid him/her. Men and women each need their own time.

She wanted to see something in fur, so her husband took her to the zoo.

Each spouse should be encouraged to enjoy his/her own activities but make sure to join together to do things they both like. Both partners must work together to find common interests, reserving time for one another. Although spontaneity is important and people should not be rigid, husbands and wives should allocate time to spend together. Fit your spouse into your busy schedule!

Partners who each have different interests must still respect the other's hobbies. A wife who accompanies her husband to the golf course but spends the entire time complaining about the waste of time is ruining her marriage.

An old couple dies and goes to heaven. There, they are greeted by an angel who shows them a magnificent home, a spectacular garden, and a luxury car. "This," he says, "is all yours."

The husband turns angrily to his wife and says, "See, if you wouldn't have kept us eating right and exercising, we could have been here years sooner."

36: Common Values and Goals

I love my husband, I love my children, but I want something more. Like a life.

—*Rosanne Barr*

Worthy values such as family and religion make a better marriage.

Values and goals are personal. One person may hope for a lot of money, while another dreams of a simple, relaxed, and tension-free life. Some people want to raise a family, while others try to avoid getting pregnant. There are people who value a close-knit relationship with their parents and siblings, while others want to get away from family. One person's goal may be to impact the world, while another wants a very private lifestyle. No one can say what is right or wrong for each individual, but every couple must share basic values and goals.

I looked up my family tree and found out I am the sap.
—Rodney Dangerfield

You start a new life with your spouse when you get married, but you don't want to do it alone. Stand on the foundation your families have given you, incorporating their good values into your new lifestyle. In order to see new lands you must leave the shoreline, but you don't want to forget where the harbor is. Remember where you came from even as you build a new life together.

Parents who love their children will give them the boat and teach them to row. They will hand over the oars, letting their children draw the map, but they will also offer a compass and be the shoreline to which the children can always row back for help. Newlyweds need the emotional support of their families. It strengthens a marriage if a couple knows their family is there to offer guidance, encouragement, and a helping hand if they need it.

Children should always feel they can turn to their families for help, because it gives them security. A good family is not there to hamper your progress or stifle your growth. They don't rule; rather, they lend support.

My wife didn't come from a fine family. She brought it along.

No one wishes you better than your family. No one cares more to see you happy, and no one takes more enjoyment in your children than your parents and relatives. It should be a source of great pride to you that you can give your family this joy. Don't deprive yourself or your families of this wonderful feeling.

Two extremely mischievous brothers, eight and ten

years old, lived in a suburban neighborhood. Whenever something went wrong in the neighborhood, it always turned out that they had a hand in it. Their parents were at their wits' end trying to control them. When they heard about a rabbi that helped these kinds of children, they asked him to speak to their sons. The rabbi agreed, saying he would meet with the younger son first. The rabbi sat the boy across from the large, impressive desk, and for five minutes they just stared at each other. Then the rabbi pointed his finger at the boy and asked, "Where is G-d?"

The boy looked under the desk, in the corners of the room, all around, but said nothing. Again, louder, the rabbi pointed at the boy and asked, "Where is G-d?" Again the boy looked all around the room but said nothing. In an even louder and firmer voice, the rabbi leaned far across the desk and put his forefinger almost to the boy's nose, asking for the third time, "Where is G-d?"

The boy panicked and ran all the way home. Finding his older brother, he dragged him upstairs to their room and into the closet where they usually plotted their mischief.

"We are in big trouble!" he said.

The older boy asked, "What do you mean 'big trouble'?"

His brother replied, "G-d is missing and they think we did it!"

It is important that *everyone* finds G-d in his/her life. A philosopher once said, "Teach a child what is wise; that is morality. Teach a child what is wise and beautiful; that is religion." A strong belief in G-d and the sanctity of marriage is a powerful tool that keeps couples morally and joyfully committed to one another.

I fear that one day I'll meet G-d, He'll sneeze, and I won't know what to say.
—*Ronnie Shakes*

A couple should share religious beliefs and direction. If G-d is a part of the home it is usually a strong, beautiful home. A couple brings G-d's presence into the world by sanctifying their marriage and building a home that is a mini-sanctuary. A primary goal of marriage is to establish a family and home that brings glory to G-d. If G-d is part of the foundation of your marriage, everything else will fall into place.

A kindergarten teacher tells her class to draw a picture. She then asks each one what they plan to draw. One little girl says she is drawing a picture of G-d.

"But no one knows what G-d looks like," says the teacher.

The little girl answers, "They will after I draw Him."

Valuing the sanctity of the institution of marriage is integral to a marriage. The commitment to continually work at making the marriage a success by being faithful, communicating well, and sharing similar goals keeps the couple growing together.

Jointly appreciating the value of religion, family, good parenting, commendable values, helping others, education, and so forth, makes you better people and better spouses.

37: Stay Emotionally Involved

A small town had one watchmaker who repaired watches. When he left the town it took the townspeople a couple of years to replace him. By that time everyone had many watches that needed repair, and the new watchmaker was given dozens of watches to fix. He divided the watches into two piles: those able to be repaired, and those he couldn't repair. When people asked how he determined which were repairable, he explained that if they were running, whether slow or fast, that meant they had been wound and he could repair them. If the watch had stopped running however, that meant no one had wound them and they were hopeless. The same holds true with marriage. As long as you keep working on your marriage, it is fixable. If you ignore your marriage, it becomes irreparable. The motto for a bride and groom should be, "We are a work in progress with a lifetime contract."

A man entered the psychiatrist's office with a chicken on his head. The psychiatrist asked, "May I help you?"

"Yes," squawked the chicken, "I want you to get this guy out from under me."

Neither the problem nor the solution is always obvious. With critical thinking one does not accept things at face value. Rather, one questions and analyzes so s/he can comprehend the situation fully. If something about your relationship feels wrong, question it to figure out what is missing in your marriage.

Sherlock Holmes and Watson go on a camping trip. Holmes wakes Watson up during the night and says, "Watson, look up. What do you deduce?"

Watson looks up at the sky and says, "I deduce that astronomically there are millions of stars in the sky. Meteorologically, the planets are aligned. Physically, the clouds are threatening a storm. Spiritually, G-d has filled the heavens with beauty. Okay Holmes, now what do you deduce?"

"I," said Holmes, "deduce that someone has stolen our tent."

Try to realistically see and evaluate what is going on in your relationship. Don't deny the existence of tension or disappointment in your relationship. Be aware of your own feelings and those of your spouse. Determine which issues result from your sensitivities and which are the result of your spouse's sensitivities, and how you can either accept or change the dynamics. Deal with the difficulties before they get blown out of proportion. Don't allow them to fester or they will become a problem that underlies, invades, and eventually erodes your relationship.

Keep your eye on your marriage as if it were the gas gauge in a car. Don't let your marriage run out of gas. Keep it refueled. Love must be constantly nurtured and renewed. It requires care, time, ingenuity, and effort.

Love often dies of neglect when spouses don't tune in to their partner's needs. They don't notice that they are growing apart, going in different directions, or growing at different speeds. If one partner is happy enough, s/he may not notice that the other is unhappy. An unhappy spouse may wallow in self-pity, unwilling or unable to draw the other one back into his/her life. Your marriage is a priority. Don't destroy it actively or passively.

Care for each other! Treat each other with kindness and sensitivity. Give to each other emotionally and physically. There is a beautiful story told about Rabbi Aryeh Levine, who once accompanied his wife to the doctor and said, "We've come to seek help because my wife's leg hurts us." Feel and share your spouse's pain, as well as his/her happiness.

Learn what your spouse needs and try to provide it. Hopefully, your spouse will do the same for you. Be aware of what is happening in one another's lives. Notice if your partner seems stressed or if something is troubling him/her. Try to find out the cause.

A plane is in trouble and about to crash. The pilot comes rushing out of the cockpit wearing a parachute. He says to the passengers, "Don't anyone panic. I am going for help." And with that he jumps out the window.

You are both in this together. Help with the workload, the worry, and the problems. Be compassionate and understanding. When one partner feels down, the other spouse should step up to the plate and be the strong, helpful, positive one. Your goal and your spouse's goal is a strong, healthy marriage, free of stressful conditions. Keep reminding one another of this.

Louis was talking to his friend Morris. "There's nothing I wouldn't do for my Beckie," he said, "and there's nothing my Beckie wouldn't do for me. And that's how we go through life – doing nothing for each other."

You and your spouse must work together to help each other achieve personal as well as common goals. A supportive wife will tell her husband, "I'll take care of the house and the kids so you can have more time for your work." Nevertheless, when she is overwhelmed because the baby is crying, she should be able to say to him, "I'd appreciate if you could stay and help tonight." If she needs him, he should help. A couple must find balance.

Felicia was upset because she had not finished her term paper for school; she felt that with all the housework and shopping she would never get her schoolwork done on time. Although Jake had work of his own to finish, he told Felicia to make a list of the things that couldn't be put off and he would help her do them. Had Jake said, "I too am so overwhelmed. What do you want from me?" there would have been two frustrated individuals. When Jake assured Felicia that he was there for her, and that she could do some of the housework after she wrote her paper, he gave Felicia the lift she needed to get both her paper and the household chores completed. Each spouse should take turns pulling the other one up.

Sometimes a spouse needs only sympathy or an understanding or forgiving ear. Sometimes a spouse needs help or a good suggestion. A good spouse tunes in, and by doing so forges a bond.

Bernie unfortunately was hit by a truck and landed in the hospital in intensive care. His best friend Shlomo came to visit him. Bernie struggled to tell Shlomo, "My wife Sadie visits me three times a day. She's so good to me. Every day, she reads to me at my bedside."

"What does she read?" asks Shlomo.

"My life insurance policy."

Too many people refuse to notice what their spouse needs, causing the partner to look elsewhere for fulfillment. A husband wants his wife to notice and appreciate him, rather than complain about finances, the kids, or being overworked. A wife also needs to be noticed and appreciated. Always be aware of those needs and try to meet them.

Stay connected, listening to each other. Go easy on one another and forgive one another. Encourage each other and relieve each other's stress. Be there for each other and side with one another.

A husband said to his wife, "Honey, I've been thinking it over since this quarrel started, and I have to say that you were right. Everything you said was right."

The wife said, "It's too late. I've changed my mind."

38: Appreciation

A husband felt his wife had ignored his homecoming, so he shouted angrily at her and stormed out. After walking around for an hour he was calmer and called the house.

"Honey, what are you making for dinner?" he asked pleasantly.

His wife answered, "Poison."

"Fine." he said. "Make only enough for one. I'm eating out."

Many individuals do not appreciate their spouse. They take their marriage for granted.

Whenever Daniel arrived home from work, the house was flying and his wife Dalia looked a mess. She was so busy with dinner and the kids that she hardly acknowledged his entrance except to call out, "Can you help with the baths?" Daniel reached a point where he was no longer excited to come home. Realizing he had to change his attitude, he developed a personal system. Every time his wife looked special or did something noteworthy he noted it on his phone memory. He compiled a list of over a hundred things and times when he truly admired her. Every evening before going home, he read his list to fortify himself and remind himself how terrific his wife was. It helped him develop an appreciation for her, and he realized that most of the time he actually admired the way she handled the children and ran the house. By lowering his expectations and increasing his awareness of his wife, he was able to improve his own mental attitude and feel more positive toward her.

A wife should make her husband glad to come home, and a husband should make his wife sad to see him leave.

Make a list. You will be surprised to find how many positive qualities you attribute to your spouse.

Cindy sounded very negative about her husband. She attended a marriage counseling session, and the group leader asked her to list some positive things about her husband. It was difficult for her to get started, but once she began, she was able to say, "He is helpful in the kitchen. He often makes dinner for the family. He does all the yard work, handles all the car maintenance, always calls if he is going to be late, pays the bills, fixes the toilets, instills trust, spends time with the kids, laughs a lot, compliments me a lot, and loves my cooking. He sweetly encouraged me through three labors and deliveries and took care of me when I was sick. He stayed by me through my mastectomy. He helped me take care of my ailing mother. My sister told me he adores me." Enumerating the good qualities in her husband made her realize they had shared a good twenty-six years.

Just as one should count his blessings rather than his problems, one should also count his/her spouse's positive traits rather than his/her negative ones. It will put things in perspective and increase your appreciation of your marriage.

At a marriage seminar a man is asked, "Can you describe your wife's favorite flower?" He gently leans over, smiles at her, and says, "Pillsbury All Purpose, isn't it?"

Some men believe that if a woman loves him, she will cook for him, clean for him, and keep the house in order. If she is unable to handle these chores, he feels she does not love him enough. But these chores are usually not a reflection of a woman's feelings for her husband. She may simply be unable to keep up with the household challenges. A home and children are a lot to manage.

Some women believe: *If my husband truly loved me he would want to earn a better living so that he might provide a better life for me.* A man can only earn what his abilities, education, opportunities, and the economy allow. Income is not a measure of love.

Another way to appreciate your spouse is to think of the thing that bothers you about him/her. *It drives me crazy that he puts his feet up on the furniture.* Now imagine him dead, *chas ve'shalom*. Your furniture is not scuffed, but are you happy without him? Would you rather have a pristine house and no husband, or scratched furniture and this guy? *She really makes me mad when I have to wait hours for her to get ready.* Now imagine she dies, *chas ve'shalom*. You can get everywhere on time, but do you want to go without her? So you want him, you want her. You need him/her to feel complete. He/she may come with flaws, but you will have to accept him/her that way because it's worth it. Unfortunately, human nature is such that most people don't appreciate what they have or whom they have until they lose it. Imagine you've lost it. Now appreciate having it.

An old man was lying on his deathbed. With only hours to live, he suddenly smelled the aroma of chocolate chip cookies coming from the kitchen. The old man pulled himself out of his bed, across the floor to the stairs, and down the stairs to the kitchen.

There, the old man's wife was baking chocolate chip cookies. With his last ounce of energy, the old man reached for a cookie.

His wife, however, quickly smacked him across the back of his hand and exclaimed, "Leave them alone! They're for the funeral!"

It is vital to continually remind yourself that you like your spouse. Tell yourself: "My spouse is my friend, my partner, my confidant. Sometimes s/he challenges me. Sometimes s/he frustrates, disappoints, and aggravates me but I value the benefits, the love, and the companionship I receive from him/her. I appreciate him/her more than I find him/her irritating." Keep telling yourself how lucky you are. Keep remembering the fun times you've had together. Keep planning the good times ahead. Appreciate the moment together.

In the beginning there was man. This created a huge demand for aspirin.

A wife wants love and affection and feels she doesn't

receive it. Her husband feels that he only gets demands and criticism. People don't recognize their own faults, yet often harp on their partner's imperfections. Once you are married, do not focus on the qualities your mate is lacking, but spotlight and appreciate his/her positive qualities.

A couple decided to divorce because the wife couldn't conceive a child. They went to Rabbi Shimon Bar Yochai, who advised them to have a separation party before they divorced. At the party the husband said, "I love you, but circumstances cause us to separate, so when you leave this house and go back to your parents' home, feel free to take whatever you most treasure." The wife plied her husband with drink until he fell asleep. Then she told her servants to carry him to her parents' house. When he awoke he said, "I don't understand." She said, "I took with me the thing I most treasure." They returned to Rabbi Shimon Bar Yochai who blessed them and told them to remain married. The wife soon conceived a child.

Work on appreciating one another. People have expectations of what they want to be like, what they want their spouse and children to be like, and how they want their lives to run. These are their dreams. *Rabbos machshavos b'lev ish, v'atzos Hashem hi takum*, Many are the thoughts of man, but G-d's plan prevails. What if life doesn't work out as perfectly as you hoped? Some people never adjust and are constantly frustrated and disappointed. Others lower their expectations and readjust their dreams so that they are attainable, and life is satisfying and fulfilling. These people realize that G-d's plan is what is best for them.

I just bought something to improve my hearing: a plane ticket out of town for my wife.

Get rid of negative feelings. Before you come home to your spouse, make sure you are calm. Drive around the block a few extra times if need be. A rabbi advised Jonathan to always have chocolate in the car so he never entered his home hungry, demanding supper immediately. He also advised him to keep a chocolate cake in the freezer so he could bring guests home without surprising and embarrassing his wife. Jonathan's wife appreciated the way he eased the pressure on her. Do whatever it takes to keep yourself from being disappointed in your spouse.

Hashem told Kayin, "*Lapetach chattas rovetz*, Sin rests at the door" (*Bereishis* 4:7). Rabbi Paysach Krohn explains this homiletically. A husband can set the tone of the household. Coming home from work, if he opens the door with a cheerful countenance and positive mood, praising his wife, he sets a good mood. But if he enters in an angry and negative way, he sets a bad tone. This holds true for the wife as well. Greeting her husband *b'seiver panim yafos*, with a pleasant face or a positive statement, sets a happy atmosphere.

Through appreciation you nurture your love.

One day my housework-challenged husband decided to wash his sweatshirt. Seconds after he stepped into the laundry room, he shouted to me, "What setting do I use on the washing machine?"

"It depends," I replied. "What does it say on your shirt?"

He yelled back, "University of North Carolina."

39: Share Your Lives

An eighty-year-old woman was arrested for shoplifting. When she went before the judge, he asked her, "What did you steal?"
She replied, "A can of peaches."

When the judge asked her why she had stolen the can of peaches, she replied that she was hungry. The judge asked her how many peaches were in the can. "Six," she said.
"Then I will give you six days in jail," the judge pronounced.
Before the judge could conclude the trial, the woman's husband asked the judge if he could say something. The judge said, "What is it?"
The husband said, "She also stole a can of peas."

We all enter marriage with a deep sense of hope and anticipation. We go into it with love in our hearts and a longing to be with our spouse. It is our task to create a life together, building a future while cherishing the past. We live in the present, but if we retain a positive feeling about the past, the marriage stays strong. As we age, and the adorable, vibrant, twenty-year-old we married becomes a balding, heavier, tired, elderly individual, the vision of the youthful person we loved creates an important bond. Additionally, appreciating your spouse's age and the knowledge and maturity s/he has gained, the mutual understanding and connection you have achieved, the laughter and tears you have shared, creates a deeper, more meaningful love. In good marriages, couples remember their shared past with nostalgia, enjoy their present, and anticipate their future.

A marriage is made up of a lifetime of memories. If resentment, anger, and irreconcilable differences have overtaken the marriage, couples will remember even their most poignant events with negativity. Rather than remembering how beautiful their wedding was, they will distort their memories, only recalling the inconsequential things that went wrong, such as the groom being late for pictures or the bride becoming too emotional. Rewriting history with a negative twist, or just forgetting past good times is a sign that a marriage is going bad. The bond is weakening, the caring is disappearing, and the couple needs help to repair their marriage and revitalize their friendship. Love is a four letter word spelled T-I-M-E. Couples must find time and energy for one another.

Wife: "Do you mind escorting me out to the garbage can, dear?"

Husband: "Why that?"

Wife: "I want to be able to tell the neighbors that we go out together once in a while."

People mistakenly think that you can connect with your partner only via a romantic vacation or a quiet dinner alone together. These are great ideas, but they will only work if you connect with each other, looking to each other for support in little ways every day.

An old man placed an order for one hamburger, French fries, and a drink. He unwrapped the hamburger and carefully cut it in half, placing one half in front of his wife. He then carefully counted out the French fries, dividing them into two piles, and neatly placed one pile in front of his wife. He took a sip of the drink, and then his wife took a sip and set the cup down between them.

As he began to eat his few bites of hamburger, the people around them whispered, "That poor old couple. All they can afford is one meal for the two of them."

As the man began to eat his fries, a young man came to the table and politely offered to buy another meal for the old couple. The old man said they were just fine; they were used to sharing everything. People closer to the table noticed the little old lady hadn't eaten a bite. She sat there watching her husband eat, and occasionally taking a turn sipping the drink. Again, the young man came over and begged them to let him buy another meal for them.

This time the old woman said, "No, thank you. We are used to sharing everything."

Finally, as the old man finished and was wiping his

face neatly with the napkin, the young man again came over to the little old lady, who had yet to eat a single bite of food and asked, "What is it you are waiting for?"

She answered, "The teeth."

Marriage makes one of two. In marriage, one plus one equals one. My father says a good marriage is a synergy where one plus one makes three, then four, and so on.

Stay involved in each other's lives. My mother quotes her mother, who always wished her to "enjoy all life's blessings together with your man" (my father). Care about each other. Make each other your priority. Don't get caught up in your own things; rather, write each other into your schedules to keep your marriage on the front burner. Follow the theory of six times six. Hug each other six times a day for six seconds, or at least give your spouse a wink, a twinkly smile, or even a thumbs-up six times during the day. It fortifies the marriage.

I know a couple that have separate bedrooms, drive different cars, and take separate vacations. They do everything they can to keep their marriage together.

Unfortunately, many couples pass each other in their own homes acting like estranged roommates. It takes effort to continually acknowledge someone's presence, especially when that person is always there. Be aware that a lifetime together consists of moments that become days and days that become years. Every moment is precious in forging and deepening your relationship. Get in the habit of saying "good morning" and "good night, dear." Say, "Sleep well." Ask, "How are things going?" or "What are you up to?"

You can notice and acknowledge one another even without major conversations. Make it a habit to ask one another every morning, "What do you have planned for the day?" In the afternoon take a moment to call and check in with one another. "How are things going?" "How was that meeting you told me about?" Discuss how the day went in the evening.

Give one another a smile, a squeeze, or an understanding nod. Give each other a knowing, tender look. Connect through eye contact or touch. Do whatever it takes to keep your spouse aware that the two of you are on the same exclusive side that belongs to the two of you alone.

Psychologists suggest you show your spouse a minimum of three to five kindnesses a day.

If you can be each other's therapists the day will be less stressful. Your tension level diminishes if you can vent to your spouse about your tough day, knowing that s/he will be understanding and sympathetic, lovingly being a shoulder for you to lean on, and taking your side and encouraging rather than accusing you.

Phil called Diane at lunchtime after a terrible confrontation with his boss. Diane listened to Phil rant about how hard he worked and how little he got paid. Then she said, "You are right. Your boss doesn't know how lucky he is to have a dedicated worker like you. It's so unfair, but I'm proud that you held yourself back from telling him what you really think of him. I am sure, given time, he will come to appreciate you and will give you that raise you want. Meanwhile, we are doing fine on your salary, so don't fret. I love you. I can't wait for you to come home."

Phil may still be frustrated with his boss, but he has

lowered his anger level and knows he is going home to a loving, supportive wife. He feels in tune with his wife. A smart wife will give her husband this kind of support, even if she is actually thinking to herself: *Why did he have to start up with his boss? He could have jeopardized his job!* If you support your spouse now, when the situation calms down, you can say, "Your boss is totally unaware of how much you contribute to the firm. Let's put our heads together and think of a strategy to make him take notice of your worth." Likewise, a smart husband will side with his wife and be there for her.

Skiing is too dangerous for me. The only black people who ski are the ones who went to Harvard. The rest of us ain't educated enough to like cold and pain.
—Bernie Mac

A newly married couple faced a problem during their first winter together. Dan wanted to go skiing, as he did every year since he was a kid. Lanie was pregnant and couldn't go skiing, and she wanted Dan to stay home with her. They consulted a *rav*, who told each one to do whatever made the other one happy. This left them baffled. The advice sounded like Dan should agree to stay home while Lanie should tell him to go skiing. The *rav* wanted them to realize that if each partner shows that s/he cares about the other's feelings and desires, whatever they actually do is inconsequential. If you take one another's feelings and opinions into consideration, you will work things out.

Remember, it's the two parts – you and your spouse – that make the marriage whole.

Women! Don't ask us men what we're thinking about

unless you are prepared to discuss such topics as baseball, the shotgun formation, or golf.

Couples should put aside fifteen to twenty minutes a day to talk to each other about bonding issues. It is ironic that so many couples gave such thought to choosing one another; share so many experiences, hopes, dreams, and challenges; created a family together; and yet don't bother talking to each other for twenty minutes out of the entire day!

Barry was passing a florist when he saw a sign in the window advertising "Say it with flowers." Entering the shop, he said to the assistant, "Wrap up one rose for me."

"Only one?" the assistant asked.

"Just one," replied Barry. "I'm a man of few words."

40: The Little Things Make a Big Marriage

A successful marriage requires falling in love many times, always with the same person.

—*Mignon McLaughlin*

It is amazing how the little things a husband and a wife do for one another add up to so much. A wife who makes her husband a cup of coffee, sews a button on his shirt, walks her husband to the door, buys him a shaver to replace the one he broke, straightens up his office, or schedules that much-needed dentist appointment for him is showing love, which evokes a loving feeling in return. Of course there are those husbands who will say, "I wanted a cold drink," "This isn't the brand shaver I planned to buy," "Don't touch my office," "I like to do my own scheduling." But even a guy like that probably appreciates the button sewn on his shirt!

A man finds himself short of breath, with his eyes bulging and turning blue. He races to the doctor, who tells him he has only three months to live. The man decides that he will travel and live it up for the next three months. He goes all out, deciding to buy a whole new wardrobe for his trip. He asks the shopkeeper for shoes size 11, a suit size 46, and two shirts size 15/34. The shopkeeper says, "You can't wear shirts size 15/34. That's much too small for you."

The man says, "That's the size I wear."

The shopkeeper says, "You can't possibly wear that size. It will be way too tight. If you wear a shirt that is so tight on you, you will find yourself short of breath with your eyes bulging, and you'll turn blue."

You may not get everything right, but make sure to get the things that really matter right. A wife may not love the flowers her husband chooses but she should appreciate the thought.

A man leaves three envelopes for his wife before he dies. After his death her friend asks what the three envelopes contained. "The first," says the wife, "had $5,000 to pay for the casket. The second envelope had $10,000 to pay for a nice funeral. The third envelope contained $25,000 to pay for a showy stone. How do you like the stone?" she asked, as she held up her finger.

Buying fur and jewelry for your wife without giving her the attention she requires, or cooking delicious meals for your husband but not offering him the encouragement he needs, will not maintain a good marriage. Couples must meet each other's real needs.

A man bought his wife a burial plot. The following year he didn't buy her anything and she complained. He answered, "You didn't use the present I bought you last year!"

Surprising her with a gift, leaving him a little love note, lending a hand when she is straightening up, bringing him a cold drink when he walks in, leaving a piece of chocolate on his pillow, holding open the door for her, talking to her when she is feeling down, giving him an encouraging smile, keeping him company while he runs on the treadmill, offering to put the kids to bed so she can go out with friends, surprising him with tickets to a concert, asking her out on a date, making him a special dinner, buying him his favorite snacks, giving her flowers are just a few of the simple things you can do that will keep your spouse in love with you.

A woman said to her husband, "Invest in diamonds."

Her husband asked, "What if their value doesn't go up?"

She answered, "Then I'll just have to wear them."

Men: Write your wife love letters or cards, remember important dates, compliment her, call her, don't cause her to worry.

Women: Wear your husband's favorite perfume, tell him he looks sharp, give him encouragement, compliment his business acumen, leave little love notes saying things like, "Thanks for helping with the dishes" or "Let's meet at eleven."

I gave $100 to my father for a present and said, "Go buy something that will make your life easier."

So he bought my mother a present.

The more you give to someone, the more you will feel needed and appreciated, and the more you will love that person and feel loved by that person.

The most effective way to remember your wife's birthday is to forget it once...

Do your best to remember the important dates that mean something to your spouse.

A woman had her portrait painted by a famous painter. When it was done he presented it to her. She said, "It is nice but the neck looks too empty. Please add a large emerald necklace." He did so and showed her the painting. She said, "It is lovely but please add large matching earrings." When the artist returned she said the painting still seemed a bit empty and asked him to add a large diamond ring and a gaudy diamond bracelet to her hand. The artist asked her why it was necessary to add all this jewelry. The woman answered, "My husband is younger than I am. When I die he will get remarried. I want his next wife to go crazy looking for this jewelry."

41: COMPROMISE

My parents have been married for fifty-five years. The secret to their longevity? Outlasting your opponent.
—*Cathy Ladman*

You are a team. You may have two minds and two opinions, but your goal is one mind-set – to make things work so both of you agree with the decision. You may not be ecstatic about the decision, but each of you can accept it.

Gloria and Robert were looking forward to their first vacation. They had two years of mileage and vacation time saved, and Robert's parents agreed to watch their baby for a week. All they had to do was pick a spot and be off. Robert chose a beautiful ski resort, while Gloria picked a warm tropical island. The battle over where to go became so intense that neither had any desire to vacation together. Gloria's mother finally came up with the solution. She suggested they drive to Vermont for Sunday and Monday so Robert could ski and then take a flight from there to the islands. By then they would both appreciate the warm weather. Their dream vacation was becoming somewhat complex and tiring because of this plan, so neither Robert nor Gloria thought it was ideal, but they both agreed to it. They had a wonderful time.

Compromise is the key word. If one person stubbornly refuses to give in, that can make the other partner stick to his position also. If one person gives in, the other will be a bit more cooperative. A compromise does not need to be equal on both sides, but each partner has to bend a little. Resentment will build up if the same person has to concede his wishes all the time. If a tree doesn't bend, it will break. So too, if one partner is totally uncooperative the relationship will suffer.

A farmer marries and is bringing his new wife home from the wedding in his horse and buggy. Suddenly, the horse stops to eat. The farmer whips the horse and says, "That's one."

As they go along, the horse whinnies and rears back. The farmer cracks the whip and says, "That's two."

They ride a bit further and the horse stops, refusing to move. The farmer says, "That's three."

With that he gets out and shoots the horse. His new wife looks on in horror.

"Why" she asks, "did you do that?"

The farmer turns to her and says, "That's one."

Some individuals refuse to ever give in. S/he will avoid

discussing issues, not even trying to understand his/her spouse's point of view. By remaining inflexible, s/he feels s/he has the upper hand and is the one in control. Other people refuse to see their partner's side of the story or adjust to his/her needs because they always believe only their point of view is accurate.

Mark insisted they live in Manhattan because it was convenient for work. Susan felt it would be better to bring up kids in the suburbs. Mark refused to even hear Susan's arguments on this subject, feeling she couldn't relate to the pressures of his job nor understand how difficult the added stress of traveling and traffic would be. Susan thought that with a house close to a railroad Mark could take the train to the city, and get work done on the train without having to deal with traffic. She was thinking of what was best for her children and her husband, but her husband wouldn't even let her speak.

A couple must find common ground. If you and your spouse are thinking about where to spend the holidays, discuss the things you both enjoy first: the foods you prefer, how you both like lying in the sun, and how you both want a place where the kids have friends. Now as a couple you are on the same page, which makes compromise much simpler when the specific choice of places is discussed.

Rabbi Paysach Krohn advises putting everything in perspective by not taking every disagreement so seriously. Remember his wonderful words *Zeh lo chashuv*, This is not important. Compromising, forgiving, and building your home into a miniature *Beis HaMikdash*, Temple, is what is important.

My parents stayed together for forty years, but that was out of spite.

—Woody Allen

42: Anger

A man is incomplete until he's married. Then he's really finished.

Keep your temper in check. Don't let stress get to you. People tend to take out all their frustrations on their spouse.

The FBI was looking for an assassin. They recruited one hundred trainees and through the process of elimination got down to fifty, then thirty, and finally three candidates. The three finalists had to take one last test in order to determine who the assassin would be. They called in the first man, handed him a pistol, and told him to go into a room, where he would find someone tied to a wooden chair. His mission was to shoot the person directly between the eyes. The first trainee entered the room and came out crying. "I just couldn't shoot. I couldn't do it. The person in the chair is my wife," he sobbed.

The FBI boss said, "Get out of here. You are no assassin." Then the second trainee was sent into the room with the same orders. He too came out wailing hysterically. "I tried but I just couldn't pull the trigger. The woman in the chair is my wife," he said.

The FBI boss said, "Get out of here. You are no assassin."

He then called in the last candidate, who happened to be a woman. She was given the same orders: "Go in the room. There will be a person tied to a chair. Shoot the person right between the eyes."

The woman entered the room and the FBI boss heard banging, knocking, and screaming. Finally the woman stumbled out and said, "I can't believe it. It was my husband, and I tried to shoot him but the gun wouldn't go off. I think it had blanks. So I had to take the wooden chair, hit him over the head, and smash him to death."

Even the best couples get angry at one another sometimes. People can be deeply in love yet still get upset about small things. When people are exhausted, disappointed, or stressed they often take out these moods on their spouses.

Rehashing past mistakes, taking revenge for a past mistake, or placing blame on your partner has a negative effect on a relationship. Couples need to focus only on the problem at hand, finding constructive ways to improve the situation. Throwing temper tantrums, refusing to talk, or walking out are not constructive ways to deal with differences.

Allowing negative feelings such as anger, disappointment, or stress to accumulate can lead to a deterioration of your marriage. If you are angry, learn to calm down. Breathing techniques, exercising, reading, listening to music, meditating, or going for a drive are all different ways of controlling anger.

Another excellent method to control anger is called self-regulation. Realize when you are moving out of your comfort zone and do things to return to your equilibrium. Teach yourself to maintain a comfortable mood. Determine what it is that makes you happy. Don't sulk or berate yourself by wallowing in self-recrimination. Don't ruminate or think in a circular way, re-experiencing the anger. Find ways to get past your frustration and anger, and regain your composure by engaging in positive, uplifting distractions. Do something that cheers you up, like eating chocolate or hitting a ball. Pat yourself on the back for even your small successes. Whatever normal activity it takes to overcome the negative feelings is acceptable. You may need to cry or shout in private in order to get your anger out. Then focus on the issue and decide to overcome it and move past it.

In a quarrel he gives in a lot. What's his word against a thousand of hers?

Couples who quarrel should examine their disagreements, noting the frequency, intensity, and duration of the arguments, and the ability each partner has to self-regulate and pull out of the quarrel.

If a couple is arguing too often, if the intensity of the argument builds too fast, or if the argument remains out of control too long, each person must question where s/he has gone wrong. Has s/he built up too much anger? Is s/he too impatient or too stubborn? Each partner must work on his/her own anger management, resentment issues, and communication techniques, and each must learn methods for self-regulation.

Last night, some hot words flew between them. She heaved some alphabet soup in his face!

Be careful how you argue. Do not attack your spouse with unforgivable insults, such as "I only married you because I was desperate." Such a statement undermines the foundation of your marriage. No matter how many apologies are offered afterward, the injured spouse feels hurt, wondering whether that statement reflects the real truth. Express your anger but do not devastate your spouse. Watch your words. Things once said can never be unsaid. If you have differences, focus on those differences in the argument but do not bring up every negative thing your spouse ever did. Try to resolve the present problem; piling on complaints only compounds the differences. Furthermore, don't embarrass your spouse by having these arguments in front of other people.

Most importantly, let it go. Discuss it, accept it, deal with it, and then don't hold a grudge. Forgive and forget.

A woman has the last word in an argument. Anything a man says after that is the beginning of a new argument.

When one partner is angry, it is important that the other partner understands the source of the frustration and tries to diffuse the tension. Two individuals who fly off the handle do not make for a calm, secure situation even if they are on the same team. If one spouse is in a lousy mood, it is unproductive for the other spouse to join in that mood. It is much better to help his/her partner by pulling out of it and presenting a positive attitude.

Stuie would often get irritable and upset with the kids. Rather than getting angry at him or joining in his irritation,

Denise would take deep breaths to calm herself and say, "Relax, honey. I'll try to get the kids to behave."

When we got married, my wife and I decided never to go to bed angry. We haven't slept in seven years.

Arguing all night is unhealthy for a marriage. Say, "I love you. We will work it out" and go to bed feeling secure that you can continue the discussion in the morning when you are rested. When people are tired they don't have the emotional energy to work out a solution.

Important words in marriage are, "Maybe you are right. Okay, let's give your way a try." Giving in does not mean giving up. It means being smart and adjusting your approach. Stubborn people erect walls between themselves.

People who are upset usually need a time-out or a little space. It's a good idea to say, "Let's give it a bit of thought and then discuss it when we are calmer."

A man may be a fool and not know it, but not if he is married.

Arguing once in a while is fine, but it should not become a way of life. Don't use it to get attention. Get attention by being loving and considerate. Everyone has an emotional bank account. Relaxing interludes, tender moments, sweet thoughts, shared accomplishments, and fulfilled dreams are your deposits. When anger, hurt, frustration, or disappointment crop up, you withdraw some of the wealth of the relationship. With enough deposits you can make a withdrawal, because a strong account can withstand some withdrawals. If the relationship is strong and a beautiful connection exists, you are continually building a positive balance. Then, if you disagree with or get upset at your spouse once in a while, your marriage will be able to bear it.

Maintain a positive balance in your emotional bank account by looking away when necessary. Use a mental filter to focus on your spouse's good points, filtering out the bad ones. By noticing, nurturing, and appreciating your spouse's positive traits, you create a positive pleasure cycle. S/he will appreciate your approval and repeat that behavior.

People often have mixed emotions. You can be angry, disappointed, or frustrated with someone and still love him/her. Your good feelings toward your spouse should outweigh your anger and help you accept and forgive his/her faults.

Never lay a hurtful hand on each other. No one should ever abuse his/her spouse physically or verbally, and no spouse should ever tolerate a partner who is an abuser. Physical abuse will only lead to a cycle of guilt, rage, and anger, besides scarring your children. Don't let yourself become a mat to be stepped on by a spouse. Draw the line. Seek help if that happens.

Fighting in front of your children is abusive to them.

The wife was a little more furious than usual, and said, "I should have listened to my mother twenty years ago."

The husband said, "Go ahead. She's still talking."

Before erupting, consider whether your anger is justified. Listen to your spouse's version and judge him/her with an open mind. There may be unknown circumstances that are causing your spouse to act this way. Consider the possibilities. Maybe your spouse is going through a tough time that he/she has not told you about, for fear of worrying you.

The wife stopped her tirade by saying, "I should have listened to my dear mother. She begged me not to marry you."

The husband said, "That's terrible – all these years I've hated her!"

Analyze your anger and understand its root cause. Is your anger disproportionate to the disagreement? Is this anger cumulative? Has it been building up over time? For example, is this one more time that your wife has not appreciated how hard you try to please her? Is this another incident where your husband embarrassed you in front of the children? Or perhaps something your spouse is in the habit of doing always bothers you, and you still have not adjusted to it. Are you overreacting because you are worried that this small transgression is a precursor to larger problems down the road? Question your spouse's reasons for acting as s/he did and question your own reason for reacting as you do.

There are different modes of conflict resolution. In the ideal situation, each spouse compromises and feels understood, and can accept his/her spouse's view. Submission, when one partner constantly gives in just to avoid confrontation; immobilization, when a couple comes to a standstill because they cannot resolve their quarrel; or running away from a conflict all lead to frustration and resentment.

When somebody says to you, "The last thing I want to do is hurt you," what they really mean is, "It's on the list. I've just got some other things to do first."

—*Mark Schiff*

Be aware of your spouse. What makes your husband happy or angry? What makes your wife depressed? People have different thresholds of tolerance. One wife may fly into a rage if her husband wears muddy shoes in the house, while another wife might just laugh at the mess.

Be careful not to confuse anger with hurt. Don't automatically think: *S/he's angry at me.* Think: *Maybe I've hurt him/her.*

Immature, insecure, unstable, anxious, or high-strung individuals need to monitor their reactions to keep them in check. The right medication for anxiety, depression, or mood stabilization may relieve many of these symptoms, making life less stressful for both partners. (Therapists agree that to prepare for the work of building a great relationship one mustn't be self-medicating or abusing drugs.)

Figure out the best way to get the reaction you want from your spouse. If you constantly berate your spouse, creating animosity and hurting your relationship, revise your approach. Threatening or instilling a feeling of guilt may work in the short run, but it usually causes resentment. In most instances, love and encouragement are better motivators. Some husbands react positively to tears, while they turn off others. Some women like a man who is soft and understanding, while others respect a tough, take-charge guy. Try to get a handle on what angers and what calms each of you, and then act appropriately.

As soon as you say, "I do," you'll discover that marriage is like a car. Both of you are sitting in the front seat, but only one of you is driving. Most marriages are more like a motorcycle than a car. Somebody has to sit in the back, and he has to yell just to be heard.

—Wanda Sylke

43: Refine Your Focus

Focus your attention on what it takes to make your spouse happy.

Ever since Eve gave Adam the apple, there has been a misunderstanding between the genders about gifts.
—*Nan Robertson*

If a woman needs your time and attention, don't give her flowers or jewelry. If a man needs encouragement or some space, making him a good dinner is nice but won't do the trick. Tune in to what your spouse needs.

Remember: A sense of humor does not mean that you tell him jokes. It means that you laugh at his.

If you are focused on your spouse's needs you will give him/her what is important to him/her whether or not you understand it, like it, or even agree with it. You may learn to like it, or just enjoy making your spouse happy.

Put things into perspective by focusing on your spouse's positive traits. Anna was very quiet, which made Max feel bored. Max decided to focus on her sweet disposition and caring attitude. Isaac was loud and aggressive but he was also generous with gifts and compliments. Susan made it a habit to look at her pretty bracelet whenever she got frustrated with him. Don't dwell on the negative.

Focus on a solution. Think and talk things out. Don't let frustration linger or anger grow. Don't analyze and rip apart every word your spouse says. See and appreciate the big picture – the total person.

Focus on problem solving rather than on what your spouse is doing wrong. Don't lay blame. Make your problems joint problems and your solutions a joint effort. Say, "We are obviously handling something wrong because I am frustrated and I am sure you are too."

Focus on what you can do to make your marriage a better and stronger one.

G-d was smart in making Adam before Eve. If He'd made Eve first, He'd still be working on Adam.

44: Trust

Believe in each other. Believe in your marriage.

Wife to husband: "When I married you, you said you had an oceangoing yacht!"

Husband: "Be quiet and keep rowing."

Give each other reason to trust one another. When a spouse can't find friendship, understanding, compassion, and respect at home, he/she will seek companionship elsewhere. When a woman needs a change, she changes her dress, her nail polish, the color of her hair, or the man in her life. When a man needs a change, he changes his car, his job, or the woman in his life. People really want to change their mirror, meaning they want to change the person who is looking back at them. They want to see themselves differently. That is why they look for someone who makes them believe that they themselves are younger, funnier, brighter, and so forth.

People search for someone who makes them feel special, needed, and loved. As people age and life seems boring and routine, as failures and challenges beset their marriage, men and women want an injection of youth and excitement in their lives. If a person feels s/he is not getting this within his/her marriage, s/he may search for someone who does make him/her feel that way. Be there for your spouse to encourage and lift him/her.

Unfortunately, as some people achieve success, they believe they deserve more recognition and greater thrills. They search for new pleasures and belittle the value of their family. Without thinking of the consequences, they can destroy a relationship that was built over a lifetime, hurting their spouse, and wrecking the family to fuel their ego and fill a shallow pleasure.

Marriage is sacred. Certainly you need change, you need excitement, and you need love. Turn to your spouse and make him/her aware of this need and work on a plan together.

Know where your marriage is heading. If the road turns a bit, adjust the steering wheel, making sure the two front tires are always headed in the same direction.

Husband to wife: "Put your coat on, I'm going to town."

Wife: "Oh, that's nice. Are you taking me for a night out?"

Husband: "No, I'm turning the heating off."

45: Forgiveness

Sidney and Judith had just returned home from a party. Judith said, "Do you realize what you did tonight, Sidney?"

"No, I don't," Sidney replied, "but I'll admit I was wrong. What did I do?"

The Torah states that we are required to attach ourselves to Hashem. Yet how can a mere mortal attach himself to the infinite? The Talmud tells us that we do this by emulating G-d's traits. Just as G-d is merciful, we must be merciful. Just as G-d is forgiving, we must be forgiving.

The best-selling novel *Love Story* is famous for the saying, "Love means never having to say you're sorry." I disagree. I believe love is being willing to say you are sorry and willing to understand and forgive. In order to have a happy marriage, you must let go of the things that are bothering you and attempt to forgive one another.

Tania told her therapist she was furious because Eli insisted his mother choose her wedding bouquet.

"Exactly how long ago was your wedding?" asked the therapist.

"Twelve years," Tania replied.

"Don't you think it's time to move on and let that anger go? If you continue to drag this baggage of bitterness and resentment, you can't enjoy your marriage."

Stay in the now, and let go of the past junk. Always move forward in a positive manner.

As Yogi Berra said, "The future is ahead of you."

As the man, you get to apologize. What does the woman get to do? She gets to forgive you. My sister, Esti Stahler, who does a comic routine, once suggested that the best way to keep a marriage strong is for husbands to call home every day and wholeheartedly say, "I'm sorry" to their wives. "Don't worry," Esti adds, "your wife will always figure out what you did wrong and why you are apologizing."

To keep your marriage strong, whenever you are wrong, admit it. When you are right, keep your mouth shut.

Admit your mistakes when you realize you are wrong, and hopefully your spouse will accept your apology graciously. Sometimes your spouse may have a difficult time forgiving you. Perhaps you've repeated the same faux pas too many times. Perhaps your misdeed is very painful. Real apologies should come with thought, feeling, regret, and a sincere promise to try to do better. If the act was unintentionally hurtful, try a major apology and a simple explanation, and pray that it helps.

Lisa prepared a surprise dinner for their three-month anniversary. Aryeh was assigned a new client and therefore worked an hour later than usual. By the time he arrived home, Lisa was in a tizzy because the food had to be rewarmed. Aryeh didn't think that coming home one hour late would cause a major upset, but in Lisa's sensitive state she could only feel that Aryeh was insensitive not to call her. It does not pay for Aryeh to keep rehashing the reasons he was late; he should just apologize.

Swallow your pride if necessary. Own up to a mistake even if you aren't convinced you are wrong. Look at the big picture. You can win the battle and lose the war; the operation can be a success and the patient can die. Likewise, you can win an argument but destroy the marriage. The goal is peace and harmony. Once in a while you can achieve this by being willing to apologize.

When you're single you think: "Should I call him?"

When you're married you think: "What should I call him?"

Sometimes there are disadvantages when one person apologizes just to keep the peace. Someone who is truly hurt and feels that his/her spouse is glibly apologizing, without listening or understanding, can be resentful. Secondly, an apology may seem to validate your spouse's point of view, which you may not want to imply. In those cases, general apologies like "I'm sorry you are disappointed," "I'm sorry you are sad," "I'm sorry you feel hurt" might be more appropriate.

Woman may forgive, but they never forget what they forgave.

"A good marriage is the union of two good forgivers" (Ruth Bell Graham). Always apologize as soon as possible. There is no reason to let anger and hurt feelings fester.

When Mira got married she thought of ten misdeeds that she would always forgive Jerry for doing. Luckily she never wrote them down. Now, every time Jerry does something that bothers her, she says to herself, "Boy, is he lucky that this is one of the things on my list." She has found a way to accept and forgive. It makes for a happy marriage.

Many people patch up their old arguments so that they look as good as new ones!

You may not always forgive your spouse, but for your own health and self-preservation, you can choose to let go of the anger. You can do this for yourself and by yourself, even if your spouse won't take responsibility. You can choose to be happy.

46: Attraction

Standards of beauty change. If Mona Lisa walked into a modeling agency today they'd say, "Sorry, we don't need a janitor."

—*Jim Gaffigan*

Attraction between couples should not be belittled. Don't allow anyone to tell you that it is not important. One should look at his/her spouse and feel something positive, whether it is a gratifyingly major flutter or a small bleep on the radar screen. You should not feel indifferent, especially when you are first married. While you cannot marry someone based on the physical attraction you feel and you must check out his/her character, think hard before you marry someone if he/she has no potential for physical attraction, even if they have other incredible qualities that appeal to you. Of course, it is also true that often, because a person's character appeals to you, you develop an attraction for him/her.

Attraction helps people tolerate more things from their partners, giving them time to adjust or change. They are also more willing to change for their spouse if they feel attracted to him/her. As time goes on, some couples replace the feeling of physical attraction with a comfort zone. Their connection may be based on a feeling of "life is okay with my partner around" or "our lives are intertwined" or even "we have a history." Of course the ideal is to keep the attraction and excitement going throughout your lifetime together.

A man succeeded to get his wife to diet by telling her, "Do you realize that there are forty pounds of you that I'm not legally married to?"

There are different levels of attraction, ranging from mild to intense. Attraction can be mental, spiritual, physical, or any combination of those. If the attraction you feel is purely physical, it can make you irrational, and it will be difficult for you to truly evaluate if this person is right for you. However, if the physical attraction is combined with a spiritual or mental attraction, it will intensify the relationship.

Attraction is not only a reaction to looks. It has to do with body language. It can be a twinkle of the eye, a bright smile, a confidence or charisma, or even a demure shyness. You can be attracted to a person's warmth, smarts, or sweetness. Attraction makes you want to be with this person because you admire or respect him/her, or because s/he makes you feel good.

Everyone is attracted to different things and a different combination of things.

Tina was attracted to Sidney because he had an air of assurance about him; this made her feel he was capable of taking control and would help determine her direction. Yet she was also drawn toward Fred, who seemed a bit insecure and made her feel like the capable one who could manage their lives.

Some individuals think they know exactly whom they will be attracted to when they are looking for a spouse. Often they do, but just as often they surprise themselves. Someone who believes s/he is searching for the super-capable type may find s/he is actually attracted to someone more disorganized, making him/her feel in control. Someone looking for an outgoing spouse may find s/he is more attracted to an introvert.

Because the rabbis recognized the importance of physical attraction, they instituted the custom that forbade a man to marry a woman without seeing her first.

She sent her picture to a lonely hearts club. They sent the picture back and said, "We're not that lonely!"

It is important to keep yourself looking good for one another. It can be difficult for a wife to look her best when her husband comes home from work. At this time of day she is usually in the middle of cooking dinner, disciplining the kids, and doing homework; the house is flying and the kids are in an uproar. It is not the opportune time to do her hair and put on her best dress. A husband should realize this and not have high expectations. Yet a wife should keep the house, the kids, and her own person basically clean and presentable at all times.

A husband should try not to arrive home dirty, sweaty, or disheveled. Straighten up, tuck yourself in, and make yourself presentable. It demonstrates respect for your wife.

A wife should acknowledge her husband's entrance and make him feel that she is happy about his arrival. Before he arrives home, she should find a moment to straighten herself up. She should hang up if she is on the phone when he walks in the door, saying, "I'll call you back. My husband just walked in." Despite how occupied or overwhelmed she may be, she should take notice of her husband and smile at his presence. He too should make an effort to enter with warm enthusiasm. When a husband shows that he feels good about coming home and his wife shows she is happy to welcome him, the attraction between them is stimulated. Taking a few minutes to ask each other about their day, to compliment one another, to laugh together, sets a good tone for the evening, no matter what stress each of you is feeling.

Marriage advice: "Don't marry a beautiful person. She may leave you. Of course, an ugly person may leave you too, but who cares?"

Each spouse should find time and energy to look good for one another on occasion. They should make an extra effort to look special sometimes. Most women spend hours dressing to go out although their looks mean nothing to the people they will meet there. Yet they look a mess when they are home with their husbands, whom they wish to keep attracted to them. This is true for men as well.

Wife: "I'm ready now. I thought you said you were ready a while ago."

Husband: "I was. But now you'll have to wait for me. I've got to shave again."

47: Pregnancy

What is a Jewish woman's idea of natural childbirth? No makeup whatsoever.

Many young girls hope to get pregnant as soon as they are married and are horrified when this is not the case. Young girls don't realize that the average time to become pregnant, once you start trying to conceive, is three to six months. If, prior to your wedding, you were taking medication to regulate your cycle, it can take an extra three months to get the medication out of your system, making the average time to conceive six to nine months. It is considered normal to conceive a child within a year of marriage.

There are people who believe that a child will be the glue that makes the marriage stick. While this works sometimes, more often it does not, and the consequences can be devastating. A divorce without any children involved is bad enough. If there are children, it is usually detrimental to them as well as to the parents.

Couples are usually ill-prepared for pregnancy. Women cannot imagine beforehand how taxing pregnancy can be. A woman's body must adjust, and some women experience extreme nausea, vomiting, weakness, and pains. In extreme cases, some women are unable to function at all.

Husbands are often overwhelmed by their wife's misery and neediness. They may also have a tough time adjusting to their wife's weight gain. Men have to be sensitive and forgiving of a wife's moods and sickness.

Husbands need to be taught that many women go through mood changes when they menstruate and when they conceive. Postpartum depression, which some women experience after delivery, can last up to two years. Thankfully, medications are now available to help with nausea, anxiety, and depression.

Couples have to be prepared for the difficulties, realizing that the beautiful baby that joins their lives at the end of this challenging period makes it all worthwhile.

Rivka suggested that Josh try his hand at changing their new baby's diaper.

"I'm busy," Josh replied. "I promise I will do the next one." The next time came around soon enough, and Rivka wasted no time asking Josh for help. Josh looked at Rivka and said innocently, "I didn't mean the next diaper, I meant the next baby."

48: Children

If your parents didn't have any children, there's a good chance that you won't either.

—Clarence Day

Many couples are ill-prepared for children. Even those who are excited about the addition to their family and those who come from a big family find that children add a challenging element to marriage. This topic is the subject of many great books and it would be irresponsible of me to discuss it in a limited amount of pages. I can only attest to the fact that children are G-d's greatest gift to man. They bring a couple unfathomable joy and unimaginable pride. They give a couple a deep, overwhelming connection and infinite purpose.

Making the decision to have a child – it's momentous. It is to decide forever to have your heart go walking outside of your body.

—Elizabeth Stone

A child needs endless love, understanding, and care. A child engenders continuous, hard, often tedious, often frustrating work and unending responsibilities. Bringing up a child is a lifetime job; shaping and molding a human being's character is a long, slow process.

A young lad watched Michelangelo mold and work a piece of sculpting clay every day. One day the lad saw that Michelangelo created the statue of David.

"Isn't it curious? he said. "How did Michelangelo know there was a boy inside that clay?"

A couple must work on themselves and their relationship in order to bring up healthy, happy, well-adjusted children. Parents must work together to mold their children.

Advice for the day: If you have a lot of tension and you get a headache, do what it says on the aspirin bottle: "Take two aspirin" and "Keep away from children."

Although each parent may have different ideas about raising and disciplining a child, they must present a united front, respecting the positive intentions of each other, being careful not to send mixed messages to their children.

A rabbi said to a precocious six-year-old boy, "So, you tell me that your mother says your prayers for you every night. That's very commendable. What does she actually say?"

The little boy replied, "Thank G-d he's in bed."

Communicating to each other about their children – what they need, how they are progressing, what to do for them, and what is best for them – should be at the top of every couple's list of discussions and interactions. As the saying goes, "To be in your child's memories tomorrow, you must be in their lives today."

I asked my mother if I was adopted. She said, "Not yet, but we placed an ad."

Children are to keep – to keep safe, keep happy, keep secure, keep loved.

49: Financial Issues

How come the most successful man is the one my wife almost married?

People use money for many different reasons. Some want enough to survive, while others want enough to thrive. Some want it to give, either to nurture a wife and family or to be charitable. Others need it for personal comfort. Some need it for security, respect, or control. Some people have been poor and feel vulnerable without money, while others have always been well-off and do not know how to survive without money. Some individuals who never had much money do not feel a need for it; others in like situation feel desperate for it. What constitutes a large fortune to one person is a pittance to another. Although we may not understand another person's need or lack of need for money, each person must understand what his/her own and his spouse's needs are, as well as how to meet or curb those needs.

Money can't buy you love, but it puts you in a great bargaining position.

The Talmud (*Eiruvin* 65b) states that we reveal our personality in three ways; one of those ways is through money. Everyone, at one time or another, is challenged by either too much or too little money; it is only the form those challenges take that is different. Money, like everything else, is part of our life test, and we need to obtain it and use it in accordance with Torah principles (*Mesillas Yesharim*, chapter 1). Couples challenged by money issues must work to be elevated rather than brought down by these tests. They must work together to navigate a solution or to develop a coping mechanism. Each test that a couple passes together is a building block in strengthening their marriage.

How couples handle their financial issues often determines the strength of a relationship. A couple's livelihood has a great impact on a marriage. Is each partner employed? Does each have the education or potential to find employment? Do both husband and wife plan to be part of the workforce? Do both or either have parents who are helping them out financially? Do both or either have money in savings or investments?

Some women expect their husbands to do well financially and judge them accordingly. Men often evaluate their own self-esteem by how much they earn and how much buying power they have. However, marrying someone for money or having your marriage dependent on money and its purchasing ability and power puts a marriage on a shaky foundation. If the money is lost, the marriage has a difficult time surviving. Powerful emotions come into play. Feeling insecure, wondering if your spouse is irresponsible, reacting with anger, feeling deprived or resentful, and feeling embarrassed about yourself for disappointing your spouse are just some of the thoughts that can enter your mind. A man's fragile ego and a woman's insecurities can become part of the scenario. The only constructive way to balance all these emotions is for a couple to discuss the issue, working it through together.

Ninety-one percent of individuals avoid speaking to their spouse about finances, but both spouses should be aware of the family expenses. This is one area where it is better to overcommunicate than undercommunicate.

There's a way of transferring funds that is even faster than electronic banking. It's called marriage.

Whether or not a young couple's parents will contribute to the couple's finances, and if so to what extent they will contribute, must be included in the equation.

A rich man is only a poor man with money.

Couples must strategize and have a plan to survive. People who were not financially responsible prior to marriage usually do not become responsible after marriage. There are couples that think they can live on love. Others believe they can live on a pittance by sacrificing worldly pleasures; some women will choose to buy a washing machine rather than receiving a ring. Every woman who wants a ring should get one, even if it is small. Every woman who finds taking care of a home and children overwhelming should have backup help when she needs it, whether it is outside help, a relative, or a husband to the rescue.

A man who doesn't earn enough money to support his family and has no other source of income – neither from his wife contributing financially, or other outside support – will probably have a stressed and frustrated family. In this case a husband and a wife must strategize to find a solution. Perhaps the husband can take on a second job such as tutoring or coaching, or possibly the wife could work to supplement the household income.

If he asks what sort of books you are interested in, tell him checkbooks.

Financial worries and disagreements are a serious cause of conflict, and therefore a husband should want his wife to feel secure in this area. A wife should not pressure a husband about his finances, and she certainly should not strain the marriage by spending more than he can afford.

Husband: "Will you love me if I lose all my money?"

Wife: "I'll not only love you, I'll also miss you."

Many people marry individuals who don't meet their financial expectations. The spouse is not accepted to the school s/he planned to attend or s/he didn't get the job s/he had hoped to get. Marriages must be able to survive these setbacks.

A person's lifestyle can change significantly when his income changes, and this can cause great tension. Sometimes people who were wealthy experience major losses. People who suddenly have too little may worry, adding excessive stress to the marriage. Couples who suddenly begin earning much more money can also feel tension. Individuals who earn more often want more – more money, more excitement, and more in a spouse.

I've got enough money for the rest of my life – unless I want to buy something.

If their finances are insufficient, the couple must discuss a plan of action for both partners to follow, either to earn more or spend less. A realistic plan, discussed with understanding and patience, will make the situation easier. Some wives feel comforted when their husbands say, "Don't worry," while other wives feel a need to get involved. A man should not feel too insecure to confide in his wife about a difficult financial situation.

Even a couple with financial security should discuss how money should be allocated, spent, and saved. One spouse may want to buy a lot of things, while the other may feel better saving some of it. One may be tight and stingy with money regardless of the amount they have, while the other may enjoy splurging. To one, a big home is a priority, while to the other charity seems the best way to spend money. Money matters must be discussed, priorities considered, compromises made, and adjustments worked out, depending on financial times and obligations.

He hung the embroidered sign in the kitchen. It read: "Bless Our Happy Home." His wife took a look and said, "It goes on the other wall, dummy."

To one person an apartment is a palace; to another it is a prison. One man needs a mansion to be happy, while another is satisfied with a small apartment. This is based on attitude and upbringing. Someone who is used to an extravagant lifestyle will have a tougher time adjusting to a financially modest one. A girl whose mother worked will probably find it easier to have a job outside the home than one whose mother spent her spare time shopping and exercising. A woman who plans to work may not expect her husband to make a great living. Some women are willing to subsidize their husband's income but expect their husband to be the main breadwinner, while others willingly carry a full load. Some men want working wives, while others want their wives to be full-time homemakers. Who you are and what type of lifestyle you want are important factors to consider when you are choosing a spouse. Ignoring this is a sure recipe for disappointment and constant fighting. You must ask yourself if you respect your spouse's attitude toward money.

A father asked the young man who had been seeing his daughter about his finances. "What will be your yearly income?"

"Fifty thousand," the young man said.

"Not too shabby," said the father. "That'll be decent enough when you add my daughter's forty thousand."

"Oh, I already counted her in the fifty."

Before a couple gets married they should discuss their needs and expectations, examining what is important to each of them and identifying their priorities. Sometimes each spouse feels the need for his/her own car, but they are both willing to live in a smaller apartment in order to afford that luxury. Some wives may offer to drive their husbands to and from the train so the couple will need to buy only one car and can therefore rent a more spacious apartment. A man may want to put aside money to join a sports club, while a woman may want money put aside for entertaining company. They may both agree to eat out less often so they can afford to hire domestic help. Everyone has his/her list of priorities and a list of things he/she is willing to sacrifice. Together a couple should construct a budget that works for the two of them.

My wife never spends more than I earn. Although I didn't know it, last year I must have earned $1,000,310,000.

Debt destroys happiness. A person should write down what he feels he owes himself. This keeps him from spending beyond his means, and is better than writing down what he owes others. As you acquire money you can carefully buy things you want. By doing this, you attain peace of mind in addition to materialistic items.

A wife may be ready to give up eating out every week but her husband may enjoy the outing and not want to give it up. By listing and comparing their desires, compromises can be worked out, and a budget, which should be flexible and open to revision, can be created. By figuring out your combined income, including any money or investments (stocks, bonds, insurance policies, commodities, options, property, and so on) and savings you each bring to the marriage, plus money that your parents continue to give you, minus any loans you may be carrying, you will get a sense of how much money you have to spend. You must then make a list of all the expenses you expect to pay. Does your income cover your expenses? If not, how can you cut down? Can you borrow some money at a rate that you can slowly pay back without incurring impossible debts? If your funds are sufficient, is there extra for saving? How can the additional funds be best invested? Financial planning or consulting financial advisers can save couples a lot of worrying and financial difficulties.

My wife has low estimates in her budget for her food. She is reasonable when it comes to clothing and the beauty parlor. She's very tight with beverages, theaters, and eating out. But she's got a

"miscellaneous" that could choke a horse!

Here is a sample starter budget:

Add

Husband's net income (less taxes)

Wife's net income (less taxes)

Savings (previous accounts, wedding money)

Outside help (from both sets of parents)

Subtract

Rent or mortgage

Home insurance

Property tax

Health care

Life insurance

Doctors' bills

Pharmacy bills

Unpaid loans

Car

Car insurance

Car maintenance

Gas

Parking

Train, taxi, or bus expenses

Utilities: gas, electric, water, Internet

Phones: home, cell phones, cable

Maintenance: plumbers, electricians, repairmen, gardening, etc.

Business expenses: office space, business expenditures

Education

Food

Clothing and accessories

Furniture

Sefarim

House needs

Baby needs

Housekeeper and babysitter

Dry cleaners

Haircuts

Glasses, lenses, makeup

Restaurants

Entertainment

Travel/vacations

Gifts

Charity

Debts

Miscellaneous

Most people spend eight hours earning money, eight hours spending money, eight hours spending more than they earn, and eight hours wondering why they can't sleep.

—*Toni Salerno*

Many times there is a disconnect between a husband and wife, with one spouse knowing only what is earned and the other knowing only what is spent. A husband may be too embarrassed to tell his wife that she is overspending, thus allowing her to put them into debt, or a wife may not be tuned in to the real situation. For a budget to work, both spouses must construct it together, determining what to spend their money on, how much to spend, and how much to save. Each partner must be aware of and agree on what is coming in and what is going out. Perhaps not every cent will be accounted for, but the overall financial picture must be understood and agreed upon by both parties. This can obviate serious conflicts.

Jake always told his wife what he was earning and gave her all the bills to pay. With this method she knew where every dollar went and she was more careful with their finances. Every couple has to find what works for them.

Disposing of credit cards and using cash or a balanced checkbook to pay for everything has kept many couples from accumulating tremendous debt by living an unrealistic lifestyle. However, it may be impractical for some couples to dispose of all their credit cards.

A family is a unit assembled to spend money the head of the family hasn't earned yet.

Of course they are worth it, but children are expensive to care for. When parents work out their finances, they must take their children's living expenses into consideration.

A successful man is one who makes more money than his wife can spend. A successful woman is one who can find such a man.

As with most marital issues, financial problems are not necessarily the fault of one or the other spouse; rather, they are due to their differences. If a man who is tight with money marries a thrifty woman he can do quite well. A woman who enjoys spending money will be fine if she marries someone who has the ability and disposition to be extravagant. The difficulty arises when the financial preferences or abilities conflict.

A man will pay $2 for a $1 item he wants. A woman will pay $1 for a $2 item she doesn't want.

There will be marital problems if the wife is tight with money but the husband enjoys spending, just as there will be problems if he is tight and she enjoys spending. Money disagreements lead to bickering and fighting, and often to verbal abuse and divorce courts.

He got his wife a gift certificate for her birthday, and she went out and exchanged it for a larger size.

When financial disagreements lead to the divorce court, the judge reviews the couple's financial situation, determining the income and savings of both partners, as well as the unnecessary living expenses. How long a couple has been married also plays a role in determining the settlement. The court looks at the added expenses each needs if they have grown accustomed to a certain lifestyle. The court also studies child support requirements to determine a settlement. Usually neither spouse is completely satisfied with this arrangement. The husband, who must usually pay for second living quarters for himself, feels he is giving his money to someone for whom he no longer cares and from whom he receives no benefit. The wife usually feels she is not receiving a sufficient amount of compensation and living expenses. In other words, the judge has forced a budget on the couple. Wouldn't it be smarter for a couple to hire a financial adviser who can help them work out a proper budget before the arguments over money begin, and the frustration and resentment accumulate?

Money is better than poverty, if only for financial reasons.

—Woody Allen

50: In-Laws

An entire book can be devoted to the art of being a mother-in-law. Being a good father-in-law, daughter-in-law, or son-in-law is also an art, as well as work.

Honolulu – it's got everything. Sand for the children, sun for the wife, sharks for the wife's mother...
—*Ken Dodd*

A good relationship between in-law parents and their married children is a wonderful ingredient that adds dimension to a young couple's healthy marriage. It is beneficial for all parties involved. Parents, who are hopefully older and wiser, should do everything they can to make their children's transition from single to married life as easy and natural as possible. Creating a balance in the relationship is not a simple matter. Parents must give guidance without being domineering, offer an opinion without forcing their children to accept that opinion, and be understanding if or when their children's logic differs from their own. Parents must be helpful and involved in their children's lives but carefully measure how much it is appropriate for them to intercede. Parents must know how much they can ask of their children, although children believe they can ask anything of their parents.

In-law parents want their son-/daughter-in-law to be good to their child. They also want him/her to join their family rather than pull their child away from the family.

I knew that my mother-in-law wasn't exactly crazy about me. On our wedding day, when we wheeled in the cake, she bit the head off the groom.

Marriage teaches men and women to look to the future, asking them to commit to each other and to devote themselves to advancing their children's prospects, which includes helping them marry and start their own family.

To be a good parent takes work. Parents must care for their children and provide for them, understand their needs and sacrifice for them. Parents must be mature, emotionally stable, and well balanced in order to educate and direct their children. They must have good values to be an example and a role model for them. Parents must put their hearts, their souls, and their energy into their children.

Mothers and fathers work hard at being good parents. Then their children marry, and once again they must learn to be good parents, not for an infant whom they can shape and control, but for a fully grown, fully formed person who is their new "daughter" or "son." The new in-law child feels the same way: *"Who are these people whom I now have to call Mom and Dad?"* Everyone agrees that this is work for both parties.

It can seem like you are walking a tightrope, especially for those newlyweds who take an instant dislike to their new in-law parents and for the in-law parents who dislike their new in-law child. If you don't get it right the first time, chances are neither side will give the other a proper chance to adjust to and reshape the relationship.

Addressing new in-laws can be the first challenge in a marriage. How many daughters- or sons-in-law are still addressing their in-law parents as "hm hm" even after years of marriage? It is best to accept that this is a universal challenge and force yourself to address your new in-law parents as Mom and Dad from the start.

A mixed emotion is watching your mother-in-law drive off a cliff in your new car.

A new daughter- or son-in-law may feel uncomfortable and insecure with her/his spouse's family. In the final analysis, this is about each person's self-esteem. Everyone deserves to feel good about his/her rightful position and relationship within a family, with his/her thoughts and opinions respected.

Like newlyweds, in-law parents can also feel insecure, despite their age and their expected level of maturity. They want love and appreciation as well. Sometimes, ironically enough, parents who are more distant are appreciated more than those parents who wish to be closely and lovingly involved in their children's lives. Parents need to understand this dynamic, realizing that the in-law relationship needs time to be established. The more insecure a person is, the harder it is to build a good relationship (see chapter 25, "The Need for Self-Esteem"). An insecure in-law child might look askance at any suggestion proposed by in-law parents, thinking they are trying to run his/her life. Until people are secure in their new relationship, this attitude is common and even understandable.

When we pray for our children to marry good spouses, we must also pray that those good spouses appreciate the family that comes along with the bride or groom. When we pray for a good spouse, we must also ask that his/her family appreciate, accept, and love us.

Two funeral cars are driving down the street followed by hundreds of men walking in the procession behind the cars. Thomas goes over to the procession and says to the first man, "Who is in the hearse? It must be someone very important."

The man says, "It's my mother-in-law. My dog bit her and she died."

"Oh," says Thomas, "I'm so sorry. But tell me, who is in the second hearse?"

The man lowers his head and quietly answers, "Oh, that one has my wife. My dog bit her and she died."

Thomas thought for a moment and said, "I'm truly sorry, but let me ask you something. Can I borrow your dog?"

"Sure," answered the man. "Get in the back of the line."

People think that if they are good to their in-law children, they can defy the rules of in-law relations and in-law difficulties. One woman claims she does everything for her daughter-in-law, Leslie. She supports the young couple, sends over dinners, and buys Leslie gifts. Nevertheless, her daughter-in-law Leslie doesn't like her. She claims, and it may be very true, that it's because Leslie is programmed to dislike her, as if all in-laws are guilty until proven innocent. A mother-in-law is usually branded as nosy, controlling, intolerable, competitive, invasive, and prone to overstep all boundaries. Unwittingly, in-laws become public enemy number one. Society has made it acceptable for people to mock their in-law relatives; indeed, it has become an expected part of the relationship. This should be changed.

Sadie was stopped by an usher at the entrance to the synagogue. The usher asked, "Are you a friend of the bride?"

Sadie quickly replied, "Of course not. I am the groom's mother."

Of course, some in-laws, like some parents, are not kind people, whereas others are kind people who display poor relationship skills, poor communication skills, poor setting of boundaries, and so on.

Most often, the snags between in-law parents and children are part of structuring the relationship. Just as a couple enters marriage with different habits, values, sensitivities, and ideas that they must work through, in-law parents and children have practices, routines, beliefs, and issues that they too must negotiate.

One mother said, "I have the best son-in-law. He treats my daughter like a queen. He brings her breakfast in bed. He straightens up the house and helps her get the kids off to school. She doesn't have to work and he supports her in real style. He is everything I dreamed of for my daughter."

The next mother-in-law said, "You are so lucky. I

have the worst daughter-in-law. She sleeps late every morning. My son has to bring her coffee, straighten up the house, and even get the kids off to school. She lazes around all day and doesn't even work, while my son slaves away trying to support her. You should count your blessings for your son-in-law, while I have to cry over the daughter-in-law my son got stuck with."

Needless to say, it all depends on your viewpoint. In-law children are looking for respect, approval, and acceptance from their in-law parents. They usually assume that their in-law parents will automatically like and appreciate them if they are "good" in-law children. Unfortunately, some in-law parents misunderstand their daughters- or sons-in-law and are too critical or demanding. They want to reshape their in-law children, refusing to accept that their in-law children's upbringing may cause them to act in a different manner than that of their family.

I'm recovering from a bad fall. My mother-in-law stayed with us in October and November.

A new mother-in-law may show up every day to help her daughter-in-law just as she did when her daughter got married. Although a daughter might appreciate that, a boy's mother should know her place and realize that a newlywed wife may feel differently and may need her space. Because couples are entitled to carve out their own lives, boundaries should be set and respected.

Parents are also entitled to set boundaries. Parents can certainly babysit when they are able to do so, but they need not be available all the time. Establishing clear boundaries in the beginning will help prevent hard feelings later if a parent has plans of his/her own and isn't always available.

Parents- and children-in-law who want to create a close friendship can do so with communication and compromise, understanding each other's needs and establishing clear boundaries. A girl may appreciate a mother-in-law who constantly buys her clothing, or she may resent her for seemingly dictating to her what to wear. It is only through discussion and understanding that each can explain her position.

"My mother-in-law is an angel."

"You are lucky. Mine is still alive."

Most people advise in-law parents to close their mouths and open their pocketbooks. It is almost universally accepted that you can say what you want to your daughter or son, but you have to tiptoe around your in-law kids, especially around a daughter-in-law. If you have something to say, think twice and perhaps three times before you say it, considering all possible repercussions.

My mother-in-law gives really exciting gifts. For my birthday she gave me a gift certificate good for four hours of free advice.

A smart mother-in-law will train herself to keep her opinion, especially her complaints, to herself. However, sometimes this can cause her to feel that she is building a wall between herself and her daughter-in-law. Never expressing one's own feelings can make a mother-in-law or daughter-in-law feel she's being controlled or manipulated. Even if the relationship looks peaceful on the surface, the players have a hard time developing a real connection. In-law parents should be allowed to tactfully yet openly speak to their in-law children. A daughter or son-in-law should also have the right to politely and respectfully inform his/her parents-in-law what s/he believes will work best for all of them, thus creating a more open, pleasant, and loving relationship.

A husband and wife had a tiff. The wife called up her mom and said, "He fought with me again. I am coming to live with you."

The mom said, "No, darling, he must pay for his mistake. I am coming to live with you."

In some instances, in-law parents and children hit it off from the start, really liking and respecting one another. Most often, forming the bonds of an in-law family relationship takes work, and everyone must be willing to learn to understand each other's needs. Then they can find a happy middle ground through sharing experiences, communicating, and compromising. A rocky beginning in the relationship is common, but it is not an appropriate status quo. Work on improving and nurturing the relationship. If you make a recognizable effort, hopefully so will everyone else involved, and you will all be happier.

Never complain about your in-law children or in-law parents to friends or other in-law relations. Look for the best in them and compliment them to their face and to others.

My wife said, "Can my mother come down for the weekend?"

So I said, "Why?"

And she said, "Well, she's been up on the roof for two weeks already."

Mrs. Grady, trying to build a good relationship, calls her

daughter-in-law every day. Rather than appreciating this, her daughter-in-law complains about it. This is a common situation. In order to be good daughters-in-law, some newly married women formulate behavior policies: *I will call my mother-in-law every Sunday.* Sometimes this works, sometimes it doesn't. It can put pressure on a daughter-in-law who must now call at a specific time. The mother-in-law may feel the relationship is a shallow one, because the daughter-in-law calls once a week yet does nothing else to advance the relationship.

Belinda thinks, *I bring the kids to see their grandmother once a week. What more can my mother-in-law want from me?* Perhaps her mother-in-law wants a friendly smile from her daughter-in-law to accompany the duty visit she is fulfilling.

I couldn't ask for a better mother-in-law, as much as I'd like to.

It is best, when feasible, to discuss issues directly with an in-law. For this to work, the relationship must be on a good footing, with both the in-law parent and the in-law child comfortable about discussing the matter.

Did you hear the one about the cannibal who got married, and at the reception toasted his mother-in-law?

Some advisers say that if one has a problem with his/her in-laws, s/he should not tell his/her spouse; likewise, a parent who has an issue with a son-/daughter-in-law should not tell his/her child. Although this can cause frustration and mounting anger, speaking to a child about his/her spouse can be dangerous, since it can cause conflict between the couple. The child feels trapped between his/her spouse and parents.

The child doesn't know how to make one happy without causing resentment in the other. Although s/he wants both people to be happy and s/he can usually understand and be sympathetic to both sides, s/he does not have the experience to negotiate this territory. S/he feels tortured and smothered by both sides, and doesn't know how to achieve a compromise without angering all parties concerned.

Other people feel that parents should be able to discuss an issue pertaining to a child's spouse with their son or daughter. They likewise maintain that a husband or wife should also be able to discuss his/her parents with his/her spouse. The criterion is that it be said in a kind, caring, and non-globally critical manner. Some sons/daughters are good at hearing and digesting complaints from their parents, either resolving the difficulties or presenting them in a calm, diplomatic way to their spouse. Or, if their spouse complains about his/her in-law parents, they know how to effectively approach the parents in a manner that still keeps the peace.

When sons/daughters must act as the go-between, presenting their parents' opinion to their new spouse, or their spouse's opinion to their parents, they must sift through the language, eliminating any harsh-sounding criticism and adding a bit of sugar. For example, Rob could say, "Ma, Alice really appreciates your calling her every morning, but she is trying to take some classes and her schedule isn't fully worked out. Maybe you can call at different times, but don't get insulted if she doesn't have time to talk to you when you do call. If she is too busy to talk on the phone, maybe we can drop by a bit more often."

One mother is so proud of her son. He goes to the

psychiatrist every day and spends the whole hour just talking about her.

In order to form a strong bond with each other, a couple must stand together. A son or daughter should help his/her parents understand his/her spouse's point of view, accepting his/her sensitivities and differences in upbringing and beliefs. Simultaneously, a child must calmly help his/her spouse understand his/her parents.

If there is a major conflict between a parent-in-law and child-in-law, a spouse or parent may be hurt because his/her spouse or child didn't side with him/her. It is a delicate situation that must be handled with care. A mature, well-adjusted in-law, be it a parent or spouse, will realize that neither parent nor child-in-law is always right or always wrong. If a husband sides with his wife during a conflict, his parents must accept that he may be siding with his wife because he agrees with her, or perhaps, in order to strengthen his marriage, he is validating rather than embarrassing his wife. If a husband sides with his parent, a wife must realize that a parent and son, having years of connection, may be on the same page and that they are not looking to hurt her or the marital relationship.

Parents must be understanding if their child decides to side with a spouse rather than his/her parents in order to maintain peace. Perhaps the child can let his/her parents know that this stance was not taken out of disrespect; it was to help the marriage. With some time and support, s/he is sure his/her spouse will understand the other viewpoint. When his/her spouse is calm and less defensive s/he can help him/her see the parent's side of the story. It goes without saying that, although a woman should feel her husband understands and supports her, she should not consistently place him in the position of fighting his own parents. Parents, in turn, should try not to put a child in the position of arguing with his/her spouse.

Communication is the key here. Differences usually occur when people take things out of context, distorting what is said or meant. A spouse who is caught in the middle should try to sort out the disagreement, helping both parties understand the other's perception of things. S/he must focus on the goal, which is peace, understanding, tolerance, acceptance, friendship, respect, and eventually love between one's spouse and one's parents.

I bought my mother-in-law a nice new chair, but she won't let me plug it in.

In-law parents are sometimes told to stay out of their daughter-in-law's life; the idea is that this way she will like them better. Although that may be true, the in-law parents are being kept out of their children's lives. A solid marriage is one where the relationship between both sets of parents and the couple is a happy one.

It is difficult to forge a solid and trusting relationship if any of the people involved are inflexible or controlling. Battles can really challenge the in-law relationship and the marriage if there are two strong-willed, overly sensitive, insecure, or selfish individuals.

However, if a mother and daughter-in-law are determined to like one another despite differences, strongly convinced about the importance of uniting the family and sharing values, they will forge a meaningful relationship that will be beneficial and rewarding for the entire family.

One passage in the Bible dictates that a married man

should never let his mother-in-law move in with him. It's the part that says, "No man should have two masters."

In some countries, India, for example, the parents usually arrange marriages, and a newly married son brings his wife to live with his parents. Since the young wife is living with her new in-laws, the boy's parents must really approve of the girl, and the girl had better like her new in-laws. I have heard though, that the fights between the daughters-in-law, who all live in the same house, can be fierce.

In the United States people believe that children should live in their own home, although most parents hope their children will live near them.

"Do you mean to tell me you've been married for five years and your mother-in-law has been to visit you only once?"

"Yeah. She came the day after we were married and never left."

Jack broke off his engagement. When he was asked why, he said, "Well, when we were looking for apartments, her mother remarked that it was rather small for three."

Sometimes a new daughter- or son-in-law feels s/he must define the relationship immediately rather than allow it to evolve. Susan said to her new in-laws, "Jeff is now my husband. We will set the policies for our home, and we would appreciate it if you keep your opinions to yourself."

From the beginning she emphasized that parenting Jeff for twenty-four years had no bearing on his life from here on. That was then. This is now. That kind of policy creates resentment because it is unfair. Although parents should respect a newly married couple's opinions, they should not be pushed aside like used furniture.

If newlyweds think about this, they realize that they will hopefully raise their own children with a value system they think is important. Imagine how they would react if their children were to eventually say to them, "Your opinions and your years of experience are inconsequential. Keep them to yourselves. We would like to have our own home without your influence."

You can always learn from the mistakes of others. The trouble is I'm always "the others"!

Some parents want to give their children the benefit of their experiences. As parents, they want to save their children from struggling through life, unwilling to watch their children learn the hard way, as they had to. But parents must allow life to happen to their children. They can't protect them all the time, nor save them from every mistake. Quite often life will play out differently for the children, although the circumstances seem similar to the parents' situation. Of course, smart children will be mindful of the lessons their parents have gained, applying them to their own situation.

I told my mother-in-law, "My house is your house." So she sold it.

Karen's mother warned her not to live in the suburbs because her husband would spend too much time traveling. She reminded Karen how worn out the commute made Karen's father feel. Karen realized that living in the suburbs had been tough for her parents, yet nevertheless she decided to move there. However, armed with her parents' experience and knowledge of the drawbacks of the suburbs, she and her husband planned that he take the train and work while commuting, rather than drive to the city. This way, he was relaxed when he came home and was able to spend time with her and the kids in a non-pressured manner. Karen made her own decision while actively listening to her mother's concerns. She took her mother's advice to make the situation work for her. She wasn't ruled by her mother but was willing to learn from her.

A great way to diffuse a tense situation is to present options. "Mom, we would love to spend some time with you, but Ben and I both need to catch up on our work. Would it be better if we came for a weekend or two consecutive Sundays? Or maybe you can come to us for the weekend instead?" This lets Mom know that there are only two free days, but the kids want to see her, and whatever works best for her is fine with them.

What did Noah say to his mother-in-law? "You take the next ark."

I cannot seem to find a mother-in-law rule that is consistent for everyone because, as in every situation, people bring their own experiences to the marriage. A girl who has a great relationship with her own mother usually has an easy time getting along with a mother-in-law. On the other hand, she does not have the same need for a mother-in-law. Her mother is quite capable of giving her any advice or help she needs, and this is easier for her to accept, since her mother makes no new demands on her; she is used to receiving advice, solicited or not, from her mother. A mother-in-law's advice may make a young or insecure girl feel as if she is being questioned, doubted, or undermined, although in most cases this is not the mother-in-law's objective.

A girl who does not have a good relationship with her own mother may feel resentful toward mothers in general. If her mother made her feel insecure, inadequate, or controlled, she may go into a marriage feeling mothers do not relate well to her and refuse to try building a relationship with her mother-in-law. She may be predisposed to dislike her mother-in-law before they even meet. Of course, there are some smart girls who think: *I never managed to have a good rapport with my mother, but I think my mother-in-law is different, and I want to start off on the right foot and give our relationship a chance.*

Sometimes a wife may resent her husband's relationship with his mother, or conversely, a mother and daughter may be so close that they unconsciously make the husband feel like a third wheel. He will therefore resent his wife's relationship with her mother. No husband appreciates if a girl confides in her mother about everything or constantly accepts her mother's advice over his. Both husband and wife should feel like the number one person in his/her spouse's life. By being aware of these possible pitfalls, people can be more careful to avoid them.

Wife: "Mother said she almost died laughing over those stories you told her."

Husband: "Where is she? I'll tell her some funnier ones."

It is unfortunate if a girl feels she doesn't need another mother, or a mother feels she doesn't need another daughter. There should always be room in people's lives to love another person. Both mother-in-law and daughter-in-law are losing out by not getting along.

Susan loved her mother, Mrs. Shiner. Iris hated her

mother-in-law, Mrs. Shiner. She was the same person, just seen from a different perspective. And there are families where one daughter-in-law raves about her terrific mother-in-law while another daughter-in-law constantly complains about her. Perhaps the same mother-in-law relates differently to her two daughters-in-law; more likely, she acts in the same manner but is perceived differently by each daughter-in-law.

Ellen and Brenda are married to two brothers. Ellen loves her mother-in-law, Carol, and appreciates that she often brings her home-cooked meals. Ellen feels that this shows that her mother-in-law is thinking about them and trying to be helpful. Brenda resents that Carol brings her meals. She says, "Doesn't Carol think I'm capable of cooking for my husband? Why does she have to be so involved in our lives? If we needed food wouldn't I ask for it?"

Each girl views her mother-in-law's behavior from the lens of her own personality. For one it is a positive and accepting viewpoint, for the other there is anger and mistrust. Is Carol truly a good mother-in-law who wants to be caring and helpful, or is she an overbearing mother-in-law who doesn't feel her daughter-in-law is capable of caring for her family? It is best to look for the positive motive in these types of behaviors.

Daughters- and sons-in-law: Be careful! Never answer the phone and call to your spouse, "It's your mother – long distance, thank goodness."

The in-law relationship is much the same as dating. The in-law children and parents have to get acquainted with each other and build trust, accepting that they are on the same team and not in a competition. Parents and spouses each play different roles. Therefore, parents don't have to relinquish their role of being a parent when their child marries. However, they do have to accept that their role has changed and that there is a new person in the equation to consider.

Most parents define their own identity by being parents to their children. They hope to stay, and indeed deserve to remain parents, even after their child marries. It usually takes some time, but with understanding, maturity, and delicacy they are able to redefine the job description once their child is married. They are able to be there for their children, their in-law children, and their grandchildren in a delicate, sensitive, loving, and giving way, not in an obtrusive and demanding way.

Learn to communicate with your in-laws in a careful, sensitive manner with the goal of growing closer by learning to understand one another through finding common ground.

A man is driving the car when his wife in the passenger seat says, "Watch the car on your right."

He continues driving when his mother-in-law in the backseat says, "Watch out for the car on the left."

After ten more orders, the man turns to his wife and asks, "Who's driving this car – you or your mother?"

A smart parent-in-law tries to remain objective and fair, not just siding with his/her own child.

Four different mothers-in-law watched their sons constantly belittle their wives for not keeping up with the household chores.

The first mother bad-mouthed her daughter-in-law, telling her son what a poor choice he had made, and that his wife was inefficient and slovenly. Of course she increased the conflict and hurt her son's marriage.

The second mother-in-law admonished her son, advising him to treat his wife respectfully and recognize her other wonderful qualities.

The third mother-in-law hired help for her daughter-in-law.

The fourth mother-in-law showed up every couple of days, quietly helping her daughter-in-law straighten up and teaching her by example how to manage her chores without being overwhelmed.

The last three mothers-in-law, each in her own way and according to her abilities and means, helped their children make their marriage work.

These days most daughters-in-law get along well with their mothers-in-law. After all, they are the cheapest babysitters.

The mother of the groom is usually the most worried – and with good reason. She is afraid she is losing a son, and she is often right. It is of utmost importance for the new wife to like her new mother-in-law and want to be part of her husband's family.

Newlyweds should be sensitive to both sets of parents and even their siblings, who are also concerned about the changing relationships within the family. They should assure everyone that they want their relationships to continue and grow. Before the wedding, the bride and groom should give family members hugs, kisses, and words of love and appreciation. Tell parents you'll call soon. Tell siblings, "Let's get together soon" or "You must come see our apartment sometime next week."

In the beginning, call your parents once a day for a quick hello. After a couple of weeks, you can skip a few days between calls if you like, but always keep both sets of parents involved in your lives.

What's the difference between in-laws and outlaws? Outlaws are wanted.

It is essential for children and parents to go into an in-law relationship with a positive and optimistic feeling. If you love your spouse, you should feel some appreciation toward his/her parents for bringing him/her up, even if you disagree with them about some things. If your spouse exhibits an undesirable behavior or attitude that you believe stems from his/her parents, don't focus on that negative behavior without acknowledging all the other wonderful traits s/he inherited. Learn to say to your spouse, "I appreciate that your father is always upbeat although I disapprove of his child-rearing policies. I am so happy you inherited his disposition." This reinforces your father-in-law's positive qualities while making your position clear.

A big game hunter went on a safari to Africa with his wife and his mother-in-law. One night he and his wife awoke to find Mama missing. After searching for hours, they were shocked to find her cowering in a clearance with a huge lion standing over her.

"Oh, what are we going to do?" the horrified wife asked.

"Nothing," answered the husband. "The lion got himself into that fix; now let him get out of it."

In the best-case scenario, people accept their in-law relationships as they do blood relatives. Ideally, parents-in-law should have the same open, honest, giving, and sharing relationship with their child-in-law that they have with their child. Just as parents love their children despite their flaws, they should accept and love their in-law children. Similarly, children should accept and love their in-laws the way they love their parents.

Adults, who are more experienced than newlyweds, should set the example, working hard to keep the relationship on a good footing. When they accept their children and their in-law children for who they are, rather than judging and analyzing every word, it will help the young couple feel comfortable. The couple will also learn not to constantly question or judge things, or wonder if there is an ulterior motive to everything their parents-in-law do.

I just came back from a pleasure trip. I took my mother-in-law to the airport.

Lena was aggravated. The advice she received from her mother-in-law, Mrs. Gold, seemed never ending. One day Mrs. Gold said, "Lena, I am so sorry. I am not telling you what to do in order to be controlling, and I don't think I know everything. Certainly I do not want to sound as if I feel you are incompetent. You are a wonderful mother, much more competent than I was when I first became a mother. Please accept my remarks as advice to help you, rather than as criticism. You are feeding the baby formula, and I am pretty sure that if he were on solid food already he wouldn't be constantly hungry and crying. I just feel the baby food will make him happier and thereby make your life easier." After hearing that, Lena was able to listen to her mother-in-law with a different attitude. Speaking about something, not in anger, but in order to understand and be understood, keeps a relationship on a good footing.

Some parents are not looking for a relationship with their in-law children. They are missing out on something special.

Most fathers- and sons-in-law can easily find something in common, whether it is learning, sports, business, or politics. They don't usually bother analyzing the quality of their relationship.

Most in-law parents would love to talk to their in-law children as they do to their own children. But just as it took years to build a relationship with your own child, it takes time and patience to forge that trust and understanding with your in-law child. A child is willing to hear things from his/her own parent that s/he is not willing to hear or tolerate from an in-law parent. A good relationship takes time to develop.

The doorbell rang this morning. When I opened the door, there was my mother-in-law on the front step. She asked, "Can I stay here for a few days?"

I answered, "Sure you can," and shut the door in her face.

Newlyweds: Remember that this is not easy for your parents. The status quo they have lived with for years is thrown off balance. They no longer have the right to talk directly to their own child without placing you, the new wife/husband, into the picture. Both spouses are happier if their new spouse treats his/her parents with respect and consideration, so both must work on avoiding fights, confrontations, blame, and guilt. Relationships take time, and it may be years before a daughter-in-law and mother-in-law gain appreciation for each other. Sometimes it just takes life – a daughter becoming a mother, a daughter-in-law becoming a mother-in-law – for true understanding and appreciation to develop. Don't give up. Work at the relationship, because the hardship caused by a poor relationship between in-law parents and children is draining on a marriage, while the advantages of a beautiful relationship between in-law parents and in-law children is unbelievably rewarding for everyone involved.

The thing I have the most trouble with is trying to discipline the little guy, because everything he does makes me laugh, and you don't want to send the wrong message. Like last week he'd somehow gotten hold of a carving knife, and he was stabbing my in-laws repeatedly. It was funny, but I had to be like, "No, that's bad."

—*Brian Kiley*

A parent's greatest sacrifice is to free his/her children to be good spouses and parents. To accomplish this, parents must have lives independent of their children's lives. If a parent has no other identity or outlet other than as a mother or father and has failed to build his/her own marriage connection, s/he is lost when a child marries and moves to a more independent stage.

Parents must give their children room to grow. This is particularly true for their married children, who need to know they are loved and supported, but are entitled to space and privacy. If you hold a bird in the palm of your hand too tightly, you will smother it. If you spread your hand too wide, the bird will fly away. But if you hold the bird softly, allowing it to move around comfortably in your hand, even if it flies away, it will always return to rest in your hand. Give your newlyweds a chance to spread their wings and they'll stay close to you.

For the holidays I bought my mother-in-law a self-complaining oven.
—*Richard Lewis*

The two sets of in-law parents should work together to help their children. Neither set should compete, trying to be the favorite parents or grandparents. Working together, they can create harmony.

I worked myself up from nothing to a state of extreme poverty.
—*Groucho Marx*

Young couples are often naive about finances, so parents should help where they can. If it is necessary, it is wonderful if parents can and do help support their children while the children work hard to achieve financial independence. Different people have different philosophies about supporting their married children. Some parents do not have the means, and therefore there is no expectation that they will help their kids monetarily. Of course they can be supportive in other ways, generously offering their time and love to help with the grandchildren. There are also various viewpoints among people who are financially secure. For example, some parents think: *We struggled on our own and finally made it. This taught us responsibility, and we think that is good for our children too.* Other parents take the opposite attitude: *We worked hard so that our children should not have to struggle like we did. We will help as often as we can.* Still others have this approach: *We will give as long as the other set of parents-in-law also help.* You will also find parents who feel: *We did everything we could for them when they were single. Now we have to look after ourselves, saving for our future.* If the couple and both sets of in-law parents all agree with one approach, things can work out without difficulty. However, different expectations can cause resentment.

There is no perfect philosophy. One set of parents may be too tight with money, while the other may overindulge their children. Some parents may choose to give a lot although they do not have much, while others have a lot but choose not to give it. Giving your children everything can rob them of feeling capable and independent. Finding a balance is the key. Parents should help by giving emotional support, a good education, and financial support to the extent that they are able to do so.

Demanding too much of a young couple is unfair. Rather, encourage and assist kids to be the most they can be.

I've got all the money I'll ever need if I die by four this afternoon.

When parents are deciding whether or not to help support a new couple financially, the couple's own financial status is important to consider. Are they finished their education? Are they already decently employed? Do they have personal savings? The parents must also assess their other financial obligations. Although parents want to and should help children meet their needs, this can be done through various means: by helping support them or by instructing them how to budget and how to earn a living independently.

It is lovely to shower your kids with some extras if you

can, but it is even more important to encourage kids to seek an education and a job in a manner that gives them the ability to earn the best living they are capable of earning.

Parents who are helping the new couple financially do not have a right to control them. Alternatively, parents who do not help financially may still voice their opinions. Parents should do what they can, and children should appreciate what their parents do, without feeling entitled to anything.

Parents and in-law parents who support you financially or emotionally, caring about you and loving you, deserve to be treated with appreciation. Show this by including them in your life and allowing them the opportunity to take pride in you and your children. Attacking, bad-mouthing, or speaking disrespectfully to them is crossing a major boundary.

A father lectured his son, "We were put here on earth to help others."

The boy said, "What are the others here for?"

Some children take a lot from their parents without appreciating them or feeling they owe anything in return. Other children are givers and want to give back to their parents by showing them appreciation, respect, and love. Some parents give a lot but demand a lot in return. Other parents give very little and also demand little.

In the ideal situation, the parents and children are all givers, working toward a giving, loving, undemanding relationship so the young couple can create a healthy family of their own in a sharing, caring environment.

My mother wants grandchildren. I said, "Mom, go for it!"

—Sue Murphy

No one has a perfect marriage, perfect children, or perfect in-laws. Everyone must appreciate what s/he has, overlooking faults and being aware that people come from different backgrounds and are brought up with different, yet acceptable, perspectives.

Your in-law children may not love you the way they love their own parents; your mother-/father-in-law may not love you the way s/he loves his/her own children. But that does not matter. The quality of in-law love, although different from the love of one's own flesh and blood, can still be beautiful, sincere, deep, and all-encompassing.

A couple drove down a country road for several miles, not saying a word. An earlier discussion had led to an argument and neither of them wanted to concede their position. As they passed a barnyard of mules, goats, and pigs, the husband asked sarcastically, "Relatives of yours?"

"Yep," the wife replied. "In-laws."

Everyone involved should work to make the in-law jokes a big joke and not the reality.

51: Commitment versus Divorce

I'm not upset about my divorce. I'm only upset I'm not a widow.

—*Rosanne Barr*

Although the Torah allows for divorce, it encourages all couples to make an effort to have the marriage succeed. Unfortunately, some people do find themselves in an unsalvageable marriage, and they ultimately suffer the pain of divorce. Hashem does not always show us the entire picture, and most often we do not understand His reasoning. In her book, *Blessings of a Broken Heart,* Sherri Mandell compares life to a tapestry in which we are able to see only the underside, which is sloppy and tangled. Hashem sees the front of the tapestry in its entirety and magnificence. It is our job to believe that Hashem is putting the thread in the appropriate place and pulling it out in a way that will create this beauty. It is our job to work on strengthening our *emunah*, belief, both in good times and bad. *Vayehi erev, vayehi boker yom echad.* G-d created both the light and the darkness, the bright, happy times and the dark, sad times. They are both part of Hashem's plan.

My wife and I drive in separate cars, go out on different nights, and take separate vacations. We do everything possible to keep our marriage together.

Although everyone should try everything possible to keep his/her marriage together, there are certain times when divorce may be unavoidable. If people are so far apart in their thinking, their beliefs, their loyalties, their values and their goals, causing constant anger, disillusionment, resentment, and fighting, it may be better to separate. If one spouse has an unmanageable diagnosis (untreated borderline, unmanaged bipolar, and the like.) that causes a dysfunctional environment for the spouse and children, divorce may be better for everyone involved. If the home life is one of anger and fighting, the children are often better off with divorced parents. Each parent can individually create a calm, loving atmosphere for their children, or one stable parent who lives alone can do this.

Divorce is usually necessary when there is physical or verbal abuse in a marriage, both of which are extremely painful and degrading. Because the abuser usually refuses counseling to modify his behavior, denying s/he has a problem, the abused person is better off breaking up the marriage. Of course, the abuser will usually go on to abuse his/her next spouse as well.

I found the resume of my husband from kindergarten. Quote: The kid is very social. Eats, sleeps, and plays aggressively. Thirty years have passed since then. Nothing has changed.

I believe there would be fewer divorces if, from the earliest possible moment, parents and educators endeavored to instill better values in their children, teaching them to be more caring, less "me" oriented, less spoiled, and more secure. Rather than hiding or ignoring the issues, parents should recognize and address their children's psychological and emotional issues before sending them into a marriage to damage themselves, a spouse, and innocent offspring.

Don't let your worries get the best of you. Remember: Moses started out as a basket case.

Going through a divorce procedure is a dark time when one must strengthen his/her faith and accept that G-d is doing what is best for him/her.

The formula for a happy marriage is the same as the one for living in California: When you find a fault, don't dwell on it.

—Jay Trachman

Unfortunately, studies show that today most divorces occur because in our disposable society, everybody wants instant gratification. If something doesn't work, we throw it away and get a new one. Just as we dispose of our used Styrofoam coffee cup, we as easily dispose of our no-longer-wanted spouses. Of course, there are times when getting rid of this cup is the healthiest move. The old saying "Through sickness and in health, for better, for worse, for richer, for poorer until death do us part" has been replaced with "Until a problem arises or I am bored with you."

One woman in her seventies said, "In my day it was put up, shut up, and go on – and that's what we all did." But current statistics show that over 50 percent of marriages end in divorce, and that over a forty-year period, chances of a first marriage ending in divorce is as great as 67 percent (*www.smartmarriages.com/before.breakup.html*).

Thankfully, statistics are much lower in the Orthodox community, but sadly, it is increasing at a very quick rate. John Gottman reports that half of all the divorces occur in the first seven years, and many couples split in the first two years of marriage. Second marriages have a 10 percent higher chance of failure than do first marriages (*www.focusonthefamily.com*).

More marriages might survive if the partners realized that sometimes the better comes after the worse.

—Doug Larson

Unfortunately, many couples want to throw in the towel as soon as they have differences. They turn everything into a disagreement and make everything seem overwhelming and stressful.

An uptight couple sought help from a rabbi who gave them a brilliant, one-word piece of advice: chill. Marriage and its responsibilities may suddenly shake up a newlywed. Keep calm. Don't be judgmental. Don't analyze every word and move your spouse makes. Don't get scared that all of life's burdens will tumble down on you. Marriage is serious, but you should still retain that wonderful feeling of dating and getting to know one another. If you discover a character flaw along the way that you were heretofore unaware of, your attitude should be: *We'll work on that*. Hopefully, you will discover many other outstanding qualities about your spouse that will offset the less appealing revelations. Work at accentuating the positive feelings and eliminating, or at least controlling, the negative ones. If you do this for your spouse and your spouse does this for you, you will both feel good about one another.

The keys to a good solid marriage are what I term "the Six Cs":

- Caring
- Communicating
- Cooperating
- Compromising
- Committing
- Creating a strong friendship

Always make sure the overriding feeling is one of respecting and liking one another. As soon as a disagreement arises, deal with it, go into "the Six Cs" mode, and then let the issue subside.

As for the secret of staying married: My wife tells me that if I ever decide to leave, she is coming with me.
—*Bon Jovi*

Sometimes, when a couple feels bored or things seem routine or monotonous, the partners are not interested in their marriage anymore. This is a terrible mistake. Both spouses must fight for the survival of the marriage. Learn what the marriage needs to make it work and thrive. Appreciate that some of the monotony may be because things are going smoothly. Challenges of marriage make the road bumpier, but dealing with them often serves to strengthen a marriage.

Get Married. Stay Married. What a concept!

If you feel related to your spouse you will treat him/her like a relative. Whenever you have a difference of opinion with your mother, or are upset with your father, or feel annoyed with your siblings, you do not decide to cut this person out of your life. You accept the relationship as a lifetime one. You may experience many emotions about him/her, but the overriding feeling is one of belonging together. Perhaps you don't feel crazy about your mother right now, but you don't negate the wonderful feelings you usually feel for her. That love is a constant, smoothing over any anger or frustration you are presently feeling.

So too, a person should continually feel an underlying love for his/her spouse, despite a temporary annoyance. By establishing a calm island of stability, a person can handle the ups and downs of the current without the fear that causes a person to rush out of the water.

Two men are talking. One said, "I got married because I was sick and tired of going to the Laundromat, eating out, and wearing torn clothes."

The other man said, "Amazing! I got divorced for the very same reason."

If you continually threaten your spouse by saying you are going to leave him/her, the marriage never takes on the glue that a good marriage requires. If you suggest giving up on the marriage instead of dealing with problems that occur, you make your spouse feel lost and unanchored. Your spouse should be your life support and you should be his/hers. Having your spouse to hold onto should give you a feeling of well-being, a feeling of *we are in this together*. When one partner suggests the possibility of divorce, the other feels like the rug has been pulled out from under him. If your marriage is steeped in insecurity, mistrust, and fear, or if you find yourself functioning out of coercion and dread, you can't act out of understanding and love. Forcing a spouse to tolerate mean or irrational behavior may work in the short term but will not allow a marriage to thrive. Mental or physical abuse erodes a marriage.

People want their marriages to be eternal, able to endure anything. That means that if they are unhappy, they have to rework their marriage. Just as a car that runs out of gas doesn't necessarily have to be thrown out, marriages often have to be refueled. The couple must figure out why there is unhappiness and dissatisfaction, remembering that they made a commitment to each other that should be upheld.

In instances where one or both refuse to change, each spouse should follow some basic steps before resorting to divorce. If you are so angry, frustrated, or tense that you can't rationally process the pros and cons of divorce, it may be advisable to temporarily go on an antidepressant or anxiety medication. It goes without saying that the decision whether or not to take medication should be made only after consulting a qualified medical professional.

I never even believed in divorce until after I got married.
—*Diana Ford*

Remember the things you liked about one another and figure out what you still offer each other. Focus on these positive traits, forcing yourself to verbalize any pleasant thoughts or feelings (see chapter 38, "Appreciation"). Recall the good memories, putting the negative aspects of your marriage into perspective and recognizing all you have built together.

Imagine life without your spouse. Realistically determine if your problems will be solved by divorce. Try to determine the effect the divorce will have on your children and how your life will have to be reorganized to accommodate the new setup. Imagine life without your children around all the time. In most instances, parents take turns being with their children.

Explore the financial consequences of a divorce. Life is much harder financially as a result of a divorce for everyone involved.

"Mr. Clark, I have reviewed this case very carefully," the divorce court judge said, "and I've decided to give your wife $775 a week."

"That's very fair, Your Honor," the husband said. "And every now and then I'll try to send her a few bucks myself."

Divorce causes a decrease in wealth that is larger than just splitting a couple's assets in half. Divorce drops each person's wealth by an average of 77 percent. It is suggested that to truly increase your wealth, get married and stay married (Jay Zagorsky, *Journal of Sociology*, Ohio State University Center for Human Resource Research, January 2006).

Just as people don't go realistically into marriage, they jump into divorce without realizing the difficult consequences, especially when children are involved.

Divorce should be the option of last resort.

Next time I feel like getting married I will just find someone I hate and buy them a house.

A single friend of mine once said, "Before anyone considers walking out on his marriage, tell him to attend a singles' event." She truly believed that would discourage most people.

Relationships don't last anymore. When I meet a guy, the first question I ask myself is, "Is this the man I want my children to spend their weekends with?"

—Rita Rudner

Each partner should identify his/her anger, disillusionment, and despair, as well as areas which s/he is willing to change, and have a mediator present the problem to the spouse to see if the couple can find some middle ground.

A man said, "I have to divorce my wife. She hasn't spoken to me in six months. His friend said, "Where are you going to find a good one like that?"

It is easy to stay married when everything is perfect, but sooner or later problems complicate everyone's lives. People experience traumas. They undergo financial difficulties. Sickness, tragedies, and life's turmoil are all trying. Little problems can make life seem overwhelming, and the romance loses its luster. Rather than being there to support each other, couples often turn from allies to enemies. People blame one another and resent that their spouse is not giving them the security and protection they crave. The equilibrium that has been created becomes jeopardized.

Remember: Marriage is the leading cause of divorce.

"I grew up in the forties and fifties with practical parents. My mother washed aluminum foil after she cooked in it, and then reused it. My father was happier getting old shoes fixed than buying new ones. The marriage was good, their dreams focused. I can see them now, Dad in trousers and T-shirt with lawn mower in hand and Mom in a housedress, the dish towel in her hand.

"It was a time of fixing things – a curtain rod, the kitchen radio, a screen door, the oven door, the hem of a dress. We kept things. It was a way of life, and sometimes it made me crazy. All that re-fixing, reheating, renewing. I wanted just once to be wasteful. Waste meant affluence. Throwing things away meant there'd be more. But then my mother died, and on that clear summer's night, in the warmth of the hospital room, I was struck with the pain of learning that sometimes there isn't any more. Sometimes, what we care about most gets all used up and goes away…never to return. So, while we have it, it's best we love it and care for it…and fix it when it's broken…and heal it when it's sick. This is true for old cars…and children with bad report cards…and dogs with bad hips…and aging parents… and grandparents…and marriage. We keep them because they are worth it, because we are worth it. Some things we keep" (Author unknown).

How can anything called "being committed" be a good thing?

People often make the terrible mistake of believing life will be better with someone else.

Research has shown that simply sticking with it – hanging in through the "for worse" and the boring or when we feel all out of love – can eventually be what gets us to the promised land (Linda J. Waite, Don Browning, William J. Doherty, Maggie Gallagher, Ye Luo, *Does Divorce Make People Happy?* Institute for American Values, 2002).

As people go through unhappy periods in their marriage, they fantasize about getting out of the marriage and finding happiness by falling in love with someone new. It turns out that the surer route to happiness – in the long run – is to fall back in love with the person with whom you have children, extended families, and a history, someone who will enjoy the grandkids with you and has been there to know what you've done for others.

The new relationship is only going to be "new" for a few years; soon enough you'll be back to wondering how to make the marriage work. Except this time you'll have to do it with the added baggage of exes, stepkids, child support, and visitation. And don't kid yourself; single life can get old, lonely, and boring.

My husband and I had a very messy divorce because there was a baby involved. Him. And I didn't want custody.

–Wendy Liebman

Max, a man married fifteen years, decided to leave his wife, Beatrice, for his glamorous secretary, Julie. He was tired of "the same old thing." His wife dressed up only when they were going out. Otherwise she looked plain and overworked and was constantly complaining. She was always busy with the kids or cleaning the house. She claimed he was too tight with money and that he was never home. He wanted "more." He married his secretary. After a few months of being married to Julie, Max noticed that she stopped getting dressed up. She was pregnant, tired, and always complaining that she was wiped out by the household chores, didn't have sufficient money to run the house, and never saw him since he was always at the office.

Max hadn't realized that marriage creates certain circumstances that should be addressed no matter who your spouse is. He should have taken his first wife out more often and given her more occasions to get dressed up and to relax and enjoy his company. He should have made sure to help her with the kids and the chores, or arrange for outside help to lighten Beatrice's burden. He should have been more generous with his money. By remaining the same type of person, Max traded in one wife for another who became the same as the first. A spouse can break up the family and destroy the home rather than try to change the situation and improve the relationship.

A young bride- and groom-to-be had just selected the wedding ring. As the girl admired the plain platinum and diamond band, she suddenly looked concerned. "Tell me," she asked the elderly salesman "is there anything special I'll have to do to take care of this ring?"

With a fatherly smile, the salesman said, "One of the best ways to protect a wedding ring is to dip it in dishwater three times a day."

Grace was sick of her husband Dan coming home late, being a tightwad with money, and generally being unhelpful. She divorced him, thinking she was punishing him. Three months later Dan was remarried and Grace had to raise their four children by herself. She still had to deal with

Dan, always fighting for child support. Although Dan had not been home enough, he was home sometimes. Even though he watched his cash, she still had convinced him to spend on certain things. Now there was a new wife who was certainly not sharing the small amount of money or time that Dan allotted her. So Grace and Dan continued to have major issues for years following the divorce.

Grace did not realize how difficult it would be to be totally alone. Nor did she envision how hard it would be for her children not to have a father in the house. And she certainly did not realize how easy it is for men, especially when they do not have full-time custody of children, to get remarried. Grace would have been better off working on her marriage and giving her husband more reason to come home. She should have encouraged his helpfulness by being more complimentary. She could have been more patient when explaining to Dan why she needed more money. They could have gone together for counseling. She could also have tried to earn money for herself so she could be more independent. Even if she was right in her estimations of Dan's shortcomings, she punished herself with the divorce more than she punished Dan.

"Why is the divorce taking so long? I want a divorce immediately!" the husband harangued the divorce lawyer.

Finally his divorce came through. The man walked right up to his ex-wife and said to her, "Will you marry me?"

His lawyer was dismayed. "Why were you in such a rush to get divorced if you want to remarry her?"

"As a first wife she is terrible, but for a second wife she is okay," the man answered.

A divorced man finds it difficult as well, even if he remarries. The courts usually force a divorced man to give his ex-wife a substantial part of his income, plus child support. The husband who was berated for being lazy, indifferent, and unsupportive usually has a new wife with the same complaints. Additionally, she will resent the time and money he spends on his original family.

Hymie is telling his friend about his recent divorce. "Yes, it's true. Sylvie divorced me for religious reasons. She worshipped money, and I didn't have any."

In a study done by Drs. Lyn Gigy and Joan Kelly, 80 percent of divorcées said their marriages ended because they gradually grew apart and lost a sense of closeness or because they no longer felt loved and appreciated. Sometimes this happens when one partner is growing while the other is stagnant, or if one spouse spirals downward.

Sammy was involved in business and interested in politics. He read many books, searching for G-d and the meaning of life. Rachie watched lots of soap operas while eating chocolate bars. She barely left the house. They soon had very little in common.

The only person who behaves sensibly is my tailor. He remeasures me every time he sees me. All the rest go on with the old measurements.

—George Bernard Shaw

Keep reevaluating. Constantly reassess your situation and yourself. Have you or your spouse changed? Is one of you growing and the other remaining stagnant?

People told Mrs. Green she had not done a good job checking out her son-in-law. She did not think she had to check him out, since her family and his had been friends for years. They lived on the same street; her husband and his father were partners; her son and her son-in-law studied together. When he married her daughter, Mrs. Green believed she knew everything about her son-in-law. She didn't know that seventeen years later he would run off with a Filipino. I told her, "Life happens. Circumstances change. People change. All the research would not have helped. It is the years since they were wed that had to be watched."

It is a sad fact that 50 percent of marriages end in divorce. But hey, the other half end in death. You could be one of the lucky ones!

—*Richard Jeni*

Be committed to the marriage. Never walk out. Discuss your differences and find a way to work through your issues. If things are difficult, you have to do them. If things are impossible you have to try a little harder.

A couple, both over ninety, goes before the judge and asks for a divorce.

"How come?" asked the judge. "You stayed together all these years. Why do you want to get divorced now? Why didn't you get divorced years ago if you were so unhappy?"

"We would have," they said, "but we wanted to wait for the kids to grow up and die."

A growing number of divorces are occurring among the elderly. This is because life expectancy has increased and quality of life has improved. Now people in their sixties are unwilling to remain in an unhappy marriage.

51: Commitment versus Divorce

Marriage is like a violin. After the music is over, you still have the strings.

Working on improving your marriage will do more for your health than spending hours working out at a gym.

Someone who asks his/her spouse for a divorce is crying, "Tell me you care. Tell me I matter."

Harry was stunned to come home from work one evening and find his wife stuffing all her belongings into a suitcase. "What on earth are you doing?" he cried.

"I can't stand it anymore!" she shrieked." "Thirty-two years we've been married, and all we do is bicker and quarrel and ignore each other. I'm leaving!"

Stunned, Harry watched his wife close the suitcase, lug it down the stairs, and proceed to walk out of the house...out of his life.

Suddenly, he was galvanized into action. Running into the bedroom and grabbing a second suitcase, he yelled back at his wife, "Sylvia, you're right. You're absolutely right, and I can't bear it either. Wait a minute. I'll go with you."

Carol complained about her husband Stan. "He is a lazy, good-for-nothing, incompetent so-and-so." Then he died and Carol cried about how much she missed him. "He used to go with me. He used to drive me. He used to listen to me." Now she realized how much a part of her life he had been.

In Hollywood a marriage is a success if it outlasts milk.

Do you ever wonder why so many Hollywood celebrities get divorced? Each knows that s/he or his/her spouse is always in demand, always being pursued by another leading man or lady. Each recognizes that they both have impossible schedules and are scarcely ever home. Each one wants to have a normal life, a spouse, a home, someone to love who loves them. However, one Hollywood marriage after another crumbles, because many of these people are self-centered individuals who are unwilling to take on the battle. They won't work at their marriages. They won't invest the time, energy, thought, planning, adjusting, understanding, and compromising that a successful marriage requires. They won't sacrifice their career or popularity. It seems that they pursue one another just for the challenge. But before a fairy tale ends with "They lived happily ever after," it should include a part that says, "and they worked very hard at their marriage."

My wife won't give me a divorce until she can find a way of doing it without making me happy.

Boredom should not be such an easily accepted reason for divorce. A twelve-year-old told me that her friend's father was leaving her mother for another woman. She told me this news with as much emotion as if she were telling me that she had found a new skirt.

I've heard individuals defend divorce, saying, "My parents were divorced and I turned out fine." It is true that a child of divorced parents can and often does turn out fine. Some even excel. Nevertheless, would these individuals, given the choice, have chosen to be brought up in a broken home?

Often the reasons why a couple marries and the reasons why a couple divorces are the same. There is a lot of overlap.

She marries a man because he is strong. Then she divorces him because he is domineering.

He marries her because she is fragile and cute and divorces her for being weak and helpless.

She marries him because he is a good provider and leaves him because all he does is work.

He marries her because she reminds him of his mother and divorces her for becoming more like her mother every day.

She marries him because he was happy and romantic. Now she divorces him because he is shiftless and frivolous.

He marries her because she was steady and sensible and divorces her for being boring and dull.

She marries him because he was the life of the party and divorces him for being a party boy.

Things you Love now	= Ten-Year Reality
Activist	Busybody
Ambitious	Workaholic
Attentive	Possessive
Confident	Arrogant
Cool	Frigid
Discerning	Snobbish
Funny	Show-off
Honest	Cynical
Laid-back	Lazy
Playful	Immature

Misses you	Restraining order
Modest	Prudish
Nonchalant	Aloof
Opinionated	Argumentative
Optimistic	Stupid
Quiet	Too quiet
Romantic	Stalker
Simple	Boring
Sincere	Brutally honest
Smart	Know-it-all
Strong-minded	Mule-headed
Supportive	Clingy
Trusting	Gullible

People's positives traits are also their negative traits; it is how they channel each quality that counts. A fun-loving guy is only fun if he makes life fun for his wife, rather than needing to be the life of the party while his wife is home alone. A soft, delicate wife is appealing, but not if she can't run a home or control her children. A man who is strong and virile is attractive, unless he is using his strength to harm his wife. Everyone has to use his/her qualities in a manner that enhances his/her relationship with his/her spouse.

When he got a divorce, he and his wife split the house. He got the outside.

52: THE MEDICAL ADVANTAGES OF MARRIAGE

A man walked over to the perfume counter and told the clerk he'd like a bottle of Chanel No. 5 for his wife's birthday.

"A little surprise, eh?" smiled the clerk.

"You bet," answered the customer. "She's expecting a cruise."

Researchers at Case Western University studied 10,000 married men and found that men who reported that they had loving wives experienced significantly less angina than those who said their wives were not loving. This was regardless of other indicators such as elevated cholesterol, high blood pressure, or diabetes (Bob Condor, Knight Ridder).

How come men die before women? Because they want to!

There is an abundance of evidence suggesting that love and marriage are good for one's health. Dr. Stephen Bogdewic, vice chairman of Family Medicine at Indiana University School of Medicine, said, "If a new drug had the same impact, virtually every doctor in the country would be recommending it" (Judy Monchuk, "Happy Marriage May Counter Work Stress," *The London Free Press,* October 26, 2004).

Do you know what the death rate is around here? One per person!

Both men and women live longer, healthier, happier, and wealthier lives when they are married (Maggie Gallagher, *The Case for Marriage*).

It has been found that a stable, happy marriage is the best protector against illness and premature death for adults, and such a marriage is the source of emotional stability and good physical health for children (Burnam and Margolinn, 1992; Dawson, 1991; Verbrugge, 1979).

If we, as a society, work diligently in every other area of life and neglect the family, it would be analogous to straightening deck chairs on the Titanic.

—*Stephen Covey*

A study of 6,000 Americans with bladder cancer found that those who were married had a better survival rate than single patients. Single patients were 265 times more likely to die during the study period than married patients, regardless of age, race, or severity of their cancer (*Reuters Health,* September 30, 2005, www.cancerpage.com).

There are multiple studies that show that positive, loving relationships protect us from stress and help us cope better with life's challenges and traumas. Researchers found that men and women in unhappy marriages suffered from increased stress levels throughout the day whether at home or at work, as well as higher blood pressure at midday at the office, raising the risk of heart attack or stroke (R. Barnett, *Annals of Behavioral Medicine*, vol. 30, 2005, 36–43).

Married men live longer than single men, but married men are a lot more willing to die.

It has been found that the mortality rates of individuals with poor social relationships are higher than for those who smoke for many years (House et al., "Social Relationships and Health," *Science* 241 [1988]: 540–44).

Marital distress is a major health hazard for adults and children. Marital instability causes depression and reduces immune system functioning in adults. Chronic marital conflict harms the emotional and physical well-being of children.

Divorce is a major health risk for American adults and children (Emery, 1982; Gottman and Katz, 1989; Kiecolt-Glaser et al., 1993).

There are well-established links between divorce and mental health problems. Adults who experience divorce more than double their risk of earlier mortality. Children who experienced parental divorce have their life expectancy shortened by four years. An unhappy marriage can increase your chance of getting ill by approximately 35 percent and can shorten your life span by an average of four years. For unknown reasons, a good marriage increases the life span and promotes better health. This may be because married couples tend to look after one another, encourage each other to have regular checkups, take medicine, and eat properly. People in happy marriages have been found to have a stronger immune system (Dawson, 1991; Cherlin et al., 1991; Doherty and Needle, 1991; Tucker et al., 1996; Schwartz et al., 1995).

I don't mind death. I just don't want to be there when it happens.

—Woody Allen

53: Don't Compare Your Marriage

The grass looks greener…but it's Astroturf.

Don't look at other marriages. Hanoch Teller, the well-known storyteller, said that someone asked him, "How come the only people who are really happy are the people I don't know well?" Everyone's life, marriage, and children look perfect to the outsider, but once you get to know the person, you find that s/he also has problems. Don't do comparative studies, because every marriage has its challenges. Everything may be perfect at this moment, but chances are they went through tough times in the past or they will unfortunately go through bumpy times in the future. Such is life.

If the grass looks greener on the other side of the fence, it's because they take better care of it.

—*Cecil Selig*

It is difficult enough to stay on top of what is happening in your own home, without trying to know what is doing in anyone else's home.

Gary and Shira were considered to be a "Barbie and Ken" couple. They looked great and dressed beautifully. They always seemed upbeat, and the story of how they met was really romantic. They were the ideal and envy of every couple. Everything seemed perfect until they announced their divorce. It seems they had not gotten along for most of their marriage, realizing quite early that it had been a mistake.

Frieda and Murray seemed to be another ideal couple. They were the parents of six lovely children. When they married off the last of their children they announced that they had stayed together for the sake of their children but were now splitting up. Everyone was flabbergasted. The parents of the children who had married into the family were shocked and felt fooled. They had all believed that their children were marrying into a very stable family. Was the home stable, or were the children suffering as they lived the lie along with the parents? Was there peace and tranquillity or fighting and frustration? Who can judge? Perhaps these were wonderful parents who made the enormous sacrifice of staying together for the sake of their children. Anyone looking at this couple thought, "What are they doing that I can copy? They have such a good marriage and close family." Meanwhile, despite six children in common, they grew apart to the point where the damage was irreparable.

Jealousy is detrimental to one's state of well-being. People who are jealous are never happy. No matter how much you have, someone will always have more, and you will never enjoy what you do have. Don't envy anyone's money, position, appearance, education, job, reputation, talent, family, and so on. Even if the other person had less it would not make you have any more. So don't envy what others have; just appreciate all the blessings G-d has given you.

Don't look at other couples and say he is earning a better living, she is keeping herself slimmer, their kids are better adjusted, and so forth. You don't know. Everything hopefully is as beautiful as it looks, but it may be that one day you will learn that unfortunately his business is on the brink of collapse, his wife is anorexic, and their son has been diagnosed with leukemia, and you have wasted your precious life being envious of these people. *Pirkei Avos*, Ethics of the Fathers, relates that a happy person is one who is happy with his lot. Happy, satisfied, appreciative individuals create a better marriage.

Getting married is very much like going to a restaurant with friends. You order what you want, and then, when you see what the other fellow has, you wish you had ordered that.

The sixth *bracha*, blessing, given to a couple at their wedding is: "*Samei'ach tesamach re'im ahuvim, k'samechachah yetzirchah b'Gan Eden mikedem*, Gladden these beloved companions as you gladdened Your creation in the Garden of Eden in the east." Because Adam and Chava were the only human beings in existence, they never doubted that they were each other's *bashert*, soul mates. They were never envious of anyone else's marriage and therefore were able to focus on and appreciate the relationship Hashem had given them.

A marriage cannot rely on a husband earning a certain amount of income or a wife remaining gorgeous or kids being perfect. It can only rely on a couple who has the right attitude of being satisfied and grateful for what they have.

Many times people are unable to earn what they had hoped to earn, or expenses are greater than they had estimated, or the market suffers deep losses, or a person loses his/her job. A person may age with worse wrinkles than s/he had anticipated, or a family may go through tragedies. A marriage must withstand change, aging, loss of looks, loss of hair, loss of hopes, and a lifetime of disappointments. Life can be extremely challenging. Couples must rise to the challenge, accept and adapt, and always look at the beauty and potential of their own marriage.

The man says to his hairstylist, "My hair is falling out. My wife asked me to ask you, what can I use to keep it in?"

The stylist replies, "Might I suggest a shoebox?"

54: Grow Old Together

David, a senior citizen, was driving through the midtown tunnel when his cell phone rang. Answering, he heard his wife urgently warning him. "David, please be careful! I just heard on the news that there's a car going the wrong way through the tunnel."

"I know," said David, "but it's not just one car. There are dozens of them."

Go through life in the same direction, always communicating and always caring about one another.

What a couple should save for old age is each other. A good marriage is compared to sipping a nice cup of coffee every morning. You may have it every day, but you still enjoy it.

Grow old together, but no matter how old you are and how long you have been married, retain the ability to enjoy one another. Share your lives, your experiences, your memories, your hopes your dreams, and your future.

Falling in love is easy but staying in love is something very special. May Hashem bless each of you with a beautiful and fulfilling marriage.

Bibliography

Aiken, Lisa. *Beyond Bashert*. New Jersey: Jason Aaronson, 1996.

Braverman, Emuna. "Dear Emuna," www.aish.com.

Doherty, William J. "The Scientific Case for Marriage and Couples: Education in Health Care," http://www.smartmarriages.com/hpmarr.html.

Emery, et al. "A Theory of Dissolution and Stability." *Journal of Family Psychology* 7, no. 1 (June 1993): 57–75.

Frand, Rabbi Yissocher. "Marriage from Caterpillar to Butterfly," www.aish.com.

Gottlieb, Lori. "The Case for Settling for Mr. Good Enough." *The Atlantic*, March 1, 2008.

Gottman, John and Silver, Nan. *The Seven Principles for Making a Marriage Work*. New York: Crown, 1999.

Gray, John. *Men Are from Mars, Women Are from Ve-*

nus. New York: HarperCollins, 1992.

Headley, Maria Dahvana. "The Year of Yes." *Newsweek*, January 2006.

Hendrix, Harville. *Getting the Love You Want*. New York: Henry Holt and Co., 1988.

House et al. "Social Relationships and Health." *Science* (1988): 241; 540–44.

Johnson, Dr. Sue. *Hold Me Tight*. New York: Little, Brown and Company, 2008.

Krohn, Rabbi Paysach. *Perspectives of the Maggid*. NewYork: Mesorah Publications, 2012.

Legato, Marianne. "Two-Track Minds." *New York Post*, November 1, 2006.

Maharal of Prague, "Field of Potential," www.aish.com, adapted from Maharal's homily delivered in Posen, Poland, Shavuos 5352/1592.

"NSAIDs Protective against Colon Cancer in Blacks and Whites." *Reuters Health*, September 30, 2005, www.cancerpage.com.

Ostrov, Shaya. *The Inner Circle: Seven Gates to Marriage*. Jerusalem: Feldheim, 2000.

Pliskin, Rabbi Zelig. *Marriage*. New York: Mesorah Publications, 1998.

Real, Terrence. *The New Rules of Marriage*. New York: Ballantin Books, 2008.

Stewart, Sara. "How Genders Think." *New York Post*, November 1, 2006.

Straus, M. and Gelles, R. *Physical Violence in American fami-*

lies. New Brunswick, N. J: Transaction Publishers, 1990.

Tjaden, P. and Thoennes, N. "Extent, Nature, and Consequences of Intimate Partner Violence." *National Institute of Justice*, 2000 NCJ 181867.

Twerski, Rabbi Dr. Abraham J. *The First Year of Marriage*. New York: Shaar Press, 2004.

Twerski, Rebbetzin Feigi. "Intimacy in Marriage," www.aish.com.

US Department of Justice, Bureau of Justice Statistics. "Violence against Women: Estimates from the Redesigned Survey," August 1995.

US Department of Justice, Bureau of Justice Statistics Crime Data Brief. "Intimate Partner Violence, 1993–2001," February 2003.

US Senate, 102nd Congress, Committee on the Judiciary. "Violence against Women: A Majority Staff Report."

Waite, Linda J. et al. "Does Divorce Make People Happy?" Institute for American Values, 2002.

Witkin, Dr. Georgia. *It's Not You, It's Me*. New York: Broadway Books, 2006.

Zagorsky, Jay. *Journal of Sociology*. Ohio State University Center for Human Resource Research, January 2006.

www.focusonthefamily.com.

www.heart-2-heart.

www.joy2meu.com/personal boundaries.html.

www.smartmarriages.com/before.breakup.html.

www.smartmarriages.com/divorcepredictor.html.